Computer Architecture

Computer Architecture

Ken Spiner

Larsen & Keller
www.larsen-keller.com

Computer Architecture
Ken Spiner
ISBN: 978-1-64172-464-7 (Hardback)

 Larsen & Keller

Published by Larsen and Keller Education,
5 Penn Plaza,
19th Floor,
New York, NY 10001, USA

Cataloging-in-Publication Data

Computer architecture / Ken Spiner.
     p. cm.
Includes bibliographical references and index.
ISBN 978-1-64172-464-7
1. Computer architecture. 2. Computer engineering. I. Spiner, Ken.
QA76.9.A73 C66 2020
004.22--dc23

For more information regarding Larsen and Keller Education and its products, please visit the publisher's website www.larsen-keller.com

Table of Contents

Preface

The set of rules and methods which describe the organization, functionality and implementation of computer systems are known as computer architecture. It is a sub-field of computer engineering. The primary goal of computer architecture is to design a computer which maximizes performance while keeping power consumption in check. It should also keep the costs low compared to the amount of expected performance and should be very reliable. There are three main subcategories within this field. These are instruction set architecture (ISA), microarchitecture and system design. The machine code which a processor reads and acts upon is defined by ISA. Microarchitecture details how a particular processor should implement the ISA. The rest of the hardware components which are in a computing system are included in system design. Computer architecture is an upcoming field of computer engineering that has undergone rapid development over the past few decades. This book is compiled in such a manner, that it will provide in-depth knowledge about the theory and applications of this field. Those in search of information to further their knowledge will be greatly assisted by this book.

A short introduction to every chapter is written below to provide an overview of the content of the book:

Chapter 1 - The set of methods and rules which define the organization, functionality and implementation of computer systems is known as computer architecture. The diverse aspects of computers and computer architecture including the Von Neumann architecture have been briefly introduced in this chapter.; **Chapter 2** - The central processing unit refers to the electronic circuit within a computer which is responsible for carrying out the varied instructions of a computer program. Some of the components of the central processing unit are the control unit and the arithmetic logic unit. The topics elaborated in this chapter will help in gaining a better perspective about these components of the central processing unit.; **Chapter 3** - Instruction set architecture is an abstract model of a computer which serves as a bridge between software and hardware. It can be classified on the basis of complexity into numerous categories such as RISC, CISC, MISC and OISC. This chapter discusses in detail these types of instruction set architecture to provide a thorough understanding of the subject.; **Chapter 4** - Memory refers to the hardware integrated circuits in computers which store information. Some of the concepts studied in relation to memory with respect to computer architecture are memory hierarchy, memory unit, cache memory and virtual memory. This chapter closely examines these key concepts of memory management to provide an extensive understanding of the subject.; **Chapter 5** - The signals or data which are received by the computer are termed as input signals and the data or signals which are sent from it to a human user or another information processing system is termed as an output system. All the diverse components of input and output systems such as the various input and output devices have been carefully analyzed in this chapter.; **Chapter 6** - A type of computing where multiple processes are executed simultaneously is known as parallel computing. Pipelining refers to a process by which instruction are accumulated from the processor through a pipeline. This chapter has been carefully written to provide an easy understanding of the varied facets of parallel computing and pipelining.

Finally, I would like to thank my fellow scholars who gave constructive feedback and my family members who supported me at every step.

Ken Spiner

Computer Architecture: An Introduction

The set of methods and rules which define the organization, functionality and implementation of computer systems is known as computer architecture. The diverse aspects of computers and computer architecture including the Von Neumann architecture have been briefly introduced in this chapter.

Computer

Computer is a device for processing, storing, and displaying information. Computer once meant a person who did computations, but now the term almost universally refers to automated electronic machinery.

Computing Basics

The first computers were used primarily for numerical calculations. However, as any information can be numerically encoded, people soon realized that computers are capable of general-purpose information processing. Their capacity to handle large amounts of data has extended the range and accuracy of weather forecasting. Their speed has allowed them to make decisions about routing telephone connections through a network and to control mechanical systems such as automobiles, nuclear reactors, and robotic surgical tools. They are also cheap enough to be embedded in everyday appliances and to make clothes dryers and rice cookers "smart." Computers have allowed us to pose and answer questions that could not be pursued before. These questions might be about DNA sequences in genes, patterns of activity in a consumer market, or all the uses of a word in texts that have been stored in a database. Increasingly, computers can also learn and adapt as they operate.

Computers also have limitations, some of which are theoretical. For example, there are undecidable propositions whose truth cannot be determined within a given set of rules, such as the logical structure of a computer. Because no universal algorithmic method can exist to identify such propositions, a computer asked to obtain the truth of such a proposition will (unless forcibly interrupted) continues indefinitely—a condition known as the "halting problem." Other limitations reflect current technology. Human minds are skilled at recognizing spatial patterns—easily distinguishing among human faces, for instance—but this is a difficult task for computers, which must process information sequentially, rather than grasping details overall at a glance. Another problematic area for computers involves natural language interactions. Because so much common knowledge and contextual information is assumed in ordinary human communication, researchers have yet to solve the problem of providing relevant information to general-purpose natural language programs.

Analog Computers

Analog computers use continuous physical magnitudes to represent quantitative information. At first they represented quantities with mechanical components, but after World War II voltages were used; by the 1960s digital computers had largely replaced them. Nonetheless, analog computers, and some hybrid digital-analog systems, continued in use through the 1960s in tasks such as aircraft and spaceflight simulation.

One advantage of analog computation is that it may be relatively simple to design and build an analog computer to solve a single problem. Another advantage is that analog computers can frequently represent and solve a problem in "real time"; that is, the computation proceeds at the same rate as the system being modeled by it. Their main disadvantages are that analog representations are limited in precision—typically a few decimal places but fewer in complex mechanisms—and general-purpose devices are expensive and not easily programmed.

Digital Computers

In contrast to analog computers, digital computers represent information in discrete form, generally as sequences of 0s and 1s (binary digits, or bits). The modern era of digital computers began in the late 1930s and early 1940s in the United States, Britain, and Germany. The first devices used switches operated by electromagnets (relays). Their programs were stored on punched paper tape or cards, and they had limited internal data storage.

Mainframe Computer

During the 1950s and '60s, Unisys (maker of the UNIVAC computer), International Business Machines Corporation (IBM), and other companies made large, expensive computers of increasing power. They were used by major corporations and government research laboratories, typically as the sole computer in the organization. In 1959 the IBM 1401 computer rented for $8,000 per month (early IBM machines were almost always leased rather than sold), and in 1964 the largest IBM S/360 computer cost several million dollars.

These computers came to be called mainframes, though the term did not become common until smaller computers were built. Mainframe computers were characterized by having (for their time) large storage capabilities, fast components, and powerful computational abilities. They were highly reliable, and, because they frequently served vital needs in an organization, they were sometimes designed with redundant components that let them survive partial failures. Because they were complex systems, they were operated by a staff of systems programmers, who alone had access to the computer. Other users submitted "batch jobs" to be run one at a time on the mainframe.

Such systems remain important today, though they are no longer the sole, or even primary, central computing resource of an organization, which will typically have hundreds or thousands of personal computers (PCs). Mainframes now provide high-capacity data storage for Internet servers, or, through time-sharing techniques, they allow hundreds or thousands of users to run programs simultaneously. Because of their current roles, these computers are now called servers rather than mainframes.

Supercomputer

The most powerful computers of the day have typically been called supercomputers. They have historically been very expensive and their use limited to high-priority computations for government-sponsored research, such as nuclear simulations and weather modeling. Today many of the computational techniques of early supercomputers are in common use in PCs. On the other hand, the design of costly, special-purpose processors for supercomputers has been supplanted by the use of large arrays of commodity processors (from several dozen to over 8,000) operating in parallel over a high-speed communications network.

Minicomputer

Although minicomputers date to the early 1950s, the term was introduced in the mid-1960s. Relatively small and inexpensive, minicomputers were typically used in a single department of an organization and often dedicated to one task or shared by a small group. Minicomputers generally had limited computational power, but they had excellent compatibility with various laboratory and industrial devices for collecting and inputting data.

One of the most important manufacturers of minicomputers was Digital Equipment Corporation (DEC) with its Programmed Data Processor (PDP). In 1960 DEC's PDP-1 sold for $120,000. Five years later its PDP-8 cost $18,000 and became the first widely used minicomputer, with more than 50,000 sold. The DEC PDP-11, introduced in 1970, came in a variety of models, small and cheap enough to control a single manufacturing process and large enough for shared use in university computer centres; more than 650,000 were sold. However, the microcomputer overtook this market in the 1980s.

Microcomputer

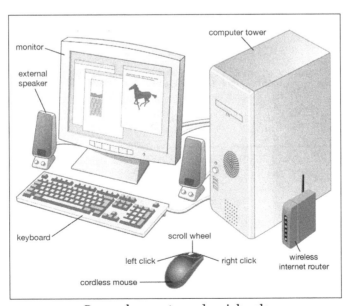

Personal computer and peripherals

A microcomputer is a small computer built around a microprocessor integrated circuit, or chip. Whereas the early minicomputers replaced vacuum tubes with discrete transistors, microcomputers (and later minicomputers as well) used microprocessors that integrated thousands or millions of transistors on a single chip. In 1971 the Intel Corporation produced the first microprocessor, the Intel 4004, which was powerful enough to function as a computer although it was produced for use in a Japanese-made calculator. In 1975 the first personal computer, the Altair, used a successor chip, the Intel 8080 microprocessor. Like minicomputers, early microcomputers had relatively limited storage and data-handling capabilities, but these have grown as storage technology has improved alongside processing power.

In the 1980s it was common to distinguish between microprocessor-based scientific workstations and personal computers. The former used the most powerful microprocessors available and had high-performance colour graphics capabilities costing thousands of dollars. They were used by scientists for computation and data visualization and by engineers for computer-aided engineering. Today the distinction between workstation and PC has virtually vanished, with PCs having the power and display capability of workstations.

Embedded Processors

Another class of computer is the embedded processor. These are small computers that use simple microprocessors to control electrical and mechanical functions. They generally do not have to do elaborate computations or be extremely fast, nor do they have to have great "input-output" capability, and so they can be inexpensive. Embedded processors help to control aircraft and industrial automation, and they are common in automobiles and in both large and small household appliances. One particular type, the digital signal processor (DSP), has become as prevalent as the microprocessor. DSPs are used in wireless telephones, digital telephone and cable modems, and some stereo equipment.

Computer Hardware

The physical elements of a computer, its hardware, are generally divided into the central processing unit (CPU), main memory (or random-access memory, RAM), and peripherals. The last class encompasses all sorts of input and output (I/O) devices: keyboard, display monitor, printer, disk drives, network connections, scanners, and more.

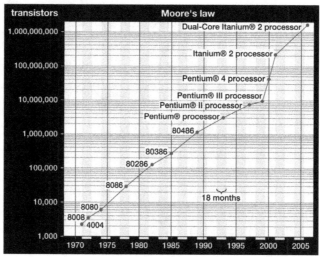

Moore's law

The CPU and RAM are integrated circuits (ICs)—small silicon wafers, or chips, that contain thousands or millions of transistors that function as electrical switches. In 1965 Gordon Moore, one of the founders of Intel, stated what has become known as Moore's law: the number of transistors on a chip doubles about every 18 months. Moore suggested that financial constraints would soon cause his law to break down, but it has been remarkably accurate for far longer than he first envisioned. It now appears that technical constraints may finally invalidate Moore's law, since sometime between 2010 and 2020 transistors would have to consist of only a few atoms each, at which point the laws of quantum physics imply that they would cease to function reliably.

Figure shows, Moore's Law: Gordon E. Moore observed that the number of transistors on a computer chip was doubling about every 18–24 months. As shown in the logarithmic graph of the number of transistors on Intel's processors at the time of their introduction, his "law" was being obeyed.

Central Processing Unit

The CPU provides the circuits that implement the computer's instruction set—its machine language. It is composed of an arithmetic-logic unit (ALU) and control circuits. The ALU carries out basic arithmetic and logic operations, and the control section determines the sequence of operations, including branch instructions that transfer control from one part of a program to another. Although the main memory was once considered part of the CPU, today it is regarded as separate. The boundaries shift, however, and CPU chips now also contain some high-speed cache memory where data and instructions are temporarily stored for fast access.

The ALU has circuits that add, subtract, multiply, and divide two arithmetic values, as well as circuits for logic operations such as AND and OR (where a 1 is interpreted as true and a 0 as false, so that, for instance, 1 AND 0 = 0;). The ALU has several to more than a hundred registers that temporarily hold results of its computations for further arithmetic operations or for transfer to main memory.

The circuits in the CPU control section provide branch instructions, which make elementary decisions about what instruction to execute next. For example, a branch instruction might be "If the result of the last ALU operation is negative, jump to location A in the program; otherwise, continue with the following instruction." Such instructions allow "if-then-else" decisions in a program and execution of a sequence of instructions, such as a "while-loop" that repeatedly does some set of instructions while some condition is met. A related instruction is the subroutine call, which transfers execution to a subprogram and then, after the subprogram finishes, returns to the main program where it left off.

In a stored-program computer, programs and data in memory are indistinguishable. Both are bit patterns—strings of 0s and 1s—that may be interpreted either as data or as program instructions and both are fetched from memory by the CPU. The CPU has a program counter that holds the memory address (location) of the next instruction to be executed. The basic operation of the CPU is the "fetch-decode-execute" cycle:

- Fetch the instruction from the address held in the program counter, and store it in a register.

- Decode the instruction: Parts of it specify the operation to be done, and parts specify the data on which it is to operate. These may be in CPU registers or in memory locations. If it is a branch instruction, part of it will contain the memory address of the next instruction to execute once the branch condition is satisfied.

- Fetch the operands, if any.

- Execute the operation if it is an ALU operation.

- Store the result (in a register or in memory), if there is one.

- Update the program counter to hold the next instruction location, which is either the next memory location or the address specified by a branch instruction.

At the end of these steps the cycle is ready to repeat, and it continues until a special halt instruction stops execution.

Steps of this cycle and all internal CPU operations are regulated by a clock that oscillates at a high frequency (now typically measured in gigahertz, or billions of cycles per second). Another factor that affects performance is the "word" size—the number of bits that are fetched at once from memory and on which CPU instructions operate. Digital words now consist of 32 or 64 bits, though sizes from 8 to 128 bits are seen.

Processing instructions one at a time, or serially, often creates a bottleneck because many program instructions may be ready and waiting for execution. Since the early 1980s, CPU design has followed a style originally called reduced-instruction-set computing (RISC). This design minimizes the transfer of data between memory and CPU (all ALU operations are done only on data in CPU registers) and calls for simple instructions that can execute very quickly. As the number of transistors on a chip has grown, the RISC design requires a relatively small portion of the CPU chip to be devoted to the basic instruction set. The remainder of the chip can then be used to speed CPU operations by providing circuits that let several instructions execute simultaneously, or in parallel.

There are two major kinds of instruction-level parallelism (ILP) in the CPU, both first used in early supercomputers. One is the pipeline, which allows the fetch-decode-execute cycle to have several instructions under way at once. While one instruction is being executed, another can obtain its operands, a third can be decoded, and a fourth can be fetched from memory. If each of these operations requires the same time, a new instruction can enter the pipeline at each phase and (for example) five instructions can be completed in the time that it would take to complete one without a pipeline. The other sort of ILP is to have multiple execution units in the CPU—duplicate arithmetic circuits, in particular, as well as specialized circuits for graphics instructions or for floating-point calculations (arithmetic operations involving non-integer numbers, such as 3.27). With this "superscalar" design, several instructions can execute at once.

Both forms of ILP face complications. A branch instruction might render preloaded instructions in the pipeline useless if they entered it before the branch jumped to a new part of the program. Also, superscalar execution must determine whether an arithmetic operation depends on the result of another operation, since they cannot be executed simultaneously. CPUs now have additional circuits to predict whether a branch will be taken and to analyze instructional dependencies. These have become highly sophisticated and can frequently rearrange instructions to execute more of them in parallel.

Main Memory

The earliest forms of computer main memory were mercury delay lines, which were tubes of mercury that stored data as ultrasonic waves, and cathode-ray tubes, which stored data as charges on the tubes' screens. The magnetic drum, invented about 1948, used an iron oxide coating on a rotating drum to store data and programs as magnetic patterns.

In a binary computer any bistable device (something that can be placed in either of two states) can represent the two possible bit values of 0 and 1 and can thus serve as computer memory. Magnetic-core memory, the first relatively cheap RAM device, appeared in 1952. It was composed of tiny, doughnut-shaped ferrite magnets threaded on the intersection points of a two-dimensional wire grid. These wires carried currents to change the direction of each core's magnetization, while a third wire threaded through the doughnut detected its magnetic orientation.

The first integrated circuit (IC) memory chip appeared in 1971. IC memory stores a bit in a transistor-capacitor combination. The capacitor holds a charge to represent a 1 and no charge for a 0; the transistor switches it between these two states. Because a capacitor charge gradually decays, IC memory is dynamic RAM (DRAM), which must have its stored values refreshed periodically (every 20 milliseconds or so). There is also static RAM (SRAM), which does not have to be refreshed. Although faster than DRAM, SRAM uses more transistors and is thus more costly; it is used primarily for CPU internal registers and cache memory.

In addition to main memory, computers generally have special video memory (VRAM) to hold graphical images, called bitmaps, for the computer display. This memory is often dual-ported—a new image can be stored in it at the same time that its current data is being read and displayed.

It takes time to specify an address in a memory chip, and, since memory is slower than a CPU, there is an advantage to memory that can transfer a series of words rapidly once the first address is specified. One such design is known as synchronous DRAM (SDRAM), which became widely used by 2001.

Nonetheless, data transfer through the "bus"—the set of a wire that connect the CPU to memory and peripheral devices—is a bottleneck. For that reason, CPU chips now contain cache memory—a small amount of fast SRAM. The cache holds copies of data from blocks of main memory. A well-designed cache allows up to 85–90 percent of memory references to be done from it in typical programs, giving a several-fold speedup in data access.

The time between two memories reads or writes (cycle time) was about 17 microseconds (millionths of a second) for early core memory and about 1 microsecond for core in the early 1970s. The first DRAM had a cycle time of about half a microsecond, or 500 nanoseconds (billionths of a second), and today it is 20 nanoseconds or less. An equally important measure is the cost per bit of memory. The first DRAM stored 128 bytes (1 byte = 8 bits) and cost about $10, or $80,000 per megabyte (millions of bytes). In 2001 DRAM could be purchased for less than $0.25 per megabyte. This vast decline in cost made possible graphical user interfaces (GUIs), the display fonts that word processors use, and the manipulation and visualization of large masses of data by scientific computers.

Secondary Memory

Secondary memory on a computer is storage for data and programs not in use at the moment. In addition to punched cards and paper tape, early computers also used magnetic tape for secondary storage. Tape is cheap, either on large reels or in small cassettes, but has the disadvantage that it must be read or written sequentially from one end to the other.

IBM introduced the first magnetic disk, the RAMAC, in 1955; it held 5 megabytes and rented for $3,200 per month. Magnetic disks are platters coated with iron oxide, like tape and drums. An arm with a tiny wire coil, the read/write (R/W) head, moves radially over the disk, which is divided into concentric tracks composed of small arcs, or sectors, of data. Magnetized regions of the disk generate small currents in the coil as it passes, thereby allowing it to "read" a sector; similarly, a small current in the coil will induce a local magnetic change in the disk, thereby "writing" to a sector. The disk rotates rapidly (up to 15,000 rotations per minute), and so the R/W head can rapidly reach any sector on the disk.

Early disks had large removable platters. In the 1970s IBM introduced sealed disks with fixed platters known as Winchester disks—perhaps because the first ones had two 30-megabyte platters, suggesting the Winchester 30-30 rifle. Not only was the sealed disk protected against dirt, the R/W head could also "fly" on a thin air film, very close to the platter. By putting the head closer to the platter, the region of oxide film that represented a single bit could be much smaller, thus increasing storage capacity. This basic technology is still used.

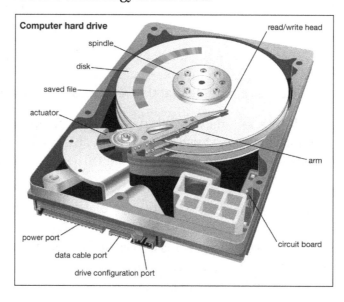

Refinements have included putting multiple platters—10 or more—in a single disk drive, with a pair of R/W heads for the two surfaces of each platter in order to increase storage and data transfer rates. Even greater gains have resulted from improving control of the radial motion of the disk arm from track to track, resulting in denser distribution of data on the disk. By 2002 such densities had reached over 8,000 tracks per centimetre (20,000 tracks per inch), and a platter the diameter of a coin could hold over a gigabyte of data. In 2002 an 80-gigabyte disk cost about $200—only one ten-millionth of the 1955 cost and representing an annual decline of nearly 30 percent, similar to the decline in the price of main memory.

Optical storage devices—CD-ROM (compact disc, read-only memory) and DVD-ROM (digital videodisc, or versatile disc)—appeared in the mid-1980s and '90s. They both represent bits as tiny pits in plastic, organized in a long spiral like a phonograph record, written and read with lasers. A CD-ROM can hold 2 gigabytes of data, but the inclusion of error-correcting codes (to correct for dust, small defects, and scratches) reduces the usable data to 650 megabytes. DVDs are denser, have smaller pits, and can hold 17 gigabytes with error correction.

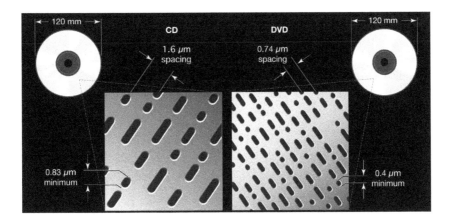

Figure shows the DVD player uses a laser that is higher-powered and has a correspondingly finer focus point than that of the CD player. This enables it to resolve shorter pits and narrower separation tracks and thereby accounts for the DVD's greater storage capacity.

Optical storage devices are slower than magnetic disks, but they are well suited for making master copies of software or for multimedia (audio and video) files that are read sequentially. There are also writable and rewritable CD-ROMs (CD-R and CD-RW) and DVD-ROMs (DVD-R and DVD-RW) that can be used like magnetic tapes for inexpensive archiving and sharing of data.

The decreasing cost of memory continues to make new uses possible. A DVD can hold a feature-length motion picture. Nevertheless, even larger and faster storage systems, such as three-dimensional optical media, are being developed for handling data for computer simulations of nuclear reactions, astronomical data, and medical data, including X-ray images. Such applications typically require many terabytes (1 terabyte = 1,000 gigabytes) of storage, which can lead to further complications in indexing and retrieval.

Peripherals

Computer peripherals are devices used to input information and instructions into a computer for storage or processing and to output the processed data. In addition, devices that enable the transmission and reception of data between computers are often classified as peripherals.

Input Devices

A plethora of devices falls into the category of input peripheral. Typical examples include keyboards, mice, trackballs, pointing sticks, joysticks, digital tablets, touch pads, and scanners.

Keyboards contain mechanical or electromechanical switches that change the flow of current through the keyboard when depressed. A microprocessor embedded in the keyboard interprets these changes and sends a signal to the computer. In addition to letter and number keys, most keyboards also include "function" and "control" keys that modify input or send special commands to the computer.

Mechanical mice and trackballs operate alike, using a rubber or rubber-coated ball that turns two shafts connected to a pair of encoders that measure the horizontal and vertical components of a user's movement, which are then translated into cursor movement on a computer monitor.

Optical mice employ a light beam and camera lens to translate motion of the mouse into cursor movement.

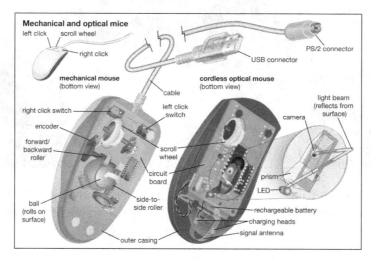

Pointing sticks, which are popular on many laptop systems, employ a technique that uses a pressure-sensitive resistor. As a user applies pressure to the stick, the resistor increases the flow of electricity, thereby signaling that movement has taken place. Most joysticks operate in a similar manner.

Digital tablets and touch pads are similar in purpose and functionality. In both cases, input is taken from a flat pad that contains electrical sensors that detect the presence of either a special tablet pen or a user's finger, respectively.

A scanner is somewhat akin to a photocopier. A light source illuminates the object to be scanned, and the varying amounts of reflected light are captured and measured by an analog-to-digital converter attached to light-sensitive diodes. The diodes generate a pattern of binary digits that are stored in the computer as a graphical image.

Output Devices

Printers are a common example of output devices. New multifunction peripherals that integrate printing, scanning, and copying into a single device are also popular. Computer monitors are sometimes treated as peripherals. High-fidelity sound systems are another example of output devices often classified as computer peripherals. Manufacturers have announced devices that provide tactile feedback to the user—"force feedback" joysticks, for example. This highlights the complexity of classifying peripherals—a joystick with force feedback is truly both an input and an output peripheral.

Early printers often used a process known as impact printing, in which a small number of pins were driven into a desired pattern by an electromagnetic printhead. As each pin was driven forward, it struck an inked ribbon and transferred a single dot the size of the pinhead to the paper. Multiple dots combined into a matrix to form characters and graphics, hence the name dot matrix. Another early print technology, daisy-wheel printers, made impressions of whole characters with a single blow of an electromagnetic printhead, similar to an electric typewriter. Laser printers have replaced such printers in most commercial settings. Laser printers employ a focused beam of light to etch patterns of positively charged particles on the surface of a cylindrical drum made of negatively charged organic, photosensitive material. As the drum rotates, negatively charged toner particles adhere to the patterns etched by the laser and are transferred to the paper. Another, less expensive printing technology developed for the home and small businesses is inkjet printing. The majority of inkjet printers operate by ejecting extremely tiny droplets of ink to form characters in a matrix of dots—much like dot matrix printers.

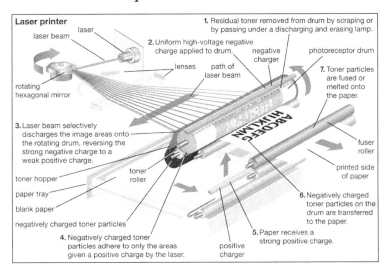

Computer display devices have been in use almost as long as computers themselves. Early computer displays employed the same cathode-ray tubes (CRTs) used in television and radar systems. The fundamental principle behind CRT displays is the emission of a controlled stream of electrons that strike light-emitting phosphors coating the inside of the screen. The screen itself is divided into multiple scan lines, each of which contains a number of pixels—the rough equivalent of dots in a dot matrix printer. The resolution of a monitor is determined by its pixel size. More recent liquid crystal displays (LCDs) rely on liquid crystal cells that realign incoming polarized light. The realigned beams pass through a filter that permits only those beams with a particular alignment to pass. By controlling the liquid crystal cells with electrical charges, various colours or shades are made to appear on the screen.

Communication Devices

The most familiar example of a communication device is the common telephone modem (from modulator/demodulator). Modems modulate, or transform, a computer's digital message into an analog signal for transmission over standard telephone networks, and they demodulate the analog signal back into a digital message on reception. In practice, telephone network components limit analog data transmission to about 48 kilobits per second. Standard cable modems operate in a similar manner over cable television networks, which have a total transmission capacity of 30 to 40 megabits per second over each local neighbourhood "loop." (Like Ethernet cards, cable modems are actually local area network devices, rather than true modems, and transmission performance deteriorates as more users share the loop.) Asymmetric digital subscriber line (ADSL) modems can be used for transmitting digital signals over a local dedicated telephone line, provided there is a telephone office nearby—in theory, within 5,500 metres (18,000 feet) but in practice about a third of that distance. ADSL is asymmetric because transmission rates differ to and from the subscriber: 8 megabits per second "downstream" to the subscriber and 1.5 megabits per second "upstream" from the subscriber to the service provider. In addition to devices for transmitting over telephone and cable wires, wireless communication devices exist for transmitting infrared, radio wave, and microwave signals.

Peripheral Interfaces

A variety of techniques have been employed in the design of interfaces to link computers and peripherals. An interface of this nature is often termed a bus. This nomenclature derives from the presence of many paths of electrical communication (e.g., wires) bundled or joined together in a single device. Multiple peripherals can be attached to a single bus—the peripherals need not be homogeneous. An example is the small computer systems interface (SCSI; pronounced "scuzzy"). This popular standard allows heterogeneous devices to communicate with a computer by sharing a single bus. Under the auspices of various national and international organizations, many such standards have been established by manufacturers and users of computers and peripherals.

Buses can be loosely classified as serial or parallel. Parallel buses have a relatively large number of wires bundled together that enable data to be transferred in parallel. This increases the throughput, or rate of data transfer, between the peripheral and computer. SCSI buses are parallel buses. Examples of serial buses include the universal serial bus (USB). USB has an interesting feature in that the bus carries not only data to and from the peripheral but also electrical power. Examples of other peripheral integration schemes include integrated drive electronics (IDE) and enhanced integrated drive electronics (EIDE). Predating USB, these two schemes were designed initially to support greater flexibility in adapting hard disk drives to a variety of different computer makers.

Microprocessor Integrated Circuits

Before integrated circuits (ICs) were invented, computers used circuits of individual transistors and other electrical components—resistors, capacitors, and diodes—soldered to a circuit board. In 1959 Jack Kilby at Texas Instruments Incorporated, and Robert Noyce at Fairchild Semiconductor Corporation filed patents for integrated circuits. Kilby found how to make all the circuit components out of germanium, the semiconductor material then commonly used for transistors. Noyce used silicon, which is now almost universal, and found a way to build the interconnecting wires as well as the components on a single silicon chip, thus eliminating all soldered connections except for those joining the IC to other components.

Design

Today IC design starts with a circuit description written in a hardware-specification language (like a programming language) or specified graphically with a digital design program. Computer simulation programs then test the design before it is approved. Another program translates the basic circuit layout into a multilayer network of electronic elements and wires.

Fabrication

The IC itself is formed on a silicon wafer cut from a cylinder of pure silicon—now commonly 200–300 mm (8–12 inches) in diameter. Since more chips can be cut from a larger wafer, the material unit cost of a chip goes down with increasing wafer size. A photographic image of each layer of the circuit design is made, and photolithography is used to expose a corresponding circuit of "resist" that has been put on the wafer. The unwanted resist is washed off and the exposed material then etched. This process is repeated to form various layers, with silicon dioxide (glass) used as electrical insulation between layers.

Between these production stages, the silicon is doped with carefully controlled amounts of impurities such as arsenic and boron. These create an excess and a deficiency, respectively, of electrons, thus creating regions with extra available negative charges (n-type) and positive "holes" (p-type). These adjacent doped regions form p-n junction transistors, with electrons (in the n-type regions) and holes (in the p-type regions) migrating through the silicon conducting electricity.

Layers of metal or conducting polycrystalline silicon are also placed on the chip to provide interconnections between its transistors. When the fabrication is complete, a final layer of insulating glass is added, and the wafer is sawed into individual chips. Each chip is tested, and those that pass are mounted in a protective package with external contacts.

Transistor Size

The size of transistor elements continually decreases in order to pack more on a chip. In 2001 a transistor commonly had dimensions of 0.25 micron (or micrometre; 1 micron = $10{-}6$ metre), and 0.1 micron was projected for 2006. This latter size would allow 200 million transistors to be placed on a chip (rather than about 40 million in 2001). Because the wavelength of visible light is too great for adequate resolution at such a small scale, ultraviolet photolithography techniques are being developed. As sizes decrease further, electron beam or X-ray techniques will become necessary. Each such advance requires new fabrication plants, costing several billion dollars apiece.

Power Consumption

The increasing speed and density of elements on chips have led to problems of power consumption and dissipation. Central processing units now typically dissipate about 50 watts of power—as much heat per square inch as an electric stove element generates—and require "heat sinks" and cooling fans or even water cooling systems. As CPU speeds increase, cryogenic cooling systems may become necessary. Because storage battery technologies have not kept pace with power consumption in portable devices, there has been renewed interest in gallium arsenide (GaAs) chips. GaAs chips can run at higher speeds and consume less power than silicon chips. (GaAs chips are also more resistant to radiation, a factor in military and space applications.) Although GaAs chips have been used in supercomputers for their speed, the brittleness of GaAs has made it too costly for most ordinary applications. One promising idea is to bond a GaAs layer to a silicon substrate for easier handling. Nevertheless, GaAs is not yet in common use except in some high-frequency communication systems.

Operating Systems

Role of Operating Systems

Operating systems manage a computer's resources—memory, peripheral devices, and even CPU access—and provide a battery of services to the user's programs. UNIX, first developed for minicomputers and now widely used on both PCs and mainframes, is one example; Linux (a version of UNIX), Microsoft Corporation's Windows XP, and Apple Computer's OS X are others.

One may think of an operating system as a set of concentric shells. At the centre is the bare processor, surrounded by layers of operating system routines to manage input/output (I/O), memory access, multiple processes, and communication among processes. User programs are located in the outermost layers. Each layer insulates its inner layer from direct access, while providing services to its outer layer. This architecture frees outer layers from having to know all the details of lower-level operations, while protecting inner layers and their essential services from interference.

Early computers had no operating system. A user loaded a program from paper tape by employing switches to specify its memory address, to start loading, and to run the program. When the program finished, the computer halted. The programmer had to have knowledge of every computer detail, such as how much memory it had and the characteristics of I/O devices used by the program.

It was quickly realized that this was an inefficient use of resources, particularly as the CPU was largely idle while waiting for relatively slow I/O devices to finish tasks such as reading and writing data. If instead several programs could be loaded at once and coordinated to interleave their steps of computation and I/O, more work could be done. The earliest operating systems were small supervisor programs that did just that: they coordinated several programs, accepting commands from the operator, and provided them all with basic I/O operations. These were known as multi-programmed systems.

A multi-programmed system must schedule its programs according to some priority rule, such as "shortest jobs first." It must protect them from mutual interference to prevent an addressing error in a program from corrupting the data or code of another. It must ensure noninterference during I/O so that output from several programs does not get commingled or input misdirected. It might also have to record the CPU time of each job for billing purposes.

Modern Types of Operating Systems

Multiuser Systems

An extension of multiprogramming systems was developed in the 1960s, known variously as multiuser or time-sharing systems. Time-sharing allows many people to interact with a computer at once, each getting a small portion of the CPU's time. If the CPU is fast enough, it will appear to be dedicated to each user, particularly as a computer can perform many functions while waiting for each user to finish typing the latest commands.

Multiuser operating systems employ a technique known as multi-processing, or multitasking (as do most single-user systems today), in which even a single program may consist of many separate computational activities, called processes. The system must keep track of active and queued processes, when each process must access secondary memory to retrieve and store its code and data, and the allocation of other resources, such as peripheral devices.

Since main memory was very limited, early operating systems had to be as small as possible to leave room for other programs. To overcome some of this limitation, operating systems use virtual memory, one of many computing techniques developed during the late 1950s under the direction of Tom Kilburn at the University of Manchester, England. Virtual memory gives each process a large address space (memory that it may use), often much larger than the actual main memory. This address space resides in secondary memory (such as tape or disks), from which portions are copied into main memory as needed, updated as necessary, and returned when a process is no longer active. Even with virtual memory, however, some "kernel" of the operating system has to remain in main memory. Early UNIX kernels occupied tens of kilobytes; today they occupy more than a megabyte, and PC operating systems are comparable, largely because of the declining cost of main memory.

Operating systems have to maintain virtual memory tables to keep track of where each process's address space resides, and modern CPUs provide special registers to make this more efficient. Indeed, much of an operating system consists of tables: tables of processes, of files and their locations (directories), of resources used by each process, and so on. There are also tables of user accounts and passwords that help control access to the user's files and protect them against accidental or malicious interference.

Thin Systems

While minimizing the memory requirements of operating systems for standard computers has been important, it has been absolutely essential for small, inexpensive, specialized devices such as personal digital assistants (PDAs), "smart" cellular telephones, portable devices for listening to compressed music files, and Internet kiosks. Such devices must be highly reliable, fast, and secure against break-ins or corruption—a cellular telephone that "freezes" in the middle of calls would not be tolerated. One might argue that these traits should characterize any operating system, but PC users seem to have become quite tolerant of frequent operating system failures that require restarts.

Reactive Systems

Still more limited are embedded, or real-time, systems. These are small systems that run the control processors embedded in machinery from factory production lines to home appliances. They interact with their environment, taking in data from sensors and making appropriate responses. Embedded systems are known as "hard" real-time systems if they must guarantee schedules that handle all events even in a worst case and "soft" if missed deadlines are not fatal. An aircraft control system is a hard real-time system, as a single flight error might be fatal. An airline reservation system, on the other hand, is a soft real-time system, since a missed booking is rarely catastrophic.

Many of the features of modern CPUs and operating systems are inappropriate for hard real-time systems. For example, pipelines and superscalar multiple execution units give high performance at the expense of occasional delays when a branch prediction fails and a pipeline is filled with unneeded instructions. Likewise, virtual memory and caches give good memory-access times on the average, but sometimes they are slow. Such variability is inimical to meeting demanding real-time schedules, and so embedded processors and their operating systems must generally be relatively simple.

Operating System Design Approaches

Operating systems may be proprietary or open. Mainframe systems have largely been proprietary, supplied by the computer manufacturer. In the PC domain, Microsoft offers its proprietary Windows systems, Apple has supplied Mac OS for its line of Macintosh computers, and there are few other choices. The best-known open system has been UNIX, originally developed by Bell Laboratories and supplied freely to universities. In its Linux variant it is available for a wide range of PCs, workstations, and, most recently, IBM mainframes.

Open-source software is copyrighted, but its author grants free use, often including the right to modify it provided that use of the new version is not restricted. Linux is protected by the Free Software Foundation's "GNU General Public License," like all the other software in the extensive GNU project, and this protection permits users to modify Linux and even to sell copies, provided that this right of free use is preserved in the copies.

One consequence of the right of free use is that numerous authors have contributed to the GNU-Linux work, adding many valuable components to the basic system. Although quality control is managed voluntarily and some have predicted that Linux would not survive heavy commercial use, it has been remarkably successful and seems well on its way to becoming the version of UNIX on mainframes and on PCs used as Internet servers.

There are other variants of the UNIX system; some are proprietary, though most are now freely used, at least non-commercially. They all provide some type of graphical user interface. Although Mac OS has been proprietary, its current version, Mac OS X, is built on UNIX.

Proprietary systems such as Microsoft's Windows 98, 2000, and XP provide highly integrated systems. All operating systems provide file directory services, for example, but a Microsoft system might use the same window display for a directory as for a World Wide Web browser. Such an integrated approach makes it more difficult for nonproprietary software to use Windows capabilities, a feature that has been an issue in antitrust lawsuits against Microsoft.

Networking

Computer communication may occur through wires, optical fibres, or radio transmissions. Wired networks may use shielded coaxial cable, similar to the wire connecting a television to a videocassette recorder or an antenna. They can also use simpler unshielded wiring with modular connectors similar to telephone wires. Optical fibres can carry more signals than wires; they are often used for linking buildings on a college campus or corporate site and increasingly for longer distances as telephone companies update their networks. Microwave radio also carries computer network signals, generally as part of long-distance telephone systems. Low-power microwave radio is becoming common for wireless networks within a building.

Local Area Networks

Local area networks (LANs) connect computers within a building or small group of buildings. A LAN may be configured as (1) a bus, a main channel to which nodes or secondary channels are connected in a branching structure, (2) a ring, in which each computer is connected to two neighbouring computers to form a closed circuit, or (3) a star, in which each computer is linked directly to a central computer and only indirectly to one another. Each of these has advantages, though the bus configuration has become the most common.

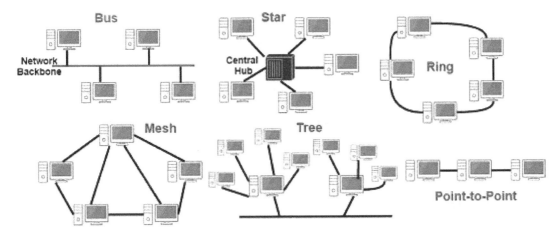

Figure shows simple bus networks, such as Ethernet, are common for home and small office configurations. The most common ring network is IBM's Token Ring, which employs a "token" that is passed around the network to control which location has sending privileges. Star networks are common in larger commercial networks since a malfunction at any node generally does not disrupt the entire network.

Even if only two computers are connected, they must follow rules, or protocols, to communicate. For example, one might signal "ready to send" and wait for the other to signal "ready to receive." When many computers share a network, the protocol might include a rule "talk only when it is your turn" or "do not talk when anyone else is talking." Protocols must also be designed to handle network errors.

The most common LAN design since the mid-1970s has been the bus-connected Ethernet, originally developed at Xerox PARC. Every computer or other device on an Ethernet has a unique 48-bit address. Any computer that wants to transmit listens for a carrier signal that indicates that a transmission is under way. If it detects none, it starts transmitting, sending the address of the recipient at the start of its transmission. Every system on the network receives each message but ignores those not addressed to it. While a system is transmitting, it also listens, and if it detects a simultaneous transmission, it stops, waits for a random time, and retries. The random time delay before retrying reduces the probability that they will collide again. This scheme is known as carrier sense multiple accesses with collision detection (CSMA/CD). It works very well until a network is moderately heavily loaded, and then it degrades as collisions become more frequent.

The first Ethernet had a capacity of about 2 megabits per second, and today 10- and 100-megabit-per-second Ethernet is common, with gigabit-per-second Ethernet also in use. Ethernet transceivers (transmitter-receivers) for PCs are inexpensive and easily installed.

A recent standard for wireless Ethernet, known as Wi-Fi, is becoming common for small office and home networks. Using frequencies from 2.4 to 5 gigahertz (GHz), such networks can transfer data at rates up to 600 megabits per second. Early in 2002 another Ethernet-like standard was released. Known as HomePlug, the first version could transmit data at about 8 megabits per second through a building's existing electrical power infrastructure. A later version could achieve rates of 1 gigabit per second.

Wide Area Networks

Wide area networks (WANs) span cities, countries, and the globe, generally using telephone lines and satellite links. The Internet connects multiple WANs; as its name suggests, it is a network of networks. Its success stems from early support by the U.S. Department of Defense, which developed its precursor, ARPANET, to let researchers communicate readily and share computer resources. Its success is also due to its flexible communication technique. The emergence of the Internet in the 1990s as not only a communication medium but also one of the principal focuses of computer use may be the most significant development in computing in the past several decades.

Computer Software

Software denotes programs that run on computers. John Tukey, a statistician at Princeton University and Bell Laboratories, is generally credited with introducing the term in 1958 (as well as coining the word bit for binary digit). Initially software referred primarily to what is now called system software—an operating system and the utility programs that come with it, such as those to compile (translate) programs into machine code and load them for execution. This software came with a computer when it was bought or leased. In 1969 IBM decided to "unbundle" its software and sell it separately, and software soon became a major income source for manufacturers as well as for dedicated software firms.

Business and Personal Software

Business software generally must handle large amounts of data but relatively little computation, although that has changed somewhat in recent years. Office software typically includes word processors, spreadsheets, database programs, and tools for designing public presentations.

A spreadsheet is a type of accounting program. Unlike specialized accounting programs (e.g., payroll and office records), an important function of spreadsheets is their ability to explore "What if?" scenarios. A spreadsheet not only holds tables of data but also defines relationships among their rows and columns. For example, if the profit on a product is defined in terms of various costs—materials, manufacturing, and shipping—it is easy to ask "What if we use cheaper materials that require more manufacturing expense."

A database is an organized collection of data, or records. Databases organize information to answer questions such as "What companies in the Southwest bought more than 100 of our products last year?" or "Which products made by Acme Manufacturing are in low supply?" Such software is often integrated so that a database report or spreadsheet table can be added to a document composed with a word processor, frequently with illustrative graphs. Today even the most trivial data can effortlessly be glorified by presenting it in a polychromatic bar chart with three-dimensional shading.

Scientific and Engineering Software

Scientific software is typically used to solve differential equations. (Differential equations are used to describe continuous actions or processes that depend on some other factors.) Although some differential equations have relatively simple mathematical solutions, exact solutions of many differential equations are very difficult to obtain. Computers, however, can be used to obtain useful approximate solutions, particularly when a problem is split into simpler spatial or temporal parts. Nevertheless, large-scale problems often require parallel computation on supercomputers or clusters of small computers that share the work.

There are numerous standard libraries of equation-solving software—some commercial, some distributed by national organizations in several countries. Another kind of software package does symbolic mathematics, obtaining exact solutions by algebraic manipulations. Two of the most widely used symbolic packages are Mathematica and Maple.

Scientific visualization software couples high-performance graphics with the output of equation solvers to yield vivid displays of models of physical systems. As with spreadsheets, visualization software lets an experimenter vary initial conditions or parameters. Observing the effect of such changes can help in improving models, as well as in understanding the original system.

Visualization is an essential feature of computer-aided engineering (CAE) and computer-aided design (CAD). An engineer can design a bridge, use modeling software to display it, and study it under different loads. CAE software can translate drawings into the precise specification of the parts of a mechanical system. Computer chips themselves are designed with CAD programs that let an engineer write a specification for part of a chip, simulate its behaviour in detail, test it thoroughly, and then generate the layouts for the photolithographic process that puts the circuit on the silicon.

Astronomical sky surveys, weather forecasting, and medical imaging—such as magnetic resonance imaging, CAT scans, and DNA analyses—create very large collections of data. Scientific computation today uses the same kinds of powerful statistical and pattern-analysis techniques as many business applications.

Internet and Collaborative Software

Among the most commonly used personal Internet software are "browsers" for displaying information located on the World Wide Web, newsreaders for reading "newsgroups" located on USENET, file-sharing programs for downloading files, and communication software for e-mail, as well as "instant messaging" and "chat room" programs that allow people to carry on conversations in real time. All of these applications are used for both personal and business activities.

Other common Internet software includes Web search engines and "Web-crawling" programs that traverse the Web to gather and classify information. Web-crawling programs are a kind of agent software, a term for programs that carry out routine tasks for a user. They stem from artificial intelligence research and carry out some of the tasks of librarians, but they are at a severe disadvantage. Although Web pages may have "content-tag" index terms, not all do, nor are there yet accepted standards for their use. Web search engines must use heuristic methods to determine the quality of Web page information as well as its content. Many details are proprietary, but they may use techniques such as finding "hubs" and "authorities" (pages with many links to and from other Web sites). Such strategies can be very effective, though the need for a Web version of card catalogs has not vanished.

A different kind of Internet use depends on the vast number of computers connected to the Internet that are idle much of the time. Rather than run a "screen-saver" program, these computers can run software that lets them collaborate in the analysis of some difficult problem. Two examples are the SETI@home project, which distributes portions of radio telescope data for analysis that might help in the search for extraterrestrial intelligence (SETI), and the "Great Internet Mersenne Prime Search" (GIMPS), which parcels out tasks to test for large prime numbers.

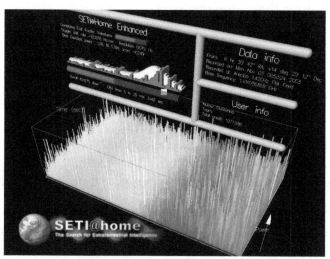

Screen shot of the SETI@home page

The Internet has also become a business tool, and the ability to collect and store immense amounts of information has given rise to data warehousing and data mining. The former is a term for unstructured collections of data and the latter a term for its analysis. Data mining uses statistics and other mathematical tools to find patterns of information.

Games and Entertainment

Computer games are nearly as old as digital computers and have steadily developed in sophistication. Chinook, a recent checkers (draughts) program, is widely believed to be better than any human player, and the IBM Deep Blue chess program beat world champion Garry Kasparov in 1996. These programs have demonstrated the power of modern computers, as well as the strength of good heuristics for strategy. On the other hand, such brute-force search heuristics have failed to produce a go-playing program that can defeat even moderately skilled players because there are too many possible moves in this Japanese game for simple quantification.

After board games, the earliest computer games were text-based adventures—in which players explored virtual worlds, sought treasure, and fought enemies by reading and typing simple commands. Such games resembled military simulation programs first used in the early 1950s. Contemporary games, however, depend on high-performance computer graphics. Played on arcade machines, special game computers for home use, or PCs, they use the same capabilities as simulation and visualization programs. A related area is computer-generated (CG) animation for films and video.

Computer Architecture

Computer architecture deals with the logical and physical design of a computer system. The *Instruction Set Architecture* (ISA) defines the set of machine-code instructions that the computer's central processing unit can execute. The *microarchitecture* describes the design features and circuitry of the central processing unit itself. The *system architecture* determines the main hardware components that make up the physical computer system and the way in which they are interconnected. The main components required for a computer system are listed below:

- Central processing unit (CPU).

- Random access memory (RAM).

- Read-only memory (ROM).

- Input / output (I/O) ports.

- The system bus.

- A power supply unit (PSU).

In addition to these core components, in order to extend the functionality of the system and to provide a computing environment with which a human operator can more easily interact, additional components are required. These could include:

- Secondary storage devices (e.g. disk drives).

- Input devices (e.g. keyboard, mouse, scanner).

- Output devices (e.g. display adapter, monitor, printer).

A distinction is usually made between the *internal* components of the system (those normally located inside the main enclosure or *case*) and the *external* components (those that connect to the internal components via an external interface. Examples of such external components usually referred to as *peripherals*, include the keyboard, video display unit (monitor) and mouse. Other peripherals can include printers, scanners, external speakers, external disk drives and webcams, to name but a few. The Internal components usually (though not always) include one or more disk drives for fixed or removable storage media (magnetic disk or tape, optical media etc.) although the core computing function does not absolutely require them. The relationship between the elements that make up the core of the system is illustrated below.

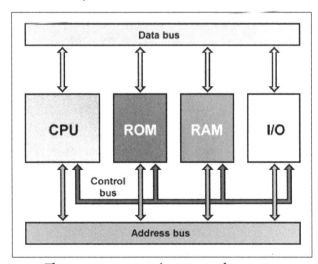

The core components in a personal computer

The core system components are mounted on a *backplane*, more commonly referred to as a *mainboard* (or *motherboard*). The mainboard is a relatively large printed circuit board that provides the electronic channels (buses) that carry data and control signals between the various components, as well as the necessary interfaces (in the form of slots or sockets) to allow the CPU, Memory cards and other components to be plugged into the system. In most cases, the ROM chip is built in to the mainboard, and the CPU and RAM must be compatible with the mainboard in terms of their physical format and electronic configuration. Internal I/O ports are provided on the mainboard for devices such as internal disk drives and optical drives.

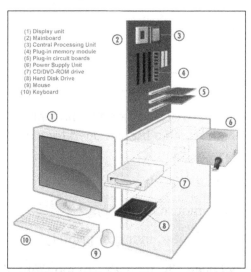

(1) Display unit
(2) Mainboard
(3) Central Processing Unit
(4) Plug-in memory module
(5) Plug-in circuit boards
(6) Power Supply Unit
(7) CD/DVD-ROM drive
(8) Hard Disk Drive
(9) Mouse
(10) Keyboard

Exploded view of personal computer system

External I/O ports are also provided on the mainboard to enable the system to be connected to external peripheral devices such as the keyboard, mouse, video display unit, and audio speakers. Both the video adaptor and audio card may be provided "on-board" (i.e. built in to the mainboard), or as separate plug-in circuit boards that are mounted in an appropriate slot on the mainboard. The main board also provides much of the control circuitry required by the various system components, allowing the CPU to concentrate on its main role, which is to execute programs.

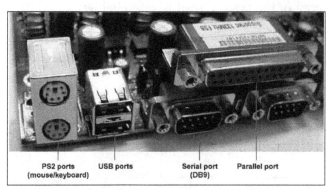

PS2 ports   USB ports   Serial port   Parallel port
(mouse/keyboard)   (DB9)

Some of the external I/O ports found on a typical IBM PC

The Von Neumann Architecture

A von Neumann architecture machine, designed by physicist and mathematician John von Neumann is a theoretical design for a stored program computer that serves as the basis for almost all modern computers. A von Neumann machine consists of a central processor with an arithmetic/logic unit and a control unit, a memory, mass storage, and input and output.

The von Neumann machine was created by its namesake, John von Neumann, a physicist and mathematician, in 1945, building on the work of Alan Turing. The design was published in a document called "First Draft of a Report on the EDVAC."

The report described the first stored-program computer. Earlier computers, such as the ENIAC, were hard-wired to do one task. If the computer had to perform a different task, it had to be re-wired, which was a tedious process. With a stored-program computer, a general purpose computer could be built to run different programs.

The theoretical design consists of:

- A central processor consisting of a control unit and an arithmetic/logic unit;

- A memory unit;

- Mass storage;

- Input and output.

The von Neumann design thus forms the basis of modern computing. A similar model, the Harvard architecture, had dedicated data address and buses for both reading and writing to memory. The von Neumann architecture won out because it was simpler to implement in real hardware.

The Fetch-Execution Cycle

This is the basic computer operating cycle. The control unit fetches an instruction from the memory and decodes it producing an operations code (op-code).

The op-code is passed to the ALU which receives the data from the memory, executes the instruction and stores the result in memory. The following describes the sequence in more detail.

Fetch Sequence

- The program counter holds the address of the next instruction to be implemented.

- The address held in the program counter is first transferred to the memory address register (MAR) which acts as a buffer holding it until it is ready to access the main memory via the address bus.

- The content of the program counter is incremented by 1 and replaced back into program counter to indicate where the next instruction is located in memory.

- At the same time, the contents of the instruction (op-code and operand) contained in the addressed main memory location specified by the MAR are transferred along the data bus to the memory data register (MDR) which also acts as a buffer.

- Contents of MDR are then transferred to current instruction register.

- Current Instruction register separates instruction into its op-code (add, load, store etc.) and its operand (the data on which it operates).

Execute Sequence

- The instruction register sends its op-code through an instruction decoder to generate its digital instruction code.

- The digital instruction, together with its operand is transferred to ALU which executes the instruction.

- The results stored in temporary accumulator.

Next Instruction

- To store the contents of accumulator in the main memory is a separate task and requires a new instruction which needs a new fetch and execute sequence like the one above to implement it.

Data Transmission

- Parallel Processing: The von Neumann scheme, as in most computers, uses parallel processing for internal data processing. It operates on the data words as a block, transmitting and processing all the bits in the word simultaneously. This speeds up the process but it uses more components to accommodate the parallel data transmission and processing channels adding to the weight and the complexity of the computer. Because of its speed advantage, parallel processing is normally used for internal data processing.

- Serial Processing: Serial processing by contrast uses a single data channel. Words are still stored as a block in registers but the bits can only be transmitted through the communications channel sequentially and processed one bit at a time. This saves on component costs but it severely restricts the processing speed.

    Serial bit transfer is however used for external network connections since, when used over long distances, it is less prone to errors and less costly than parallel transmission.

The Communications Bus

A computer bus is a set of parallel electrical tracks interconnecting the components within the computer. The von Neumann architecture combines signals from three separate buses, the control bus, the address bus, and the data bus which carries both data and instructions, into a single systems bus. All data traffic with the CPU thus takes place across this single internal communications bus.

- The data bus carries data and instructions to and from the main memory. Its width, that is its number of wires, determines the possible word length.

- The width of the address bus determines how many addresses the computer can access. It is unidirectional from CPU to the memory. The CPU generates addresses for storing data in the main memory which it loads onto the address bus as required.

The von Neumann architecture has only one bus which is used for both data transfers and instruction fetches, and therefore, data transfers and instruction fetches must be scheduled - they cannot be performed simultaneously. This is often known as the von Neumann bottleneck.

The Operating System (OS)

Early computers didn't have what we would recognize today as an operating system. They were single user machines with programs from different users being processed sequentially in batches. In response to the need for more efficient use of expensive computing resources, in 1959, operating systems were developed to allow multiple users to access the computer simultaneously. The object of the initial systems was time sharing, but this was soon expanded to allow for the computer's overall resources and capability to be extended with file management and multiple programs, subroutines and input and output devices from which the users could choose.

Operating systems are now essential systems software that manages the computer's hardware and software resources providing common processing, communications, interfacing and security services for computer programs. They are specific to a particular machine type and are not usually accessible to the user.

References

- Computer, technology: britannica.com, retrieved 19 may, 2019

- Architecture, computer-hardware, computing: technologyuk.net, retrieved 28 april, 2019

- Von-neumann-architecture, definition: techopedia.com, retrieved 21 july, 2019

- Computer-architecture: mpoweruk.com, retrieved 7 may, 2019

2

The Central Processing Unit

The central processing unit refers to the electronic circuit within a computer which is responsible for carrying out the varied instructions of a computer program. Some of the components of the central processing unit are the control unit and the arithmetic logic unit. The topics elaborated in this chapter will help in gaining a better perspective about these components of the central processing unit.

The central processing unit (CPU) is the unit which performs most of the processing inside a computer. To control instructions and data flow to and from other parts of the computer, the CPU relies heavily on a chipset, which is a group of microchips located on the motherboard.

The CPU has two components:

- Control Unit: Extracts instructions from memory and decodes and executes them.

- Arithmetic Logic Unit (ALU): Handles arithmetic and logical operations.

To function properly, the CPU relies on the system clock, memory, secondary storage, and data and address buses.

This term is also known as a central processor, microprocessor or chip. The CPU is the heart and brain of a computer. It receives data input, executes instructions, and processes information. It communicates with input/output (I/O) devices, which send and receive data to and from the CPU. Additionally, the CPU has an internal bus for communication with the internal cache memory, called the backside bus. The main bus for data transfer to and from the CPU, memory, chipset, and AGP socket is called the front-side bus.

The CPU contains internal memory units, which are called registers. These registers contain data, instructions, counters and addresses used in the ALU's information processing.

Some computers utilize two or more processors. These consist of separate physical CPUs located side by side on the same board or on separate boards. Each CPU has an independent interface, separate cache, and individual paths to the system front-side bus. Multiple processors are ideal for intensive parallel tasks requiring multitasking. Multicore CPUs are also common, in which a single chip contains multiple CPUs.

CPU Operations

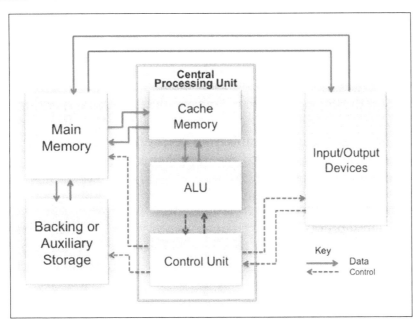

The primary functions of a processor are fetch, decode and execute:

- Fetch: Is the operation which receives instructions from program memory from systems RAM.

- Decode: Is where the instruction is converted to understand which other parts of the CPU are needed to continue the operation. This is performed by the instruction decoder.

- Execute: Is where the operation is performed. Each part of the CPU that is needed is activated to carry out the instructions.

Types

Most processors today are multi-core, which means that the IC contains two or more processors for enhanced performance, reduced power consumption and more efficient simultaneous processing of multiple tasks. Multi-core set-ups are similar to having multiple, separate processors installed in the same computer, but because the processors are actually plugged into the same socket, the connection between them is faster.

Most computers may have up to two-four cores; however, this number can increase up to 12 cores, for example. If a CPU can only process a single set of instructions at one time, then it is considered as a single-core processor. If a CPU can process two sets of instructions at a time it is called a dual-core processor; four sets would be considered a quad-core processor. The more cores, the more instructions at a time a computer can handle.

Some processors use multi-threading, which uses virtualized processor cores. Virtualized processor cores are called vCPUs. These are not as powerful as physical cores but can be used to improve performance in virtual machines (VMs). However, adding unnecessary vCPUs can hurt consolidation ratios, so there should be about four-six vCPUs per physical core.

Control Unit

Control Unit is the part of the computer's central processing unit (CPU), which directs the operation of the processor. It was included as part of the Von Neumann Architecture by John von Neumann. It is the responsibility of the Control Unit to tell the computer's memory, arithmetic/logic unit and input and output devices how to respond to the instructions that have been sent to the processor. It fetches internal instructions of the programs from the main memory to the processor instruction register, and based on this register contents, the control unit generates a control signal that supervises the execution of these instructions.

A control unit works by receiving input information to which it converts into control signals, which are then sent to the central processor. The computer's processor then tells the attached hardware what operations to perform. The functions that a control unit performs are dependent on the type of CPU because the architecture of CPU varies from manufacturer to manufacturer. Examples of devices that require a CU are:

- Control Processing Units(CPUs)

- Graphics Processing Units(GPUs)

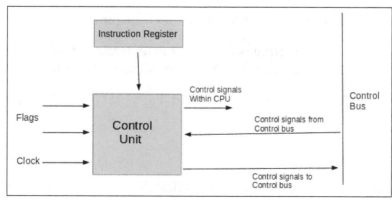

Block Diagram of the Control Unit

Functions of the Control Unit

1. It coordinates the sequence of data movements into, out of, and between a processor's many sub-units.

2. It interprets instructions.

3. It controls data flow inside the processor.

4. It receives external instructions or commands to which it converts to sequence of control signals.

5. It controls many execution units (i.e. ALU, data buffers and registers) contained within a CPU.

6. It also handles multiple tasks, such as fetching, decoding, execution handling and storing results.

Types of Control Unit

There are two types of control units: Hardwired control unit and Micro-programmable control unit.

Hardwired Control Unit

In the Hardwired control unit, the control signals that are important for instruction execution control are generated by specially designed hardware logical circuits, in which we cannot modify the signal generation method without physical change of the circuit structure. The operation code of an instruction contains the basic data for control signal generation. In the instruction decoder, the operation code is decoded. The instruction decoder constitutes a set of many decoders that decode different fields of the instruction opcode.

As a result, few output lines going out from the instruction decoder obtains active signal values. These output lines are connected to the inputs of the matrix that generates control signals for executive units of the computer. These matrixes implements logical combinations of the decoded signals from the instruction opcode with the outputs from the matrix that generates signals representing consecutive control unit states and with signals coming from the outside of the processor, e.g. interrupt signals. The matrices are built in a similar way as a programmable logic arrays.

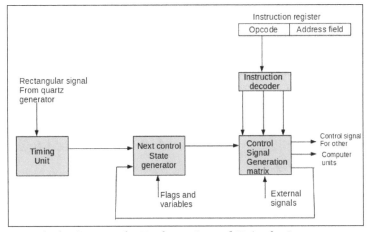

Block Diagram of a Hardware Control Unit of a Computer

Control signals for an instruction execution have to be generated not in a single time point but during the entire time interval that corresponds to the instruction execution cycle. Following the structure of this cycle, the suitable sequence of internal states is organized in the control unit.

A number of signals generated by the control signal generator matrix are sent back to inputs of the next control state generator matrix. This matrix combines these signals with the timing signals, which are generated by the timing unit based on the rectangular patterns usually supplied by the quartz generator. When a new instruction arrives at the control unit, the control units are in the initial state of new instruction fetching. Instruction decoding allows the control unit enters the first state relating execution of the new instruction, which lasts as long as the timing signals and other input signals as flags and state information of the computer remain unaltered. A change of any of the earlier mentioned signals stimulates the change of the control unit state.

This causes that a new respective input is generated for the control signal generator matrix. When an external signal appears, (e.g. an interrupt) the control unit takes entry into a next control state that is the state concerned with the reaction to this external signal (e.g. interrupt processing). The values of flags and state variables of the computer are used to select suitable states for the instruction execution cycle.

The last states in the cycle are control states that commence fetching the next instruction of the program: sending the program counter content to the main memory address buffer register and next, reading the instruction word to the instruction register of computer. When the ongoing instruction is the stop instruction that ends program execution, the control unit enters an operating system state, in which it waits for a next user directive.

Microprogrammable Control Unit

The fundamental difference between these unit structures and the structure of the hardwired control unit is the existence of the control store that is used for storing words containing encoded control signals mandatory for instruction execution.

In microprogrammed control units, subsequent instruction words are fetched into the instruction register in a normal way. However, the operation code of each instruction is not directly decoded to enable immediate control signal generation but it comprises the initial address of a microprogram contained in the control store.

- With a single-level control store: In this, the instruction opcode from the instruction register is sent to the control store address register. Based on this address, the first microinstruction of a microprogram that interprets execution of this instruction is read to the microinstruction register. This microinstruction contains in its operation part encoded control signals, normally as few bit fields. In a set microinstruction field decoders, the fields are decoded. The microinstruction also contains the address of the next microinstruction of the given instruction microprogram and a control field used to control activities of the microinstruction address generator.

The last mentioned field decides the addressing mode (addressing operation) to be applied to the address embedded in the ongoing microinstruction. In microinstructions along with conditional addressing mode, this address is refined by using the processor condition flags that represent the status of computations in the current program. The last microinstruction in the instruction of the given microprogram is the microinstruction that fetches the next instruction from the main memory to the instruction register.

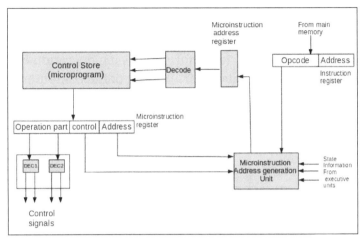

Microprogammed Control Unit with a single level control store

- With a two-level control store: In this, in a control unit with a two-level control store, besides the control memory for microinstructions, a nano-instruction memory is included. In such a control unit, microinstructions do not contain encoded control signals. The operation part of microinstructions contains the address of the word in the nano-instruction memory, which contains encoded control signals. The nano-instruction memory contains all combinations of control signals that appear in microprograms that interpret the complete instruction set of a given computer, written once in the form of nano-instructions.

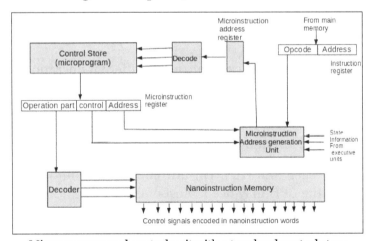

Microprogrammed control unit with a two-level control store

In this way, unnecessary storing of the same operation parts of microinstructions is avoided. In this case, microinstruction word can be much shorter than with the single level control store. It gives a much smaller size in bits of the microinstruction memory and, as a result, a much smaller size of the entire control memory. The microinstruction memory contains the control for selection of consecutive microinstructions, while those control signals are generated at the basis of nano-instructions. In nano-instructions, control signals are frequently encoded using 1 bit/ 1 signal method that eliminate decoding.

Arithmetic Logic Unit

Inside a computer, there is an Arithmetic Logic Unit (ALU), which is capable of performing logical operations (e.g. AND, OR, Ex-OR, Invert etc.) in addition to the arithmetic operations (e.g. Addition, Subtraction etc.). The control unit supplies the data required by the ALU from memory, or from input devices, and directs the ALU to perform a specific operation based on the instruction fetched from the memory. ALU is the "calculator" portion of the computer.

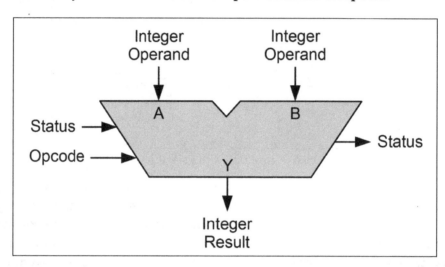

An arithmetic logic unit (ALU) is a major component of the central processing unit of the computer system. It does all processes related to arithmetic and logic operations that need to be done on instruction words. In some microprocessor architectures, the ALU is divided into the arithmetic unit (AU) and the logic unit (LU).

An ALU can be designed by engineers to calculate many different operations. When the operations become more and more complex, then the ALU will also become more and more expensive and also takes up more space in the CPU and dissipates more heat. That is why engineers make the ALU powerful enough to ensure that the CPU is also powerful and fast, but not so complex as to become prohibitive in terms of cost and other disadvantages.

ALU is also known as an Integer Unit (IU). The arithmetic logic unit is that part of the CPU that handles all the calculations the CPU may need. Most of these operations are logical in nature. Depending on how the ALU is designed, it can make the CPU more powerful, but it also consumes more energy and creates more heat. Therefore, there must be a balance between how powerful and complex the ALU is and how expensive the whole unit becomes. This is why faster CPUs are more expensive, consume more power and dissipate more heat.

Different operation as carried out by ALU can be categorized as follows –

- Logical operations: These include operations like AND, OR, NOT, XOR, NOR, NAND, etc.

- Bit-Shifting Operations: This pertains to shifting the positions of the bits by a certain number of places either towards the right or left, which is considered a multiplication or division operations.

- Arithmetic operations: This refers to bit addition and subtraction. Although multiplication and division are sometimes used, these operations are more expensive to make. Multiplication and subtraction can also be done by repetitive additions and subtractions respectively.

The three fundamental attributes of an ALU are its operands and results, functional organization, and algorithms.

Operands and Results

The operands and results of the ALU are machine words of two kinds: *arithmetic words,* which represent numerical values in digital form, and *logic words,* which represent arbitrary sets of digitally encoded symbols. Arithmetic words consist of digit vectors (strings of digits).

- Operator: Operator is arithmetic or logical operation that is performed on the operand given in instructions.

- Flag: ALU uses many types of the flag during processing instructions. All these bits are stored in status or flag registers.

Functional Organization of an ALU

A typical ALU consists of three types of functional parts: storage registers, operations logic, and sequencing logic.

Arithmetic Logical Unit (ALU) Architecture

ALU is formed through the combinational circuit. The combinational circuit used logical gates like AND, OR, NOT, XOR for their construction. The combinational circuit does not have any memory element to store a previous data bit. Adders are the main part of the arithmetic logic unit to perform addition, subtraction by 2's complement.

Control unit generates the selection signals for selecting the function performed by ALU.

Registers: Registers are a very important component in ALU to store instruction, intermediate data, output, and input.

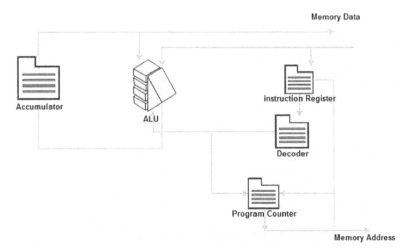

Logic Gates

Logic gates are building a block of ALU. Logic gates are constructed from diode, resistors or transistors. These gates are used in Integrated circuit represent binary input as 'ON' and 'OFF' state. Binary number 0 is represented by 'OFF' and Binary Number '1' is represented by 'ON' state in an integrated circuit.

- OR gate: OR gate can take two or more inputs. The output of OR gate is always 1 if any of the inputs is 1 and 0 if all the inputs are false. OR gate performs an addition operation on all operand given in instructions. It can be expressed as X=A+B or X=A+B+C.

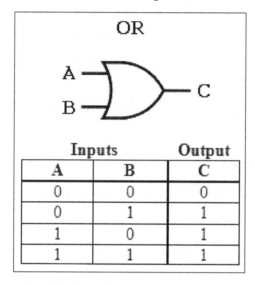

Inputs		Output
A	B	C
0	0	0
0	1	1
1	0	1
1	1	1

- AND gate: AND gate takes two or more inputs. The output of AND gate is 1 if all inputs are 1. AND gate gives 0 results if any one of input in given data is 0. AND gate performs multiplication option on all inputs operands. It is represented by '.' symbol. We can write it as- X=A.B or X=A.B.C.

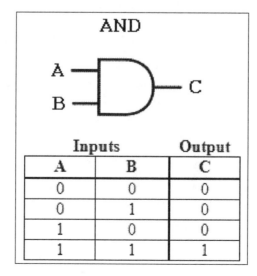

Inputs		Output
A	B	C
0	0	0
0	1	0
1	0	0
1	1	1

- NOT gate: NOT gate is used to reverse the result of gates or reverse Boolean state from 0 to 1 and 1 to 0. NOT gate is also used with 'AND' and 'OR' gate. While using with AND or 'OR' gate, NOT gate is representing an as small circle in front of both gates. After using NOT gate, AND gates convert into NAND or 'OR' gate convert into NOR.

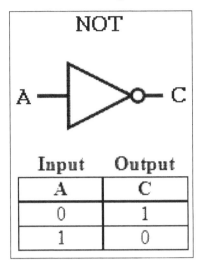

- Registers: Registers provide fast memory access as a comparison to cache, RAM, hard disk. They are built on CPU. Register are small in size. Processing Intermediate data stored in registers. A number of registers used for specific purpose. ALU used four general purpose register. All these four registers are 16-bit register is divided into registers. 16-bit register implies that register can store maximum 16 bit of data.

- Accumulator: Accumulator is 16 bit by default and general purpose register. By default means that any operand in instruction does not specify a particular register for holding the operand. That time operand will automatically store in AC. AC is used as two separate registers of 7 bit AL and AH. AC located inside the ALU. Intermediate data and result after execution will store in AC. AC used MBR to deal with memory.

- Program Counter: PC stands for program counter. *It is 16-bit register.* It counts the number of instruction left for execution. It acts as a pointer for instructions and also known as Instruction pointer register. PC holds the address of next instruction to be executed. When an instruction is fetched from the register. Register get automatically incremented by one and point to the address of next instruction.

- Flag register: It is also known as a Status register or Program Status register. Flag register holds the Boolean value of status word used by the process.

- Auxiliary Flag: If two numbers are to be added such that if in the beginning of higher bit there is a carry. This is known as auxiliary bit.

- Carry bit: Carry bit is indicate the most significant borrow or carry bit by subtracting a greater number than a smaller number or adding two numbers.

- Sign bit: Sign bit is a most significant bit in 2's complement to show that result is negative or positive. It is also known as negative bit. If the final carry over here after the sum of last most significant bit is 1, it is dropped and the result is positive.

- If there is no carry over here then 2's complement will negative and negative bit set as 1.

- Overflow bit: Overflow bit used to indicate that stack is overflow or not after processing the instruction. It is set to be 1 means that stack is overflow if it is 0 then its reverse to happen.

- Parity bit: Parity bit represent odd or even set of '1' bits in given string. It is used as error detecting code. Parity bit has two types: Even parity bit and an Odd parity bit.

  In Even parity bit, we count the occurrence of I's in the string. If a number of 1 bit is odd in counting than we will add even parity bit to make it even or if the number of 1 bit are even then even parity bit is 0.

Data	Number of 1 bits	Even Parity Bit	Data including Even Parity Bit
1010111	5	1	11010111

- Memory Address Register: Address register holds the address of memory where data is residing. CPU fetches the address from the register and access the location to acquire data. In the same way, MAR is used to write the data into memory.

- Data Register: Data registers also Known as Memory Data Register. It holds the content or instruction fetched from memory location for reading and writing purpose. It is 16-bit register means that can store 2^{16} bytes of data. From Data, register instruction moves in Instruction register and data content moves to AC for manipulation.

- Instruction register: Instruction holds the instruction to be executed. Control unit of CPU fetch the instruction, decode it and execute the instruction by accessing appropriate content. IR is 16-bit register. It has two fields – Opcode and operand.

  PC holds the address of the instruction to be executed. Once the address is fetched it gets incremented by 1.PC hold the address of next instructions. In this situation, IR holds the address of the current instruction.

- Input/output register: Input register holds the input from input devices and output register hold the output that has to give to output devices.

References

- What-is-cpu, introduction-to-computer, fundamental: ecomputernotes.com, retrieved 15 january, 2019

- Processor, definition: techtarget.com, retrieved 1 august, 2019

- Introduction-of-control-unit-and-its-design: geeksforgeeks.org

- Arithmetic-logic-unit-alu: tutorialspoint.com, retrieved 13 july, 2019

- What-is-arithmetic-and-logic-unit-alu, introduction-to-computer, fundamental: ecomputernotes.com, retrieved 8 august, 2019

3

Instruction Set Architecture

Instruction set architecture is an abstract model of a computer which serves as a bridge between software and hardware. It can be classified on the basis of complexity into numerous categories such as RISC, CISC, MISC and OISC. This chapter discusses in detail these types of instruction set architecture to provide a thorough understanding of the subject.

Instruction Set

An instruction set (used in what is called ISA or Instruction Set Architecture) is code that the computer processor (CPU) can understand. The language is 1s and 0s, or machine language. It contains instructions or tasks that control the movement of bits and bytes within the processor.

But if it's 1s and 0s, how do we actually communicate with the processor? Systems programmers use assembly language, which is a type of programming language. The statements are assembled into machine language - into the instructions that the processor can understand. Assembly language is a lot like machine language with labels - because binary alone would quickly get hard to keep track of.

What makes up an instruction set? When we start talking about 1s and 0s, machine language, assembly language, and registers, it might all become murky. Let's start with the overall structure of an instruction and go from there.

The instruction set consists of a limited set of unique codes that let the processor know what to do next, along with some basic rules of how to express them.

Elements of an Instruction

Each instruction must have elements that contain the information required by the CPU for execution. These elements are as follows:

- Operation code: Specifies the operation to be performed (e.g. ADD, I/O). The operation is specified by a binary code, known as the operation code, or opcode.

- Source operand reference: The operation may involve one or more source operands, that is, operands that are inputs for the operation.

- Result operand reference: The operation may produce a result.

- Next instruction reference: This tells the CPU where to fetch the next instruction after the execution of this instruction is complete.

The next instruction to be fetched is located in main memory or, in the case of a virtual memory system, in either main memory or secondary memory (disk). In most cases, the next instruction to be fetched immediately follows the current instruction. In those cases, there is no explicit reference to the next instruction. Source and result operands can be in one of three areas:

- Main or virtual memory: As with next instruction references, the main or virtual memory address must be supplied.

- CPU register: With rare exceptions, a CPU contains one or more registers that may be referenced by machine instructions. If only one register exists, reference to it may be implicit. If more than one register exists, then each register is assigned a unique number, and the instruction must contain the number of the desired register.

- I/O device: The instruction must specify (the I/O module and device for the operation. If memory-mapped I/O is used, this is just another main or virtual memory address.

Instruction Cycle State Diagram

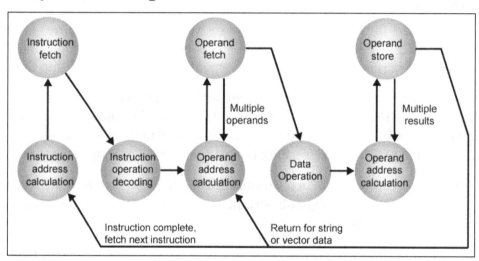

Instruction cycle state diagram

Instruction Representation

Within the computer, each instruction is represented by a sequence of bits. The instruction is divided into fields, corresponding to the constituent elements of the instruction. During instruction execution, an instruction is read into an instruction register (IR) in the CPU. The CPU must be able to extract the data from the various instruction fields to perform the required operation.

It is difficult for both the programmer and the reader of textbooks to deal with binary representations of machine instructions. Thus, it has become common practice to use a symbolic representation of machine instructions. Opcodes are represented by abbreviations, called mnemonics that indicate the operation. Common examples include:

ADD	Add
SUB	Subtract
MPY	Multiply

DIV	Divide
LOAD	Load data from memory
STOR	Store data to memory

Operands are also represented symbolically.

For example, the instruction ADD R, Y:

May mean add the value contained in data location Y to the contents of register R. In this example, Y refers to the address of a location in memory, and R refers to a particular register. Note that the operation is performed on the contents of a location, not on its address.

Simple Instruction Format

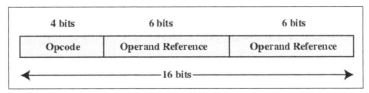

A simple instruction format

Instruction Types

Consider a high-level language instruction that could be expressed in a language such as BASIC or FORTRAN. For example,

X = X+Y

This statement instructs the computer lo add the value stored in Y to the value Stored in X and put the result in X. How might this be accomplished with machine instructions? Let us assume that the variables X and Y correspond lo locations 513 and 514. If we assume a simple set of machine instructions, this operation could be accomplished with three instructions:

- Load a register with the contents of memory location 513.

- Add the contents of memory location 514 to the register.

- Store the contents of the register in memory location 513.

As can be seen, the single BASIC instruction may require three machine instructions. This is typical of the relationship between a high-level language and a machine language. A high-level language expresses operations in a concise algebraic form, using variables. A machine language expresses operations in a basic form involving the movement of data to or from registers.

With this simple example to guide us, let us consider the types of instructions that must be included in a practical computer. A computer should have a set of instructions that allows the user to formulate any data processing task. Another way to view it is to consider the capabilities of a high-level programming language. Any program written in a high-level language must be translated into machine language to be executed. Thus, the set of machine instructions must be sufficient to express any of the instructions from a high-level language. With this in mind we can categorize instruction types as follows:

- Data processing: Arithmetic and logic instructions.

- Data storage: Memory instructions.

- Data movement: I/O instructions.

- Control: Test and branch instructions.

Number of Addresses

What is the maximum number of addresses one might need in an instruction? Evidently, arithmetic and logic instructions will require the most operands. Virtually all arithmetic and logic operations are either unary (one operand) or binary (two operands). Thus, we would need a maximum of two addresses to reference operands. The result of an operation must be stored, suggesting a third address. Finally, after completion of an instruction, the next instruction must be fetched, and its address is needed.

This line of reasoning suggests that an instruction could plausibly be required to contain four address references: two operands, one result and the address of the next instruction. In practice, four-address instructions are extremely rare. Most instructions have one, two, or three operand addresses, with the address of the next instruction being implicit (obtained from the program counter).

Three addresses: Operand 1, Operand 2, Result

Example: a = b + c

- Three-address instruction formats are not common, because they require a relatively long instruction format to hold the three address references.

- Two addresses: One address doubles as operand and result.

Example: a = a + b

- The two-address formal reduces the space requirement but also introduces some awkwardness. To avoid altering the value of an operand, a MOVE instruction is used to move one of the values to a result or temporary location before performing the operation.

- One address: A second address must be implicit. This was common in earlier machines, with the implied address being a CPU register known as the accumulator. or AC. The accumulator contains one of the operands and is used to store the result.

- Zero addresses: Zero-address instructions are applicable to a special memory organization, called a Stack. A stack is a last-in-first-out set of locations.

The number of addresses per instruction is a basic design decision.

- Fewer addresses: Fewer addresses per instruction result in more primitive instructions, which require a less complex CPU. It also results in instructions of shorter length. On the other hand, programs contain more total instructions, which in general results in longer execution times and longer, more complex programs.

- Multiple-address instructions: With multiple-address instructions, it is common to have multiple general-purpose registers. This allows some operations to be performed solely on registers. Because register references are faster than memory references, this speeds up execution.

Design Decisions

One of the most interesting and most analyzed, aspects of computer design is instruction set design. The design of an instruction set is very complex, because it affects so many aspects of the computer system. The instruction set defines many of the functions performed by the CPU and thus has a significant effect on the implementation of the CPU. The instruction set is the programmer's means of controlling the CPU. Thus, programmer requirements must be considered in designing the instruction set. The most important design issues include the following:

- Operation repertoire: How many and which operations to provide, and how complex operations should be performed.

- Data types: The various types of data upon which operations are performed.

- Instruction format: Instruction length (in bits), number of addresses, size of various fields, and so on.

- Registers: Number of CPU registers that can be referenced by instructions, and their use.

- Addressing: The mode or modes by which the address of an operand is specified.

Types of Operands

Machine instructions operate on data. The most important general categories of data are:

- Addresses.

- Numbers.

- Characters.

- Logical data.

Numbers

All machine languages include numeric data types. Even in nonnumeric data processing, there is a need for numbers to act as counters, field widths, and so forth. An important distinction between numbers used in ordinary mathematics and numbers stored in a computer is that the latter are limited. Thus, the programmer is faced with understanding the consequences of rounding, overflow and underflow.

Three types of numerical data are common in computers:

- Integer or fixed point.

- Floating point.

- Decimal.

Characters

A common form of data is text or character strings. While textual data are most convenient for human beings, they cannot, in character form, be easily stored or transmitted by data processing and communications systems. Such systems are designed for binary data. Thus, a number of codes have been devised by which characters are represented by a sequence of bits. Perhaps the earliest common example of this is the Morse code. Today, the most commonly used character code in the International Reference Alphabet (IRA), referred to in the United States as the American Standard Code for Information Interchange (ASCII). IRA is also widely used outside the United States. Each character in this code is represented by a unique 7-bit pattern, thus, 128 different characters can be represented. This is a larger number than is necessary to represent printable characters, and some of the patterns represent control characters. Some of these control characters have to do with controlling the printing of characters on a page. Others are concerned with communications procedures. IRA-encoded characters are almost always stored and transmitted using 8 bits per character. The eighth bit may be set to 0 or used as a parity bit for error detection. In the latter case, the bit is set such that the total number of binary 1s in each octet is always odd (odd parity) or always even (even parity).

Another code used to encode characters is the Extended Binary Coded Decimal Interchange Code (EBCDIC). EBCDIC is used on IBM S/390 machines. It is an 8-bit code. As with IRA, EBCDIC is compatible with packed decimal. In the case of EBCDIC, the codes 11110000 through 11111001 represent the digits 0 through 9.

Logical Data

Normally, each word or other addressable unit (byte, half-word, and soon) is treated as a single unit of data. It is sometimes useful, however, to consider an n-bit unit as consisting 1-bit items of data, each item having the value 0 or I. When data are viewed this way, they are considered to be logic data.

There are two advantages to the bit-oriented view:

- First, we may sometimes wish to store an array of Boolean or binary data items, in which each item can take on only the values I (true) and II (fake). With logical data, memory can be used most efficiently for this storage.

- Second, there are occasions when we wish to manipulate the bits of a data item.

Types of Operations

The number of different opcodes varies widely from machine to machine. However, the same general types of operations are found on all machines. A useful and typical categorization is the following:

- Data transfer.

- Arithmetic.

- Logical.

- Conversion.

- I/O.

- System control.

- Transfer of control.

Data Transfer

The most fundamental type of machine instruction is the data transfer instruction. The data transfer instruction must specify several things.

- The location of the source and destination operands must be specified. Each location could be memory. A register, or the lop of the stack.

- The length of data to be transferred must be indicated.

- As with all instructions with operands, the mode of addressing for each operand must be specified.

In term of CPU action, data transfer operations are perhaps the simplest type. If both source and destination are registers, then the CPU simply causes data to be transferred from one register to another; this is an operation internal to the CPU. If one or both operands are in memory, then (he CPU must perform some or all of following actions:

- Calculate the memory address, based on the address mode.

- If the address refers to virtual memory, translate from virtual to actual memory address.

- Determine whether the addressed item is in cache.

- If not, issue a command lo the memory module.

Example:

Operation mnemonic	Name	Number of bits transferred	Description
L	Load	32	Transfer from memory in register
LH	Load half-word	16	Transfer from memory to register
ST	Store	32	Transfer from register to memory
STH	Store half-word	16	Transfer from register to memory

Arithmetic

Most machines provide the basic arithmetic operations of add, subtract, multiply, and divide. These are invariably provided for signed integer (fixed-point) numbers, often they are also provided for floating-point and packed decimal numbers.

Other possible operations include a variety of single-operand instructions: for example:

- Absolute: Take the absolute value of the operand.

- Negate: Negate the Operand.

- Increment: Add 1 to the operand.

- Decrement: Subtract 1 from the operand.

Logical

Most machines also provide a variety of operations for manipulating individual bits of a word or other addressable units, often referred to as "bit twiddling." They are based upon Boolean operations.

Some of the basic logical operations that can be performed on Boolean or binary data are AND, OR, NOT, XOR. These logical operations can be applied bitwise to n-bit logical data units. Thus, if two registers contain the data:

(R1) - 10100101 (R2) - 00001111

then

(R1) AND (R2) – 00000101

In addition lo bitwise logical operations, most machines provide a variety of shifting and rotating functions such as shift left, shift right, right rotate, left rotate.

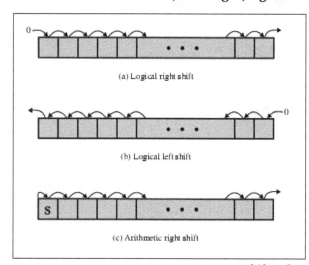

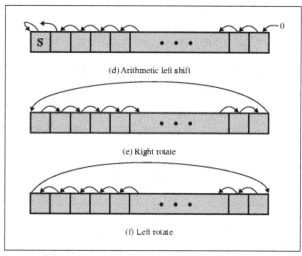

(a) Logical right shift

(b) Logical left shift

(c) Arithmetic right shift

(d) Arithmetic left shift

(e) Right rotate

(f) Left rotate

Shift and rotate operations

Conversion

Conversion instructions are those that change the format or operate on the format of data. An example is converting from decimal to binary.

Input/Output

As we saw, there are a variety of approaches taken, including isolated programmed IO, memory-mapped programmed I/O, DMA, and the use of an I/O processor. Many implementations provide only a few I/O instructions, with the specific actions specified by parameters, codes, or command words.

System Controls

System control instructions are those that can he executed only while the processor is in a certain privileged state or are executing a program in a special privileged area of memory, typically, these instructions are reserved for the use of the operating system.

Some examples of system control operations are as follows. A system control instruction may read or alter a control register. Another example is an instruction to read or modify a storage protection key, such us is used in the S/390 memory system. Another example is access to process control blocks in a multiprogramming system.

Transfer of Control

For all of the operation types discussed so far. The next instruction to be performed is the one that immediately follows, in memory, the current instruction. However, a significant fraction of the instructions in any program have as their function changing the sequence of instruction execution. For these instructions, the operation performed by the CPU is to update the program counter to contain the address of some instruction in memory.

There are a number of reasons why transfer-of-control operations are required. Among the most important are the following:

1. In the practical use of computers, it is essential to be able to execute each instruction more than once and perhaps many thousands of times. It may require thousands or perhaps millions of instructions to implement an application. This would be unthinkable if each instruction had to be written out separately. If a table or a list of items is to be processed, a program loop is needed. One sequence of instructions is executed repeatedly to process all the data.

2. Virtually all programs involve some decision making. We would like the computer to do one thing if one condition holds, and another thing if another condition holds. For example, a sequence of instructions computes the square root of a number. At the start of the sequence, the sign of the number is tested, if the number is negative, the computation is not performed, hut an error condition is reported.

3. To compose correctly a large or even medium-size computer program is an exceedingly difficult task. It helps if there are mechanisms for breaking the task up into smaller pieces that can be worked on one at a time.

We now turn to a discussion of the most common transfer-of-control operations found in instruction sets: branch, skip, and procedure call.

Branch Instruction

A branch instruction, also called a jump instruction, has as one of its operands the address of the next instruction to be executed. Most often, the instruction is a conditional branch instruction. That is, the branch is made (update program counter to equal address specified in operand) only if a certain condition is met. Otherwise, the next instruction in sequence is executed (increment program counter as usual).

Skip Instructions

Another common form of transfer-of-control instruction is the skip instruction. The skip instruction includes an implied address. Typically, the skip implies that one instruction be skipped; thus, the implied address equals the address of the next instruction plus one instruction-length.

Procedure Call Instructions

Perhaps the most important innovation in the development of programming languages is the procedure; a procedure is a self-contained computer program that is incorporated into a larger program. At any point in the program the procedure may he invoked, or called. The processor is instructed to go and execute the entire procedure and then return to the point from which the call took place.

The two principal reasons for the use of procedures are economy and modularity. A procedure allows the same piece of code to be used many times. This is important for economy in programming effort and for making the most efficient use of storage space in the system (the program must be stored). Procedures also allow large programming tasks to be subdivided into smaller units. This use of modularity greatly eases the programming task.

The procedure mechanism involves two basic instructions: a call instruction that branches from the present location to the procedure, and a return instruction that returns from the procedure to the place from which it was called. Both of these are forms of branching instructions.

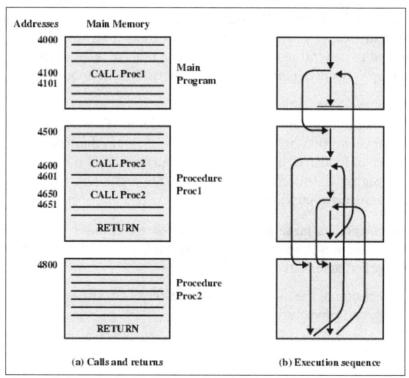

(a) Calls and returns   (b) Execution sequence

Nested Procedures

The figure illustrates the use of procedures to construct a program. In this example, there is a main program starting at location 4000. This program includes a call to procedure PROC1, starting at location 4500. When this call instruction is encountered, the CPU suspends execution of the main program and begins execution of PROC1 by fetching the next instruction from location 4500. Within PROC1, there are two calls to PRoC2 at location 4800. In each case, the execution of PROC1 is suspended and PROC2 is executed. The RETURN statement causes the CPU to go back to the calling program and continue execution at the instruction after the corresponding CALL instruction. This behavior is illustrated in the right of this figure.

Several points are worth noting:

- A procedure can be called from more than one location.

- A procedure call can appear in a procedure. This allows the nesting of procedures to an arbitrary depth.

- Each procedure call is matched by a return in the called program.

Because we would like to be able to call a procedure from a variety of points, the CPU must somehow save the return address so that the return can take place appropriately. There are three common places for storing the return address:

- Register.

- Start of called procedure.

- Top of stack.

Instruction Formats

Computer perform task on the basis of instruction provided. An instruction in computer comprises of groups called fields. This field contains different information as for computers everything is in 0 and 1 so each field has different significance on the basis of which a CPU decide what so perform. The most common fields are:

- Operation field which specifies the operation to be performed like addition.

- Address field which contain the location of operand, i.e., register or memory location.

- Mode field which specifies how operand is to be founded.

An instruction is of various lengths depending upon the number of addresses it contains. Generally CPU organization is of three types on the basis of number of address fields:

- Single Accumulator organization.

- General register organization.

- Stack organization.

In first organization operation is done involving a special register called accumulator. In second on multiple registers are used for the computation purpose. In third organization the work on stack basis operation due to which it does not contain any address field. It is not necessary that only a single organization is applied a blend of various organizations is mostly what we see generally.

On the basis of number of address instruction are classified as note that we will use X = (A+B)*(C+D) expression to showcase the procedure:

Zero Address Instructions

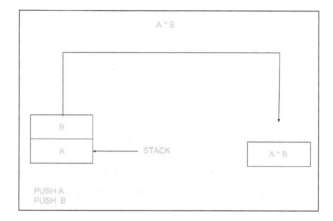

A stack based computer do not use address field in instruction. To evaluate a expression first it is converted to revere Polish Notation i.e. Post fix Notation.

```
Expression: X = (A+B)*(C+D)
```

```
Postfixed : X = AB+CD+*
```

```
TOP means top of stack
```

```
M[X] is any memory location
```

PUSH	A	TOP = A
PUSH	B	TOP = B
ADD		TOP = A+B
PUSH	C	TOP = C
PUSH	D	TOP = D
ADD		TOP = C+D
MUL		TOP = (C+D)*(A+B)
POP	X	M[X] = TOP

One Address Instructions

This uses an implied ACCUMULATOR register for data manipulation. One operand is in accumulator and other is in register or memory location. Implied means that the CPU already knows that one operand is in accumulator so there is no need to specify it.

opcode	operand/address of operand	mode

Expression: X = (A+B)*(C+D)

AC is accumulator

M[] is any memory location

M[T] is temporary location

LOAD	A	AC = M[A]
ADD	B	AC = AC + M[B]
STORE	T	M[T] = AC
LOAD	C	AC = M[C]
ADD	D	AC = AC + M[D]
MUL	T	AC = AC * M[T]
STORE	X	M[X] = AC

Two Address Instructions

This is common in commercial computers. Here two addresses can be specified in the instruction. Unlike earlier in one address instruction the result was stored in accumulator here result can be stored at different location rather than just accumulator, but require more number of bit to represent address.

opcode	Destination address	Source address	mode

Here destination address can also contain operand.

Expression: X = (A+B)*(C+D)

R1, R2 are registers

M[] is any memory location

MOV	R1, A	R1 = M[A]
ADD	R1, B	R1 = R1 + M[B]
MOV	R2, C	R2 = C
ADD	R2, D	R2 = R2 + D
MUL	R1, R2	R1 = R1 * R2
MOV	X, R1	M[X] = R1

Three Address Instructions

This has three address field to specify a register or a memory location. Program created are much short in size but number of bits per instruction increase. These instructions make creation of program much easier but it does not mean that program will run much faster because now instruction only contain more information but each micro operation (changing content of register, loading address in address bus etc.) will be performed in one cycle only.

opcode	Destination address	Source address	Source address	mode

```
Expression: X = (A+B)*(C+D)

R1, R2 are registers

M[] is any memory location
```

ADD	R1, A, B	R1 = M[A] + M[B]
ADD	R2, C, D	R2 = M[C] + M[D]
MUL	X, R1, R2	M[X] = R1 * R2

An instruction format defines the different component of an instruction. The main components of an instruction are opcode (which instruction to be executed) and operands (data on which instruction to be executed). Here are the different terms related to instruction format:

- Instruction set size: It tells the total number of instructions defined in the processor.

- Opcode size: It is the number of bits occupied by the opcode which is calculated by taking log of instruction set size.

- Operand size: It is the number of bits occupied by the operand.

- Instruction size: It is calculated as sum of bits occupied by opcode and operands.

Now we will discuss different types of problems based on instruction format:

Type 1

Given instruction set size and operands size and their count, find the size of the instruction. In this type of questions, you will be given the size of instruction set, number of operands and their size; you have to find out the size of the instruction.

Example: Consider a processor with 64 registers and an instruction set of size twelve. Each instruction has five distinct fields, namely, opcode, two source register identifiers, one destination register identifier, and a twelve-bit immediate value. Each instruction must be stored in memory in a byte-aligned fashion. If a program has 100 instructions, the amount of memory (in bytes) consumed by the program text is _____.

(A) 100

(B) 200

(C) 400

(D) 500

Solution: It can be approached as:

- The instruction consists of opcode and operands. Given the instruction set of size 12, 4 bits are required for opcode ($2^4 = 16$).

- As there are total 64 registers, 6 bits are required for identifying a register.

- As the instruction contains 3 registers (2 source + 1 designation), $3 * 6 = 18$ bit are required for register identifiers.

- 12 bits are required for immediate value as given.

- Total bits for an instruction = $4 + 18 + 12 = 34$ bits.

- For 100 instructions, number of bits = $34 * 100 = 3400$ bits = $3400/8$ bytes = 425 bytes.

- As memory must be greater than or equal to 425, correct option is (D).

Type 2

Given instruction size, opcode size and size of some operands, find the size and maximum value of remaining operands. In this type of questions, you will be given the size of instruction, size of opcode, number of operands and size of some operands; you have to find out the size or maximum value of remaining operands.

Example: A processor has 40 distinct instructions and 24 general purpose registers. A 32-bit instruction word has an opcode, two registers operands and an immediate operand. The number of bits available for the immediate operand field is_____.

Solution: It can be approached as:

- As the processor has 40 instructions, number of bits for opcode = 6 ($2^6 = 64$).

- As the processor has 24 register, number of bits for one register = 5 ($2^5 = 32$).

- Total bits occupied by 2 registers and opcode = $6 + 5 + 5 = 16$.

- As instruction size given is 32 bits, remaining bit left for operand = $32-16 = 16$ bits.

Example: A machine has a 32-bit architecture, with 1-word long instructions. It has 64 registers, each of which is 32 bits long. It needs to support 45 instructions, which have an immediate operand in addition to two register operands. Assuming that the immediate operand is an unsigned integer, the maximum value of the immediate operand is _____.

Solution: It can be approached as:

- As machine has 32-bit architecture, therefore, 1 word = 32 bits = instruction size.

- As the processor has 64 register, number of bits for one register = 6 ($2^6 = 64$).

- As the processor has 45 instructions, number of bits for opcode = 6 ($2^6 = 64$).

- Total bits occupied by 2 registers and opcode = $6 + 6 + 6 = 18$.

- As instruction size given is 32 bits, remaining bit left for immediate operand = 32-18 = 14 bits.

- Maximum unsigned value using 14 bits = $2^{14} - 1 = 16383$ which is the answer.

Type 3

Instruction format with different categories of instruction. In this type of questions, you will be given different categories of instructions. You have to find maximum possible instructions of a given type.

Example: A processor has 16 integer registers (R0, R1, ..., R15) and 64 floating point registers (F0, F1, ..., F63). It uses a 2 byte instruction format. There are four categories of instructions: Type-1, Type-2, Type-3, and Type 4. Type-1 category consists of four instructions, each with 3 integer register operands (3Rs). Type-2 category consists of eight instructions, each with 2 floating point register operands (2Fs). Type-3 category consists of fourteen instructions, each with one integer register operand and one floating point register operand (1R+1F). Type-4 category consists of N instructions, each with a floating point register operand (1F).

The maximum value of N is _____.

Solution: It can be approached as:

- As machine has 2 byte = 16 bits instruction format, therefore, possible encodings = 2^{16}.

- As the processor has 16 integer register, number of bits for one integer register = 4 ($2^4 = 16$).

- As the processor has 64 floating point register, number of bits for one floating point register = 6 ($2^6 = 64$).

- For type-1 category having 4 instructions each having 3 integer register operands ($4*3 = 12$ bits) will consume $4 * 2^{12} = 2^{14}$ encodings.

- For type-2 category having 8 instructions each having 2 floating point register operands ($2*6 = 12$ bits) will consume $8 * 2^{12} = 2^{15}$ encodings.

- For type-3 category having 14 instructions each having 1 integer register and 1 floating point register operands ($4 + 6 = 10$ bits) will consume $14 * 2^{10} = 14336$ encodings.

- For type-4 category instructions, number of encodings left = $2^{16} - 2^{14} - 2^{15} - 14336 = 2048$.

- For type-4 category having N instructions each having 1 floating point register operand (6 bits) will consume $N * 2^6 = 2048$ (calculated from previous step). Therefore, N = 32.

Instruction Cycle

An instruction cycle, also known as fetch-decode-execute cycle is the basic operational process of a computer. This process is repeated continuously by CPU from boot up to shut down of computer.

Each phase of Instruction Cycle can be decomposed into a sequence of elementary micro-operations.

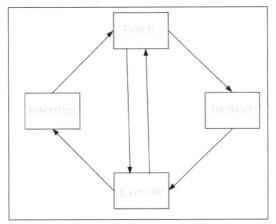

The Indirect Cycle

The Indirect Cycle is always followed by the Execute Cycle. The Interrupt Cycle is always followed by the Fetch Cycle. For both fetch and execute cycles, the next cycle depends on the state of the system.

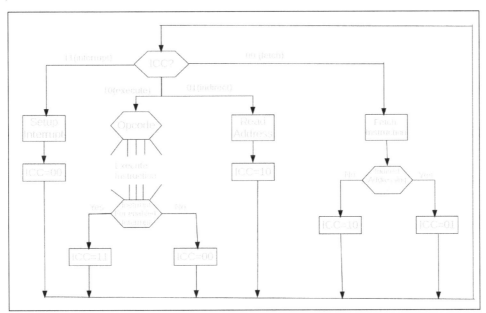

Flowchart for instruction cycle

We assumed a new 2-bit register called *Instruction Cycle Code* (ICC). The ICC designates the state of processor in terms of which portion of the cycle it is in:-

- 00 : Fetch Cycle
- 01 : Indirect Cycle
- 10 : Execute Cycle
- 11 : Interrupt Cycle

At the end of the each cycle, the ICC is set appropriately. The above flowchart of *Instruction Cycle* describes the complete sequence of micro-operations, depending only on the instruction sequence and the interrupt pattern (this is a simplified example). The operation of the processor is described as the performance of a sequence of micro-operation.

Different Instruction Cycles

The Fetch Cycle

At the beginning of the fetch cycle, the address of the next instruction to be executed is in the *Program Counter* (PC).

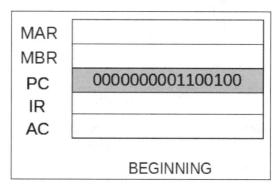

BEGINNING

- Step 1: The address in the program counter is moved to the memory address register (MAR), as this is the only register which is connected to address lines of the system bus.

MAR   0000000001100100
MBR
PC   0000000001100100
IR
AC

FIRST STEP

- Step 2: The address in MAR is placed on the address bus, now the control unit issues a READ command on the control bus, and the result appears on the data bus and is then copied into the memory buffer register (MBR). Program counter is incremented by one, to get ready for the next instruction. (These two actions can be performed simultaneously to save time).

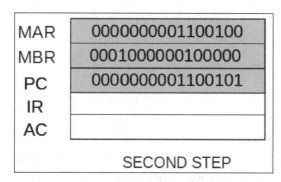

SECOND STEP

- Step 3: The content of the MBR is moved to the instruction register (IR).

MAR	0000000001100100
MBR	0001000000100000
PC	0000000001100100
IR	0001000000100000
AC	

FIRST STEP

Thus, a simple *Fetch Cycle* consists of three steps and four micro-operations. Symbolically, we can write these sequences of events as follows:

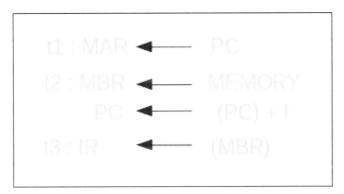

Here 'I' is the instruction length. The notation (t1, t2, t3) represents successive time units. We assume that a clock is available for timing purposes and it emits regularly spaced clock pulses. Each clock pulse defines a time unit. Thus, all time units are of equal duration. Each micro-operation can be performed within the time of a single time unit.

- First time unit: Move the contents of the PC to MAR.

- Second time unit: Move contents of memory location specified by MAR to MBR. Increment content of PC by I.

- Third time unit: Move contents of MBR to IR.

(Second and third micro-operations both take place during the second time unit.)

The Indirect Cycles

Once an instruction is fetched, the next step is to fetch source operands. *Source Operand* is being fetched by indirect addressing (it can be fetched by any addressing mode; here it's done by indirect addressing). Register-based operands need not be fetched. Once the opcode is executed, a similar process may be needed to store the result in main memory. Following *micro-operations* takes place:

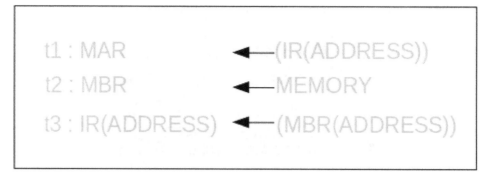

- Step 1: The address field of the instruction is transferred to the MAR. This is used to fetch the address of the operand.

- Step 2: The address field of the IR is updated from the MBR.(So that it now contains a direct addressing rather than indirect addressing).

- Step 3: The IR is now in the state, as if indirect addressing has not been occurred.

(Now IR is ready for the execute cycle, but it skips that cycle for a moment to consider the *Interrupt Cycle*.)

The Execute Cycle

The other three cycles (*Fetch, Indirect and Interrupt*) are simple and predictable. Each of them requires simple, small and fixed sequence of micro-operation. In each case same micro-operation are repeated each time around.

Execute Cycle is different from them. Like, for a machine with N different opcodes there are N different sequence of micro-operations that can occur. Let's take a hypothetical example:

Consider an add instruction:

Here, this instruction adds the content of location X to register R. Corresponding micro-operation will be:

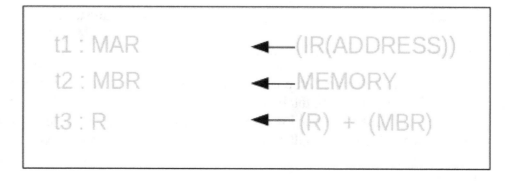

We begin with the IR containing the ADD instruction.

- Step 1: The address portion of IR is loaded into the MAR.

- Step 2: The address field of the IR is updated from the MBR, so the reference memory location is read.

- Step 3: Now, the contents of R and MBR are added by the ALU.

Let's take a complex example:

Here, the content of location X is incremented by 1. If the result is 0, the next instruction will be skipped. Corresponding sequence of micro-operation will be:

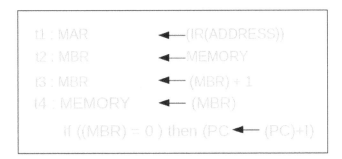

Here, the PC is incremented if (MBR) = 0. This test (is MBR equal to zero or not) and action (PC is incremented by 1) can be implemented as one micro-operation.

This test and action micro-operation can be performed during the same time unit during which the updated value MBR is stored back to memory.

The Interrupt Cycle

At the completion of the Execute Cycle, a test is made to determine whether any enabled interrupt has occurred or not. If an enabled interrupt has occurred then Interrupt Cycle occurs. The nature of this cycle varies greatly from one machine to another.Let's take a sequence of micro-operation:

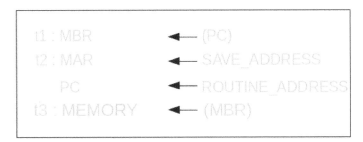

- Step 1: Contents of the PC is transferred to the MBR, so that they can be saved for return.

- Step 2: MAR is loaded with the address at which the contents of the PC are to be saved. PC is loaded with the address of the start of the interrupt-processing routine.

- Step 3: MBR, containing the old value of PC, is stored in memory.

(In step 2, two actions are implemented as one micro-operation. However, most processor provide multiple types of interrupts, it may take one or more micro-operation to obtain the save_address and the routine_address before they are transferred to the MAR and PC respectively).

Addressing Modes

The addressing modes in computer architecture actually define how an operand is chosen to execute an instruction. It is the way that is used to identify the location of an operand which is specified in an instruction.

Whenever an instruction executes, it requires operands to be operated on. An instruction field consisting of opcode and operand. Where operand means the data and opcode means the instruction itself. In case of operations like addition or subtraction, they require two data. So, they are called binary instruction. On the other hand, the increment or decrement operations need only one data and are so called unary instruction. Now the question is how these data can be obtained.

Consider an example that you want to buy a product from an online shopping site say Amazon. Now you can pay it either by using cash on delivery, by net banking, by debit/credit card, by UPI etc. So, in different ways, you can make payment to Amazon. This is the various payment modes available. But here we are discussing the addressing modes in computer architecture that means how an instruction can access operands to be operated on using various modes.

The various addressing modes in computer architecture can be classified as below. We have some other addressing modes too, but these are the prime addressing modes in computer architecture.

Addressing modes in computer architecture:

- Implicit

- Immediate

- Direct

- Indirect

- Register

- Register Indirect

- Displacement

  o Relative

  o Base register

        ◦   Indexing

- Stack

Implicit Addressing Mode

The term implicit addressing mode means here we are not mentioning clearly in details that from where the instruction can get the operand. But by default, the instruction itself knows from where it is supposed to access the operand. For example, CMA stands for complement accumulator. The meaning of the CMA instruction is whatever the value present in the accumulator will be replaced by its 1's complement.

In this instruction CMA or along with this instruction, we are not mentioning any operand. So here it knows that the operand has to be accessed from the accumulator implicitly. This is known as implicit addressing modes.

Immediate Addressing Mode

In the immediate addressing mode, the instruction contains two fields. One for the opcode and another field contains the operand itself. That means in this addressing mode, there is no need to go anywhere to access the operand because of the instruction itself containing the operand. This is known as immediate addressing mode.

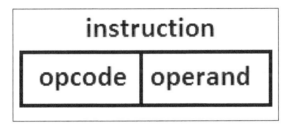

Direct Addressing Mode

In the direct addressing mode, the instruction will have the two parts. One part will contain the opcode and another one will contain the address of the memory location at where the operand can be found.

Here A is the address of the operand. That means at the Ath location in the memory, the operand can be found.

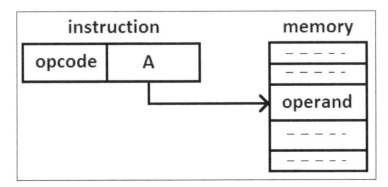

Indirect Addressing Mode

Indirect addressing mode contains the opcode and address field. But unlike direct addressing mode, it doesn't contain the address of the operand but contains the address of a memory location in which the actual address of the operand can be found.

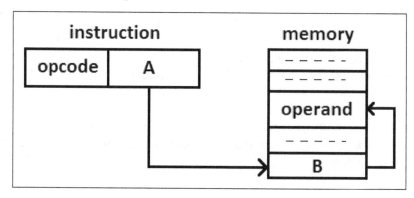

Here A contains the address of the location B in memory and B contains the actual address of the operand in memory.

Register Addressing Mode

In case of register addressing mode, the instruction will have the opcode and a register number. Depending upon the register number, one of the registers will be selected from the available sets of registers by default automatically.

The unique identification of the register can be done by the register number which is mentioned in the instruction. In that register, the operand can be found.

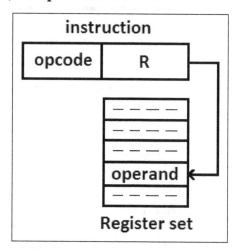

Register Indirect Addressing Mode

In the register indirect addressing mode, the instruction will contain the opcode as well as a register number. Depending upon the register number mentioned in the instruction, the corresponding register will be accessed from the set of registers. But here the register doesn't contain the operand but will contain the address of the operand in the memory at where the operand can be found.

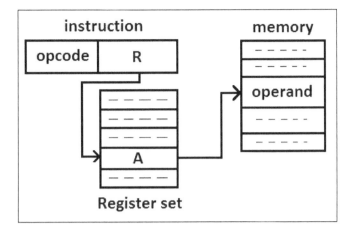

Suppose in memory, the operand is in the Ath location. Now, this address A will be stored in the register and the register number says R will be mentioned in the instruction. This is called register addressing mode.

Displacement Addressing Mode

In the displacement addressing mode, the instruction will be having three fields. One for the opcode, one for the register number and the remaining one for an absolute address.

At first, depending upon the register number the register will be selected from the register set. After that its content will be added with the absolute address and the new address formed will be the actual physical address of the operand in the memory.

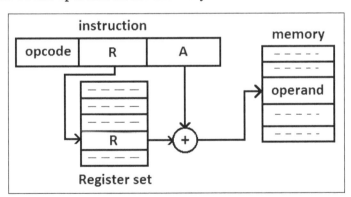

Displacement addressing mode in computer architecture can be categorized into 3 different modes.

1. Relative

2. Base register

3. Indexing

In case of relative addressing mode, the register used will be a program counter.

In the base addressing mode, the register will contain the base address and the absolute field will be the offset or displacement from the base address. After adding both the actual physical address of the operand can be obtained and mapping this address in the memory we can access the operand.

For example, if the base address is 3000 and the offset is 20, then after adding both i.e. 3020 will be the actual address of the operand.

In case of Indexing mode, the absolute field will contain the starting base address of the memory block and the register field will contain the index value. Adding both will give the actual physical address of the operand.

Stack Addressing Mode

In case of stack addressing mode, the instruction knows the topmost data should be the operand. If the instruction is a unary instruction then it will select the topmost data as the operand and if the instruction is a binary instruction then it will select the topmost two data as the operands from the top of the stack.

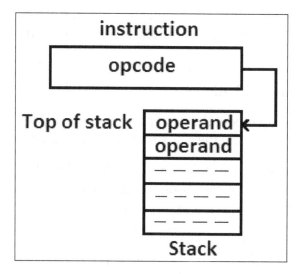

These are the basic and primary addressing modes in computer architecture. Apart from these modes, we have some other addressing modes in computer architecture including auto-increment, auto-decrement mode. But above mentioned are the most important addressing modes in computer architecture or computer organization.

Program Control Instructions

Program control instructions change or modify the flow of a program. The most basic kind of program control is the unconditional branch or unconditional jump. Branch is usually an indication of a short change relative to the current program counter. Jump is usually an indication of a change in program counter that is not directly related to the current program counter (such as a jump to an absolute memory location or a jump using a dynamic or static table), and is often free of distance limits from the current program counter.

The penultimate kind of program control is the conditional branch or conditional jump. This gives computers their ability to make decisions and implement both loops and algorithms beyond simple formulas.

Most computers have some kind of instructions for subroutine call and return from subroutines.

There are often instructions for saving and restoring part or all of the processor state before and after subroutine calls. Some kinds of subroutine or return instructions will include some kinds of save and restore of the processor state.

Even if there are no explicit hardware instructions for subroutine calls and returns, subroutines can be implemented using jumps (saving the return address in a register or memory location for the return jump). Even if there is no hardware support for saving the processor state as a group, most (if not all) of the processor state can be saved and restored one item at a time.

NOP, or no operation, takes up the space of the smallest possible instruction and causes no change in the processor state other than an advancement of the program counter and any time related changes. It can be used to synchronize timing (at least crudely). It is often used during development cycles to temporarily or permanently wipe out a series of instructions without having to reassemble the surrounding code.

Stop or halt instructions bring the processor to an orderly halt, remaining in an idle state until restarted by interrupt, trace, reset, or external action.

Reset instructions reset the processor. This may include any or all of: setting registers to an initial value, setting the program counter to a standard starting location (restarting the computer), clearing or setting interrupts, and sending a reset signal to external devices.

Jump (JMP) Instruction

Jump (JMP) instruction allows the programmer to skip sections of a program and branch to any part of the memory for the next instruction. Jump is two types:

- Unconditional Jump

- Conditional Jump

Unconditional Jump (JMP XXX)

It does not depend any condition or numerical tests. Three types:

- Short Jump

- Near Jump

- Far jump

• Short and near jump are often called intra-segment jump and far jumps are often called intersegment jump.

• Short jump and near jump follows a distance or displacement to jump where as far jump follows an address (segment + offset) to jump.

Short Jump (JMP 1byte-displacement)

- Short jump is a two-byte instruction.

- Instead of a jump address, it jumps by following a 8-bit (one byte) signed displacement.

- It allows jumps or branches to memory location within +127 and -128 bytes from the address following the jump.

- The displacement is sign-extended and added to the instruction pointer (IP) to generate the jump address within the current code segment.

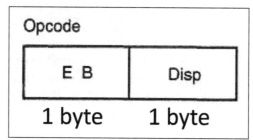

JMP disp: Here disp is 8-bit signed displacement or distance

Example: JMP 04H.

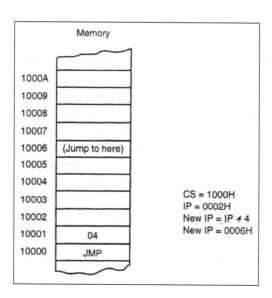

Near Jump (JMP 2byte-displacement)

- Near jump is similar to short jump, except that the distance is farther.

- Near jump is a three-byte instruction.

- Displacement is 16-bit (2 byte) signed displacement.

- It allows jumps or branches to memory location within $\pm 32\ K\ bytes$ of current code segment.

$$2^{16} = 65536 = 64\ K\ byte \left(\frac{65536}{1024} \right) = -32K\ byte\ to + 32K\ byte.$$

- The signed displacement added to the instruction pointer (IP) to generate the jump address.

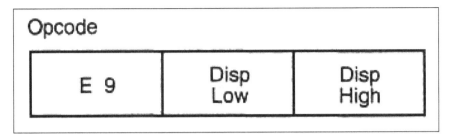

Example: JMP 0002H.

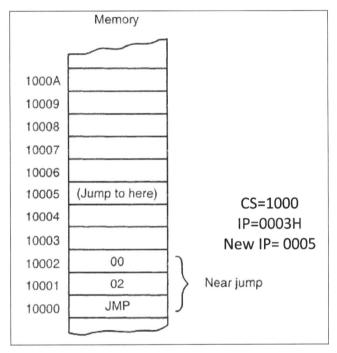

Far Jump (JMP 4byte-displacement)

- A far jump instruction obtains a new segment and offset address to accomplish the jump.

- It is a 5 byte instruction.

- Byte 2 and 3 contain new offset address. Byte 4 and 5 contains new segment address.

- It allows jumps or branches to any memory location of any memory segment. That's why far jump is called intersegment jump.

Opcode

E A	IP Low	IP High	CS Low	CS High

Example: JMP 0127: A300.

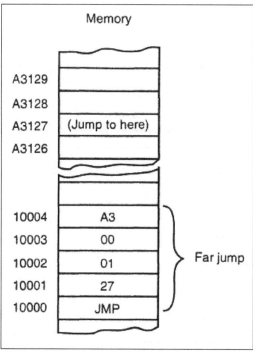

Jump to CSX10+IP = A300X10+0127 = A3127

Conditional Jump

- A conditional jump instruction allows the programmer to make decision based upon numerical tests.

- The conditional jump instructions are always short jump in 8086.

- Conditional jump instructions test the following flag bits: sign (S), zero (O), carry (C), parity (P) and overflow (O).

- If the condition under test is true, a branch to the label associated with the jump instruction occurs. If the condition is false, the next sequential step in the program executes. For example, a JC will jump if the carry bit is set.

Example of some common conditional jump.

Assembly language	Tested Condition	Operation
JNE or, JNZ	Z=0	Jump if not equal or jump if not zero
JE or JZ	Z=1	Jump if equal or jump if zero
JNO	O=0	Jump if no overflow
JNP or JPO	P=0	Jump if no parity of jump if parity odd
JP or JPE	P=1	Jump if parity or jump if parity even

LOOP

- The loop instruction is a combination of a decrement CX and the JNZ conditional jump.

- In the 8086 through the 80286 processor, LOOP decrement CX, if CX!=0, it jumps to the address indicated by the label. If CX becomes 0, the next sequential instruction executes.

Example: Using LOOP instruction write assembly language program to find out the sum of following series.

        1+2+3+............................+100

Solution:

        No of terms=100, No of addition needed=99 (63H)

        MOV CX, 63H

        MOV AX, 01H

        MOV BX, 02H

        SUM: ADC AX, BX

            ADD BX,01H

            LOOP SUM

Procedures

A procedure is a group of instructions (subroutine or function) that usually perform a specific task.

Advantages

- It is reusable section of the software that is stored in memory once, but used as often as necessary.

- It saves memory space.

- Makes easier to develop software.

Disadvantages

- It takes the compiler a small amount of time to link the procedure and return from it.

How Procedure Links with Main Program

- The CALL instruction links to the procedure and the RET (return) instruction return from the procedure.

- The CALL instruction pushes the address (return address) of the instruction following the CALL on the stack. The RET instruction removes an address from the stack so the program return to the instruction following the CALL.

- A procedure begins with the PROC directive and ends with the ENDP directive. The PROC directive is followed by the type of procedure: NEAR (intra-segment) or FAR (intersegment).

Format of Procedure	Example:
XXX PROC NEAR/FAR	SUMS PROC NEAR
....	ADD AX,BX
....	ADD AX,CX
....	ADD AX,DX
RET	RET
XXX ENDP	SUMS ENDP

N.B

- XXX is the name of level (both level name should be same).

- To call a procedure in main program write: CALL XXX.

CALL Instruction

The CALL instruction transfers the flow of the program to the procedure. The CALL instruction differs from a jump instruction because a CALL saves a return address on the stack.

Whenever a CALL instruction executes it:

- Pushes the IP or, CS:IP on the stack.

- Changes the value of IP or, CS:IP.

- Jumps to the procedure by new IP or, CS:IP address.

Table: Difference between JMP and CALL instruction.

JMP	CALL
Doesn't use stack	Uses stack
Doesn't return to the next instruction of JMP	Must return to the next instruction of CALL

Types of CALL

- Near CALL

- Far CALL

Table: Difference between Near CALL and Far Call.

Near CALL	Far CALL
1. Procedure located within the same code segment (±32KB)	1. Procedure located in the entire memory (1 MB)
2. 3-byte instruction	2. 5-byte instruction
3. Only IP content is replaced by (IP±displacement)	3. Both CS and IP contents are replaced by new CS and IP address
4. Stack stores only return IP address (2 byte)	4. Stack stores the return CS and IP address. (4 byte)

RET Instruction

- The return (RET) instruction removes a 16-bit number (near return) from the stack and places it into IP or removes a 32-bit number (far return) and places it into IP and CS.

- The near and far return instructions are both defined in the procedure's PROC directive, which automatically selects the proper return instruction.

Interrupts

- An interrupt is either a hardware-generated CALL (externally derived from a hardware signal) or a software-generated CALL (internally derived from the execution of an instruction or some other internal event) that allow normal program execution to be interrupted (stopped).

- In response to an interrupt, the microprocessor stops execution its current program and calls a procedure called interrupt service procedure (ISP).

- An IRET instruction at end of the interrupt-service procedure returns execution to the interrupted program.

Instruction: INT nn; where nn indicates interrupt vector number (0 to 255) Each INT instruction is 2-byte long. 1st byte contain opcode and 2nd byte contains vector type number. (exception: INTO and INT3 both are 1-byte instruction).

Types

The 8086 interrupts can be classified into three types. These are:

- Predefined interrupts.

- User-defined software interrupts.

- User-defined hardware interrupts.

Interrupt Vectors

- Interrupt vector is the 4 byte long (CS:IP) address of interrupt service procedure stored in the first 1024 bytes (out of 1Mbytes) of the memory (00000-003FFH). This memory location (1024 byte) is known as interrupt vector table.

- There are 256 different interrupt vectors, and each vector contains 4 byte address of ISP. The first two bytes contain the IP and last two byte contains the CS.

Instruction: INT nn; where nn indicates interrupt vector number.

Finding Address of ISP

For the interrupt type nn (Instruction INT nn), the table address for IP=4×nn and the table address for CS=4×nn+2.

Assign Interrupt Types

- Types 0 to 4 are for the predefined interrupts.

- Types 5 to 31 are reserved by intel for future use.

- Types 32 to 255 are available for maskable interrupts.

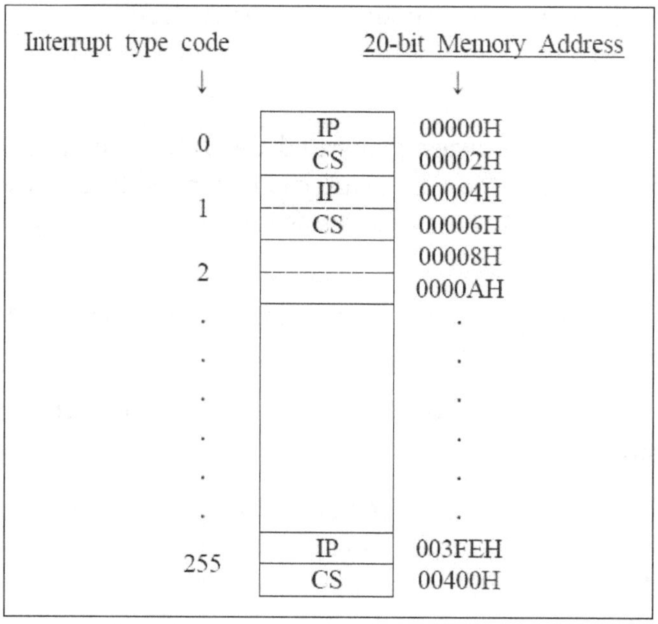

8086 interrupt vector table/pointer table

Example: Find the physical address of interrupt service procedure for the following interrupt instructions:

- INT 01H

- INT FFH

Interrupt vector table is given.

Solution:

Address for IP = 4 × 1 = 00004H

Address for CS = 4 × 1 + 2 = 00006H

So, IP= AC5EH and CS= C83AH

Physical address = CS × 10+IP

$\qquad$ = (C83AH × 10+AC5EH)

$\qquad$ = D2FFEH

Address for IP = 4 × FF = 003FCH

Address for CS = 4 × FF + 2 = 003FEH

So, IP= 5A99H and CS= 9800H

Physical address = CS × 10+IP

$\qquad$ = (5A99H × 10+9800H)

$\qquad$ = 64190H

12	00000H
34	00001H
65	00002H
F2	00003H
5E	00004H
AC	00005H
3A	00006H
C8	00007H
99	00008H
45	00009H
99	003FCH
5A	003FDH
00	003FEH
98	003FFH

Predefined Interrupts (0 to 4)

The predefined interrupts (it is defined by the manufacturer) include:

- Division zero (type 0)
- Single step (type 1)
- Nonmaskable interrupt pin (type 2)
- Breakpoint interrupt (type 3) and
- Interrupt on overflow (type 4).

Type 0 (divided by zero): The 8086 is automatically interrupted whenever a division by zero is attempted.

Type 1 (Single step execution): Once TF is set to one, the 8086 automatically generates a TYPE 1 interrupt after execution of each instruction.

Type 2 (NMI pin): The nonmaskable interrupt is initiated via the 8086 NMI pin. It is edge triggered (LOW to HIGH) and must be active for two clock cycles to guarantee recognition. It is normally used for catastrophic failures such as power failure.

INT 3 (Break Point Interrupt)-type 3

- When a break point interrupt inserted (it is inserted by INT 3 instruction), the system executes the instruction up to break point.
- Unlike the single step feature which stops execution after each instruction, the break point features executes all the instruction up to the inserted breakpoint and then stop execution.
- It is a 1-byte instruction.

INTO (Interrupt on Overflow)-type 4

- Interrupt on overflow (INTO) is a conditional software interrupt that tests the overflow flag (O).
- If O=0, the INTO instruction performs no operation.

And if O=1, INTO call procedure whose address is stored in interrupt vector with type number 4.

Consequences of Software Interrupt Instruction (INT Instruction)

Whenever a software interrupt executes it:

- Pushes flags onto stack.
- Clears the T and I flag bits.
- Pushes CS onto stack.
- Fetches new CS from vector table.

- Pushes IP onto stack.

- Fetches new IP from vector table.

- Jumps to service procedure pointed by new CS:IP.

IRET Instruction

The interrupt return instruction (IRET) is used only with software and hardware interrupt service procedure.

It is a special return instruction which perform following task:

- POP stack data back into the IP.

- POP stack data back into CS.

- POP stack data back into the flag register.

Why We Need to Clear T and I Flag in Case of Software Interrupt?

- I flag controls the external hardware interrupt. During software interrupt I flag is cleared to prevent hardware interrupt, because microprocessor does not allow hardware and software interrupt simultaneously.

- T flag is cleared to stop debugging so that no debugging occurs during interrupt.

Miscellaneous Control Instruction

Controlling the Carry Flag Bit

- STC= Sets the carry flag.

- CLC= Clears the carry flag.

- CMC= Complements the carry flag.

HLT (Halt) Instruction

HLT instruction stops the execution of the program. There are three ways to exit of HLT state:

- By an interrupt.

- By a hardware reset.

- A DMA operation.

NOP

- It just takes time to execute NOP instruction but performs no operation.

- Used to insert time delay.

WAIT Instruction

- Wait instruction monitors the $\overline{TEST}$ pin of 8086 microprocessor. If WAIT instruction executes while $\overline{TEST}$ pin is 1(high), nothing will happen.

- If WAIT instruction executes while $\overline{TEST}$ pin is low microprocessor waits until $\overline{TEST}$ pin becomes 1(high).

CLD (Clear Direction Flag)

- This instruction resets the direction flag to 0. No other flags are affected.

- If the direction flag is reset, SI and DI will automatically be incremented when one of the string instructions, such as MOVS, CMPS or, SCAS executes.

CLI (Clear Interrupt Flag)

- This instruction resets the interrupt flag without affecting other flag bits.

- If the interrupt flag is reset, the 8086 will not respond to an interrupt signal on its INTR input.

RISC

The microcontroller architecture that utilizes small and highly optimized set of instructions is termed as the Reduced Instruction Set Computer or simply called as RISC. It is also called as LOAD/STORE architecture.

In the late 1970s and early 1980s, RISC projects were primarily developed from Stanford, UC-Berkley and IBM. The John Coke of IBM research team developed RISC by reducing the number of instructions required for processing computations faster than the CISC. The RISC architecture is faster and the chips required for the manufacture of RISC architecture is also less expensive compared to the CISC architecture.

Typical Features of RISC Architecture

- Pipelining technique of RISC, executes multiple parts or stages of instructions simultaneously such that every instruction on the CPU is optimized. Hence, the RISC processors have Clock per Instruction of one cycle, and this is called as One Cycle Execution.

- It optimizes the usage of register with more number of registers in the RISC and more number of interactions within the memory can be prevented.

- Simple addressing modes, even complex addressing can be done by using arithmetic and logical operations.

- It simplifies the compiler design by using identical general purpose registers which allows any register to be used in any context.

- For efficient usage of the registers and optimization of the pipelining uses, reduced instruction set is required.

- The number of bits used for the opcode is reduced.

- In general there are 32 or more registers in the RISC.

Advantages of RISC Processor Architecture

- Because of the small set of instructions of RISC, high-level language compilers can produce more efficient code.

- RISC allows freedom of using the space on microprocessors because of its simplicity.

- Instead of using Stack, many RISC processors use the registers for passing arguments and holding the local variables.

- RISC functions uses only a few parameters, and the RISC processors cannot use the call instructions, and therefore, use a fixed length instructions which are easy to pipeline.

- The speed of the operation can be maximized and the execution time can be minimized.

- Very less number of instruction formats (less than four), a few number of instructions (around 150) and a few addressing modes (less than four) are needed.

Disadvantages of RISC Processor Architecture

- With the increase in length of the instructions, the complexity increases for the RISC processors to execute due to its character cycle per instruction.

- The performance of the RISC processors depends mostly on the compiler or programmer as the knowledge of the compiler plays a major role while converting the CISC code to a RISC code; hence, the quality of the generated code depends on the compiler.

- While rescheduling the CISC code to a RISC code, termed as a code expansion, will increase the size. And, the quality of this code expansion will again depend on the compiler, and also on the machine's instruction set.

- The first level cache of the RISC processors is also a disadvantage of the RISC, in which these processors have large memory caches on the chip itself. For feeding the instructions, they require very fast memory systems.

CISC

The CISC approach attempts to minimize the number of instructions per program, sacrificing the number of cycles per instruction. Computers based on the CISC architecture are designed to decrease the memory cost. Because, the large programs need more storage, thus increasing the memory cost and large memory becomes more expensive. To solve these problems, the number of instructions per program can be reduced by embedding the number of operations in a single instruction, thereby making the instructions more complex.

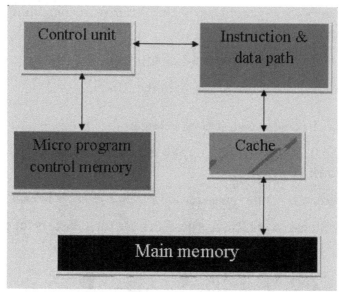

CISC Architecture

- MUL loads two values from the memory into separate registers in CISC.

- CISC uses minimum possible instructions by implementing hardware and executes operations.

- Instruction Set Architecture is a medium to permit communication between the programmer and the hardware. Data execution part, copying of data, deleting or editing is the user commands used in the microprocessor and with this microprocessor the Instruction set architecture is operated.

The main keywords used in the above Instruction Set Architecture are as below:

Instruction Set

Group of instructions given to execute the program and they direct the computer by manipulating the data. Instructions are in the form – Opcode (operational code) and Operand. Where, opcode is the instruction applied to load and store data, etc. The operand is a memory register where instruction applied.

Addressing Modes

Addressing modes are the manner in the data is accessed. Depending upon the type of instruction applied, addressing modes are of various types such as direct mode where straight data is accessed or indirect mode where the location of the data is accessed. Processors having identical ISA may be very different in organization. A processor with identical ISA and nearly identical organization is still not nearly identical.

CPU performance is given by the fundamental law:

$$\text{CPU Time} = \frac{\text{Second}}{\text{Program}} = \frac{\text{Instructions}}{\text{Program}} \times \frac{\text{Cycles}}{\text{Instructions}} \times \frac{\text{Second}}{\text{Cycles}}$$

Thus, CPU performance is dependent upon Instruction Count, CPI (Cycles per instruction) and Clock cycle time. And all three are affected by the instruction set architecture.

Table: Instruction Count of the CPU

	Instruction Count	CPI	Clock
Program	X		
Compiler	X	X	
Instruction Set Architecture	X	X	X
Microarchitecture		X	X
Physical Design			X

This underlines the importance of the instruction set architecture. There are two prevalent instruction set architectures.

Examples of CISC Processors

- IBM 370/168: It was introduced in the year 1970. CISC design is a 32 bit processor and four 64-bit floating point registers.

- VAX 11/780: CISC design is a 32-bit processor and it supports many numbers of addressing modes and machine instructions which is from Digital Equipment Corporation.

- Intel 80486: It was launched in the year 1989 and it is a CISC processor, which has instructions varying lengths from 1 to 11 and it will have 235 instructions.

Characteristics of CISC Architecture

- Instruction-decoding logic will be Complex.

- One instruction is required to support multiple addressing modes.

- Less chip space is enough for general purpose registers for the instructions that are ooperated directly on memory.

- Various CISC designs are set up two special registers for the stack pointer, handling interrupts, etc.

- MUL is referred to as a "complex instruction" and requires the programmer for storing functions.

Advantages of CISC Architecture

- Microprogramming is easy assembly language to implement, and less expensive than hard wiring a control unit.

- The ease of micro coding new instructions allowed designers to make CISC machines upwardly compatible.

- As each instruction became more accomplished, fewer instructions could be used to implement a given task.

Disadvantages of CISC Architecture

- The performance of the machine slows down due to the amount of clock time taken by different instructions will be dissimilar.

- Only 20% of the existing instructions are used in a typical programming event, even though there are various specialized instructions in reality which are not even used frequently.

- The conditional codes are set by the CISC instructions as a side effect of each instruction which takes time for this setting – and, as the subsequent instruction changes the condition code bits – so, the compiler has to examine the condition code bits before this happens.

MISC

Minimal instruction set computer (MISC) is a processor architecture with a very small number of basic operations and corresponding opcodes. Such instruction sets are commonly stack-based rather than register-based to reduce the size of operand specifiers.

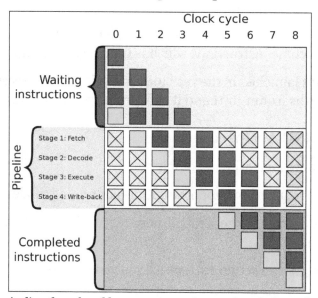

Generic 4-stage pipeline the colored boxes represent instructions independent of each other

Such a stack machine architecture is inherently simpler since all instructions operate on the topmost stack entries.

As a result of the stack architecture is an overall smaller instruction set, a smaller and faster instruction decode unit with overall faster operation of individual instructions.

Separate from the stack definition of MISC architecture, is the MISC architecture being defined with respect to the number of instructions supported.

- Typically a minimal instruction set computer is viewed as having 32 or fewer instructions, where NOP, RESET and CPUID type instructions are generally not counted by consensus due to their fundamental nature.

- 32 instructions is viewed as the highest allowable number of instructions for a MISC, as 16 or 8 instructions are closer to what is meant by "Minimal Instructions".

- A MISC CPU cannot have zero instructions as that is a zero instruction set computer.

- A MISC CPU cannot have one instruction as that is a one instruction set computer.

- The implemented CPU instructions should by default not support a wide set of inputs, so this typically means an 8-bit or 16-bit CPU.

- If a CPU has an NX bit, it is more likely to be viewed as being CISC or RISC.

- MISC chips typically don't have hardware memory protection of any kind unless there is an application specific reason to have the feature.

- If a CPU has a microcode subsystem, that excludes it from being a MISC system.

- The only addressing mode considered acceptable for a MISC CPU to have is load/store, the same as for RISC CPUs.

- MISC CPUs can typically have between 64 KB to 4 GB of accessible addressable memory-but most MISC designs are less than 1 megabyte.

Also, the instruction pipelines of MISC as a rule tend to be very simple. Instruction pipelines, branch prediction, out-of-order execution, register renaming and speculative execution broadly exclude a CPU from being classified as a MISC architecture system.

Disadvantages

Disadvantages of MISC design are:

- Instructions tend to have more sequential dependencies, reducing overall instruction-level parallelism.

- Optimal features like Instruction pipelines, branch prediction, out-of-order execution, register renaming and speculative execution do not form a part hence, has lower performance.

OISC

OISC is the *One Instruction Set Computer* (by analogy with RISC and CISC), a machine providing only one instruction. The abbreviation URISC (Ultimate RISC) has been used in some publications with the same meaning as OISC.

In some implementations the instruction is subtract and branch unless positive, abbreviated *subleq* (subtract and branch if less or equal to zero), or sometimes subtract and branch if negative (SBN), which only differ by zero-inclusion. Some languages use a memory mapped instruction pointer (as in RSSB). Branching is done by writing to IP in these implementations. More advanced memory mapping allows complex functionality such as arithmetic but with the benefit of having a simple copy operation (MOVE).

The subtract-and-branch-unless-positive operation usually has three parameters. *Subleq (a,b,c)* (Subleq) subtracts *a* from *b*, stores the result in *b*, and then transfers control to the address in *c* if the result was non-positive.

The simplest known OISC is arguably BitBitJump. Its instruction has 3 operands as in Subleq, but the meaning is: copy the bit addressed by *a* to the bit addressed by *b* and jump to the address *c*. BitBitJump has a "big brother" ByteByteJump that copies 1 byte at a time instead of 1 bit. Both of these machines belong to a larger class of machines, WordWordJump, that copy *b* bits at a time but have address operands of size *n*b*, where $n \geq 2$ (e.g. 32-bit addresses and 8-bit data for a 32-bit WordWordJump machine). It is this feature that allows BitBitJump, ByteByteJump and similar machines to perform arithmetic and conditional jumps through the use of self-modifying code.

Some OISC languages are Turing-complete, making them Turing tarpits, while others are bounded-storage machines, more akin to physical CPUs. Turing-completeness requires the OISC to be defined with sufficient abstraction with respect to both addressing scheme and operand size. For example, Subleq uses absolute addressing and does not specify its operand size, so it is TC. BitBitJump, on the other hand, is defined to use bounded operand size and absolute addressing, so it is only a bounded storage machine. It is not known whether either of these languages with bounded operand size could achieve TC-ness by revising them to use *relative addressing*. It seems likely, however, because *relative addressing* is the Turing machine property.

Any OISC language belongs to either one of the two groups: with memory mapping (MOVE, RSSB) or without (Subleq, SBN, BitBitJump, ByteByteJump). Note, that a language from the second group may have an extension with memory mapped special addresses, but those addresses are not required for computations; they are used for IO or any other system calls.

Machine Architecture

In a Turing-complete model, each memory location can store an arbitrary integer, and – depending on the model – there may be arbitrarily many locations. The instructions themselves reside in memory as a sequence of such integers.

There exists a class of universal computers with a single instruction based on bit manipulation such as bit copying or bit inversion. Since their memory model is finite, as is the memory structure used in real computers, those bit manipulation machines are equivalent to real computers rather than to Turing machines.

Currently known OISCs can be roughly separated into three broad categories:

- Bit-manipulating machines.
- Transport triggered architecture machines.
- Arithmetic-based Turing-complete machines.

Bit-manipulating Machines

Bit-manipulating machines are the simplest class.

BitBitJump

A bit copying machine, called BitBitJump, copies one bit in memory and passes the execution unconditionally to the address specified by one of the operands of the instruction. This process turns out to be capable of universal computation (i.e. being able to execute any algorithm and to interpret any other universal machine) because copying bits can conditionally modify the code that will be subsequently executed.

Toga Computer

Another machine, called the Toga Computer, inverts a bit and passes the execution conditionally depending on the result of inversion.

Multi-bit Copying Machine

Yet another bit operating machine, similar to BitBitJump, copies several bits at the same time. The problem of computational universality is solved in this case by keeping predefined jump tables in the memory.

Transport Triggered Architecture

Transport triggered architecture (TTA) is a design in which computation is a side effect of data transport. Usually, some memory registers (triggering ports) within common address space perform an assigned operation when the instruction references them. For example, in an OISC using a single memory-to-memory copy instruction, this is done by triggering ports that perform arithmetic and instruction pointer jumps when written to.

Arithmetic-based Turing-complete Machines

Arithmetic-based Turing-complete machines use an arithmetic operation and a conditional jump. Like the two previous universal computers, this class is also Turing-complete. The instruction operates on integers which may also be addresses in memory.

Currently there are several known OISCs of this class, based on different arithmetic operations:

- Addition (addleq, add and branch if less than or equal to zero).
- Decrement (djn, decrement and branch (jump) if nonzero).
- Increment (p1eq, plus 1 and branch if equal to another value).
- Subtraction (subleq, subtract and branch if less than or equal to zero).
- Subtraction when possible (Arithmetic machine).

Instruction Types

Common choices for the single instruction are:

- Subtract and branch if less than or equal to zero;
- Subtract and branch if negative;

- Subtract if positive else branch;

- Reverse subtract and skip if borrow;

- Move (used as part of a transport triggered architecture);

- Subtract and branch if non zero (SBNZ a, b, c, destination);

- Cryptoleq (heterogeneous encrypted and unencrypted computation).

Only *one* of these instructions is used in a given implementation. Hence, there is no need for an opcode to identify which instruction to execute; the choice of instruction is inherent in the design of the machine, and an OISC is typically named after the instruction it uses (e.g., an SBN OISC, the SUBLEQ language, etc.). Each of the above instructions can be used to construct a Turing-complete OISC.

Subtract and Branch if not Equal to Zero

The SBNZ a, b, c, d instruction ("*subtract and branch if not equal to zero*") subtracts the contents at address *a* from the contents at address *b*, stores the result at address *c*, and then, *if the result is not 0*, transfers control to address *d* (if the result is equal to zero, execution proceeds to the next instruction in sequence).

Subtract and Branch if Less than or Equal to Zero

The subleq instruction ("*subtract and branch if less than or equal to zero*") subtracts the contents at address a from the contents at address b, stores the result at address b, and then, *if the result is not positive*, transfers control to address c (if the result is positive, execution proceeds to the next instruction in sequence).

Pseudocode:

```
subleq a, b, c   ; Mem[b] = Mem[b] - Mem[a]

                 ; if (Mem[b] ≤ 0) goto c
```

Conditional branching can be suppressed by setting the third operand equal to the address of the next instruction in sequence. If the third operand is not written, this suppression is implied.

A variant is also possible with two operands and an internal accumulator, where the accumulator is subtracted from the memory location specified by the first operand. The result is stored in both the accumulator and the memory location, and the second operand specifies the branch address:

```
subleq2 a, b     ; Mem[a] = Mem[a] - ACCUM

                 ; ACCUM = Mem[a]

                 ; if (Mem[a] ≤ 0) goto b
```

Although this uses only two (instead of three) operands per instruction, correspondingly more instructions are then needed to effect various logical operations.

Synthesized Instructions

It is possible to synthesize many types of higher-order instructions using only the subleq instruction.

Unconditional branch:

```
JMP c
                subleq Z, Z, c
```

Addition can be performed by repeated subtraction, with no conditional branching; e.g., the following instructions result in the content at location a being added to the content at location b:

```
ADD a, b
                subleq a, Z

                subleq Z, b

                subleq Z, Z
```

The first instruction subtracts the content at location a from the content at location Z (which is 0) and stores the result (which is the negative of the content at a) in location Z. The second instruction subtracts this result from b, storing in b this difference (which is now the sum of the contents originally at a and b); the third instruction restores the value 0 to Z.

A copy instruction can be implemented similarly; e.g., the following instructions result in the content at location b getting replaced by the content at location a, again assuming the content at location Z is maintained as 0:

```
MOV a, b
                subleq b, b

                subleq a, Z

                subleq Z, b

                subleq Z, Z
```

Any desired arithmetic test can be built. For example, a branch-if-zero condition can be assembled from the following instructions:

```
BEQ b, c
                subleq b, Z, L1

                subleq Z, Z, OUT

        L1: subleq Z, Z

                subleq Z, b, c

        OUT: ...
```

Subleq2 can also be used to synthesize higher-order instructions, although it generally requires more operations for a given task. For example, no fewer than 10 subleq2 instructions are required to flip all the bits in a given byte:

```
NOT a

            subleq2 tmp             ; tmp = 0 (tmp = temporary register)

            subleq2 tmp

            subleq2 minus_one       ; acc = -1

            subleq2 a               ; a' = a + 1

            subleq2 Z               ; Z = - a - 1

            subleq2 tmp             ; tmp = a + 1

            subleq2 a               ; a' = 0

            subleq2 tmp             ; load tmp into acc

            subleq2 a               ; a' = - a - 1 ( = ~a )

            subleq2 Z               ; set Z back to 0
```

Emulation

The following program (written in pseudocode) emulates the execution of a subleq-based OISC:

```
int memory[], program_counter, a, b, c

 program_counter = 0

 while (program_counter >= 0):

     a = memory[program_counter]

     b = memory[program_counter+1]

     c = memory[program_counter+2]

     if (a < 0 or b < 0):

         program_counter = -1

     else:

         memory[b] = memory[b] - memory[a]

         if (memory[b] > 0):

             program_counter += 3
```

```
        else:

            program_counter = c
```

This program assumes that memory[] is indexed by *nonnegative* integers. Consequently, for a subleq instruction (a, b, c), the program interprets a < 0, b < 0, or an executed branch to c < 0 as a halting condition.

Compilation

There is a compiler called Higher Subleq written by Oleg Mazonka that compiles a simplified C program into subleq code.

Subtract and Branch if Negative

The subneg instruction ("*subtract and branch if negative*"), also called SBN, is defined similarly to subleq:

```
subneg a, b, c    ; Mem[b] = Mem[b] - Mem[a]

                  ; if (Mem[b] < 0) goto c
```

Conditional branching can be suppressed by setting the third operand equal to the address of the next instruction in sequence. If the third operand is not written, this suppression is implied.

Synthesized Instructions

It is possible to synthesize many types of higher-order instructions using only the subneg instruction. For simplicity, only one synthesized instruction is shown here to illustrate the difference between subleq and subneg.

Unconditional branch:

```
JMP c

                subneg POS, Z, c

                . . .

            c: subneg Z, Z
```

where Z and POS are locations previously set to contain 0 and a positive integer, respectively.

Unconditional branching is assured only if Z initially contains 0 (or a value less than the integer stored in POS). A follow-up instruction is required to clear Z after the branching, assuming that the content of Z must be maintained as 0.

A variant is also possible with four operands – subneg4. The reversal of minuend and subtrahend eases implementation in hardware. The non-destructive result simplifies the synthetic instructions.

```
subneg4 s, m, r, j    ; subtrahend, minuend, result and jump addresses

                      ; Mem[r] = Mem[m] - Mem[s]

                      ; if (Mem[r] < 0) goto j
```

Arithmetic Machine

In an attempt to make Turing machine more intuitive, Z. A. Melzac consider the task of computing with positive numbers. The machine has an infinite abacus, an infinite number of counters (pebbles, tally sticks) initially at a special location S. The machine is able to do one operation:

Take from location X as many counters as there are in location Y and transfer them to location Z and proceed to next instruction. If this operation is not possible because there is not enough counter in Y, then leave the abacus as it is and proceed to instruction T.

This essentially a subneg where the test is done before rather than after the subtraction, in order to keep all number positive and mimic a human operator computing on a real world abacus.

Pseudocode:

```
command X, Y, Z, T    ; if (Mem[Y] < Mem[X]) goto T

                      ; Mem[Z] = Mem[Y] - Mem[X]
```

After giving a few programs: multiplication, gcd, computing the nth prime number, representation in base b of an arbitrary number, sorting in order of magnitude, Melzac shows explicitly how to simulate an arbitrary Turing machine on his Arithmetic Machine.

He mentions that it can easily be shown using the elements of recursive functions that every number calculable on the Arithmetic Machine is computable. A proof of which was given by Lambek on an equivalent two instruction machine: X+ (increment X) and X- else T (decrement X if it not empty, else jump to T).

Reverse Subtract and Skip if Borrow

In a *reverse subtract and skip if borrow* (RSSB) instruction, the accumulator is subtracted from the memory location and the next instruction is skipped if there was a borrow (memory location was smaller than the accumulator). The result is stored in both the accumulator and the memory location. The program counter is mapped to memory location 0. The accumulator is mapped to memory location 1.

Example

To set x to the value of y minus z:

```
# First, move z to the destination location x.

 RSSB temp # Three instructions required to clear acc, temp

 RSSB temp
```

```
RSSB temp

RSSB x     # Two instructions clear acc, x, since acc is already clear

RSSB x

RSSB y     # Load y into acc: no borrow

RSSB temp # Store -y into acc, temp: always borrow and skip

RSSB temp # Skipped

RSSB x     # Store y into x, acc

 # Second, perform the operation.

RSSB temp # Three instructions required to clear acc, temp

RSSB temp

RSSB temp

RSSB z     # Load z

RSSB x     # x = y - z
```

- If the value stored at "temp" is initially a negative value and the instruction that executed right before the first "RSSB temp" in this routine borrowed, then four "RSSB temp" instructions will be required for the routine to work.

- If the value stored at "z" is initially a negative value then the final "RSSB x" will be skipped and thus the routine will not work.

Transport Triggered Architecture

A transport triggered architecture uses only the *move* instruction, hence it was originally called a "move machine". This instruction moves the contents of one memory location to another memory location combining with the current content of the new location:

```
move a to b ; Mem[b] := Mem[a] (+, -, *, /, ...) Mem[b]
```

sometimes written as:

```
a -> b ; Mem[b] := Mem[a] (+, -, *, /, ...) Mem[b]
```

The operation performed is defined by the destination memory cell. Some cells are specialized in addition, some other in multiplication, etc. So memory cells are not simple store but coupled with an arithmetic logic unit (ALU) setup to perform only one sort of operation with the current value of the cell. Some of the cells are control flow instructions to alter the program execution with jumps, conditional execution, subroutines, if-then-else, for-loop, etc.

A commercial transport triggered architecture microcontroller has been produced called MAXQ, which hides the apparent inconvenience of an OISC by using a "transfer map" that represents all possible destinations for the *move* instructions.

Cryptoleq

Cryptoleq processor made at NYU Abu Dhabi

Cryptoleq is a language consisting of one instruction, the eponymous, is capable of performing general-purpose computation on encrypted programs and is a close relative to Subleq. Cryptoleq works on continuous cells of memory using direct and indirect addressing, and performs two operations O_1 and O_2 on three values A, B, and C:

```
Cryptoleq a, b, c       [b] = O1([a],[b]) ;

                        IP = c,   if O2[b] ≤ 0

                        IP = IP + 3, otherwise
```

where, a, b and c are addressed by the instruction pointer, IP, with the value of IP addressing a, IP + 1 point to b and IP + 2 to c.

In Cryptoleq operations O_1 and O_2 are defined as follows:

$$O_1(x, y) = x_{N^2}^{-1} y \bmod N^2$$

$$O_2(x) = \left\lfloor \frac{x-1}{N} \right\rfloor$$

The main difference with Subleq is that in Subleq, $O_1(x,y)$ simply subtracts y from x and $O_2(x)$ equals to x. Cryptoleq is also homomorphic to Subleq, modular inversion and multiplication is homomorphic to subtraction and the operation of O_2 corresponds the Subleq test if the values were unencrypted. A program written in Subleq can run on a Cryptoleq machine, meaning backwards compatibility. Cryptoleq though, implements fully homomorphic calculations and since the model is be able to do multiplications. Multiplication on an encrypted domain is assisted by a unique function G that is assumed to be difficult to reverse engineer and allows re-encryption of a value based on the O_2 operation:

$$G(x,y) = \begin{cases} \tilde{0}, & \text{if } O_2(\overline{x}) \leq 0 \\ \tilde{y}, & \text{otherwise} \end{cases}$$

where, $\tilde{y}$ is the re-encrypted value of y and $\tilde{0}$ is encrypted zero. x is the encrypted value of a variable, let it be m, and $\overline{x}$ equals $Nm+1$.

The multiplication algorithm is based on addition and subtraction, uses the function G and does not have conditional jumps nor branches. Cryptoleq encryption is based on Paillier cryptosystem.

NISC

A no-instruction-set-computer (NISC) processor in combination with a program counter, program memory and data memory comprises a controller coupled to the program memory; and a datapath coupled to the controller and to the data memory, characterized in that computer code compiles directly into the controller and the datapath. The datapath comprises a plurality of storage elements, a plurality of functional units and a plurality of busses. The plurality of storage elements and functional units are selectively coupled together by the plurality of busses. The datapath collectively generate datapath output and status signals and have a data memory input. The controller has no instruction set and computer code runs directly on the controller. The processor is combined with a compiler which is arranged and configured to operate a parse tree. Under control of the compiler the controller covers the parse tree with control words stored in the program memory.

NISC Benefits

NISC architecture has several benefits:

1. The distinction between SW and HW implementation disappears. For HW implementation the control words are in ROM or gate logic, while for SW implementation they are in a RAM.

2. Since DP can be pipelined by introducing any number of stages and since DP can have any level of parallelism, it is difficult to outperform NISC.

3. Since there is no instruction set, NISC eliminates the last stage of interpretation between C code and HW. C code runs directly on HW (DP).

4. NISC can emulate any instruction set, since NISC control word can execute any operation as long as DP resources in DP are available. Therefore, any legacy code can be executed on a properly defined NISC by converting legacy instructions into NISC control words through a table look up.

5. The NISC compiler uses the High-Level Synthesis algorithms for covering parse tree with control words.

6. Since NISC is a sufficient component for any computation, only one compiler is needed worldwide. Hopefully, such a compiler will be in public domain.

7. Similarly, only one NISC processor, although in different versions and with different parameters, is needed worldwide. That uniqueness will simplify education, design, trade, maintenance, testing and many other aspects of system design, in similar fashion as gate libraries led to standardization of digital design.

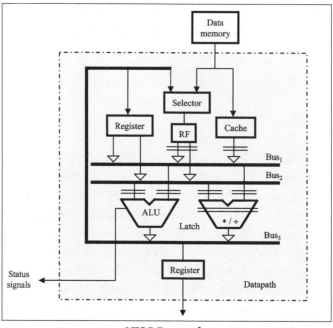

NISC Datapath

NISC Datapath

Any C program can be executed on a NISC processor, which consists of a Controller and the Datapath. Datapath consists of a set of storage elements (registers, register files, memories), set of functional units (ALUs, multipliers, shifters, custom functions) and set of busses. All these components may be allocated in different quantities and types and connected arbitrarily through busses. Each component may take one or more clock cycles to execute, each component may be pipelined and each component may have input or output latches or registers. The entire Datapath can be pipelined in several stages in addition to components being pipelined themselves. The Controller defines the state of the processor and issues the control signals for the Datapath.

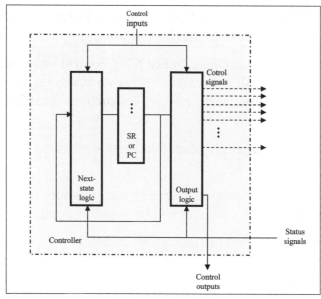

NISC Controller (HW)

NISC Controller (Fixed Implementation)

NISC controller generates a sequence of control words in order to execute a computation specified by the C program. If the sequence is short and it will not change over time, the Controller can be implemented with gates and a state register (SR). This implementation can be easily specified by a finite-state machine model (FSM).

The controller has Control inputs and outputs from the external environment and provides outputs to the external environment. It also gets the status signals from the Datapath and provides the control signals, collectively called control word to the Datapath. The Controller consists of a State register (SR), Nextstate logic and Output logic. SR stores the present state of the processor which is equal to the present state of the FSM model describing the operation of the Controller. The Next-state logic computes the next state to be loaded into the SR, while the Output logic generates the Control signals and the Control outputs. The Next-state and Output logic are combinatorial circuits that are implemented with gates.

The SR, Next-state and Output logic can be redefined and reconfigured if the Controller is implemented on a FPGA.

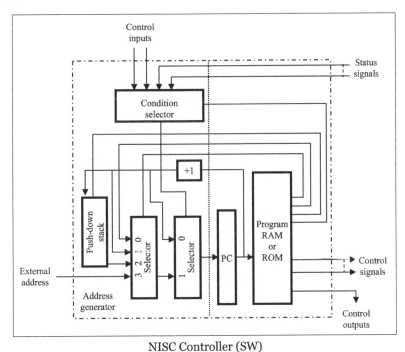

NISC Controller (SW)

NISC Controller (Programmable Implementation)

In the programmable version of the NISC Controller the State Register is called a Program Counter (PC) while Output logic is implemented by a Program memory (PM). PM can be writable if we use a RAM or fixed if we use a ROM. The next-state logic is replaced by an Address generator, which computes the next PM address from several sources. It can just increment the present address or generate a new address from a jump address in the PM, from external sources (OS), or from the push-down stack (subroutine return). The proper address is selected by a mixture of output control signals and status signals from the Datapath. Although the Controller shown in the figure is sufficient for any computation it can be made more sophisticated while implementing the same functionality. For example, the PM can include a cache for speed up if a large PM is required.

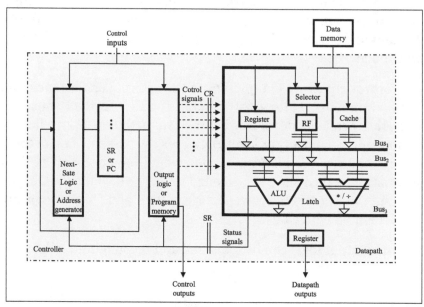

NISC Processor

However, the main characteristic of the programmable controller is that new program can be loaded dynamically and executed, thus making NISC programmable like any other processor.

NISC Processor

NISC processor is the combination of Controller and Datapath. Controller can be fixed or programmable. Datapath can be reprogrammable and reconfigurable. Reprogrammable means that Datapath can be extended or reduced by adding or omitting some components, while reconfigurable means that Datapath can be reconnected with the same components. Either way we make changes we must recompile the original code.

In order to speed up the NISC pipelining, we may insert a Control register (CR) and the Status register (SR) between the Controller and the Datapath.

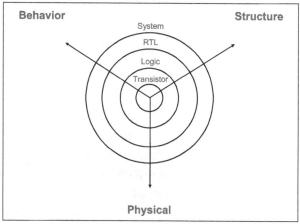

Y Chart (Types of models and levels of abstractions)

Y-Chart

In order to explain the relationship between different abstraction levels, design models and design methodologies or design flows for a NISC processor, we will use Y-Chart. The Y-Chart makes the assumption that each design, no matter how complex, can be modeled in three basic ways emphasizing different properties of the same design.

Therefore, Y-Chart has three axes representing design behavior (function, specification), design structure (connected components, block diagram), and physical design (layout, boards, packages). Behavior represents a design as a black box and describes its outputs in terms of its inputs and time. The black-box behavior does not indicate in anyway how to implement the black box or what its structure is. That is given on the structure axis, where black box is represented as a set of components and connections. Although, behavior of the black box can be derived from its component behaviors such an obtained behavior may be difficult to understand. Physical design adds dimensionality to the structure. It specifies size (height and width) of each component, the position of each component, each port and each connection on the silicon substrate or board or any other container.

Y-Chart can also represent design on different abstraction levels identified by concentric circles around the origin. Usually, four levels are used: Transistor, Logic, Register-transfers and System levels. The name of the abstraction level is derived by the main component used in the structure on this abstraction level. Thus, the main components on Transistor level are N or P-type transistors, while on Logic level they are gates and flip-flops. On the Register-transfers level the main components are registers, register files and functional units such as ALUs, while on the System level they are processors, memories and buses.

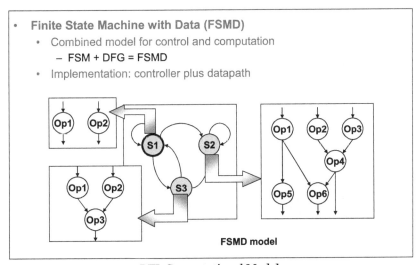

RTL Computational Models

RTL Computational Model

The RTL behavior or computational model is given by a Finite-state-machine with Data (FSMD). It combines finite-state-machine (FSM) model for Controller and data-flow-graph (DFG) for Datapath. FSM has a set of states and a set of transitions from one state into other depending on the value of some of the input signals. In each state FSMD executes a set of expressions represented by a DFG. FSMD model is clock-accurate if each state takes a single clock-cycle.

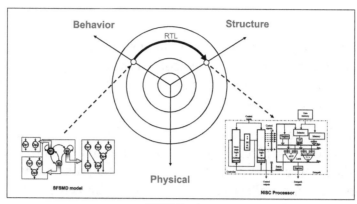

NISC Design

It should be noted that FSMD model encapsulates the definition of the state-based (Moore-type) FSM in which the output is stable during duration of each state. It also encapsulates the definition of the input-based (Mealy-type) FSM with the following interpretation: Input-based FSM transitions to a new state and outputs data conditionally on the value of some of FSM inputs. Similarly, FSMD executes set of expressions depending on the value of some FSMD inputs. However, if the inputs change just before the clock edge there may be not enough time to execute the expressions associated with that particular state. Therefore, designers should avoid this situation by making sure the input values change only early in the clock period or they must insert a state that waits for the input value change. In this case if the input changes too late in the clock cycle, FSMD will stay in the waiting state and proceed with a normal operation in the next clock cycle.

NISC Design

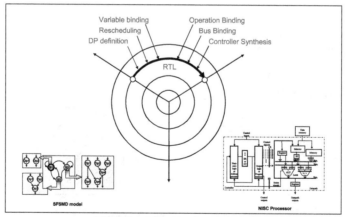

NISC Compilation (Back-end)

NISC design starts with the FSMD model in the behavior axes of the Y-chart and ends up with a custom NISC processor containing any number and type of components connected as required by the FSMD model. Note, that FSMD model can be obtained easily from a programming language code such as C by grouping all the consecutive statements into basic blocks (BB) and introducing two states for each if statement or loop statement, where each state executes a BB. Such a FSMD is sometimes called Super-state FSMD (SFSMD) since each BB may be considered to be executed in one super state. This generation is very simple. Note that each BB will be partitioned into several states during synthesis, where the number of states depends on the resources allocated to the NISC processor.

NISC Compilation (Back-end)

NISC design consists of Datapath definition, generation of control-word sequence, and design of the Controller (fixed or programmable), that executes the functionality specified by the FSMD model. It consists of several tasks:

(a) Definition of the Datapath as a set of components and connections from the RTL library.

(b) Binding of variables, operations and register transfers to storage elements, functional units and busses.

(c) Rescheduling of computation in each state since some components may need more or less than one clock cycle, and computation must satisfy the Datapath pipelining constraints.

(d) Synthesis of programmable or fixed controller.

(e) Generation of control-word sequence for downloading to the Controller RAM.

Any of the above tasks can be performed manually or automatically.

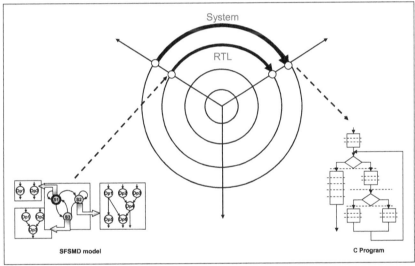

NISC Compilation (Front-end)

NISC Compilation (Front-end)

The NISC processor definition and compilation follows the task of system design, in which the system components and their connectivity as well as partitioning or mapping of system functionality onto different components is performed. Therefore, for each NISC component in the system the C code that executes on that component is known.

NISC compilation consists of parsing that C code and constructing from the parse tree the well-known Control-Data Flow Graph (CDFG). CDFG consists of three objects: if statements, loop statements, and basic blocks (BB) of assignment statements without ifs or loops. Each if and loop statement needs two states in the FSMD while BB can be executed in one or more states depending on the availability of resources in the Datapath. Such a CDFG is equivalent to the Super-state FSMD (SFSMD) which is the starting point for the NISC Back-end.

ZISC

Zero instruction set computer (ZISC) is a computer architecture based on two fundamental ideas:

- Pattern matching.

- Absence of micro instructions.

It has been jointly developed by IBM in Paris and by Guy Paillet, Chairman of Sunnyvale, CA-based Silicon Recognition, Inc.

These chips are known for being thought of as comparable to the neural networks, being marketed for the number of "synapses" and "neurons".

A typical program in an assembly language consists of code which operates on data. The code is normally made up of a sequence of commands/instructions, and typically, most of those commands will take arguments.

The OISC (One Instruction Set Computer) concept maintains this construction. However, it only has one sort of instruction/command, which is therefore entirely defined by its arguments. Most OISC commands are moderately, but not excessively, complex and take many arguments. OISCs also commonly use techniques such as self-modifying code and memory-mapping important registers, in order to gain more functionality from their instruction.

A ZISC takes this concept to its extreme. In addition to having only one commands, that command takes no arguments. As such, any program necessarily consists of that one command repeated indefinitely; any two programs are thus equivalent, and in fact the program itself is entirely implicit. In order to program in a ZISC, you obviously cannot write the program; instead, you initialize memory.

Pretty much any language which reads commands from memory can be interpreted as a ZISC. This is easiest to see using OISCs as an example.

For example, ByteByteJump, when interpreted as an OISC, has command *b = *a; goto *c;. The ZISC interpretation of the language is more complex, as it has to include the semantics of fetching a memory-mapped instruction from memory: with a 3-word-per-address configuration, its ZISC operation is:

```
*(ip[3] * 65536 + ip[4] * 256 + ip[5]) = *(ip[0] * 65536 + ip[1] * 256 +
ip[2]); ip = ip[7] * 65536 + ip[8] * 256 + ip[9];
```

Typically, a language that is designed as a ZISC would have a much simpler operation.

Advantages of Zero Instruction Set Computer ZISC

One Instruction Set Computer (OISC) is a common choice for interpreter golf competitions, because only needing to implement one instruction keeps the size of the interpreter low. However, they suffer the overhead of handling the code and data separately (even if they are in the same physical memory array, you nonetheless tend to need separate registers for handling the instruction pointer and for handling any data being manipulated).

A ZISC arrangement simplifies the problem still further as there is no need to keep track of command arguments.

References

- Instruction-set-of-a-processor-definition-components, lesson, academy: study.com, retrieved 23 june, 2019

- Computer-organization-instruction-formats-zero-one-two-three-address-instruction: geeksforgeeks.org, retrieved 12 april, 2019

- Computer-organization-problem-solving-instruction-format: geeksforgeeks.org, retrieved 24 march , 2019

- Addressing-modes-in-computer-architecture-diagram-examples: csetutor.com, retrieved 7 may, 2019

- What-is-risc-and-cisc-architecture-and-their-workings: elprocus.com, retrieved 18 april, 2019

- Minimal-instruction-set-computer: wikiwand.com, retrieved 21 may, 2019

- Minimal-instruction-set-computer-misc: opengenus.org, retrieved 26 july, 2019

- Catsoulis, john (2005), designing embedded hardware (2 ed.), o'reilly media, pp. 327–333, isbn 978-0-596-00755-3

Memory Management

Memory refers to the hardware integrated circuits in computers which store information. Some of the concepts studied in relation to memory with respect to computer architecture are memory hierarchy, memory unit, cache memory and virtual memory. This chapter closely examines these key concepts of memory management to provide an extensive understanding of the subject.

Memory

Computer memory is a device that is used to store data or programs (sequences of instructions) on a temporary or permanent basis for use in an electronic digital computer. Computers represent information in binary code, written as sequences of 0s and 1s. Each binary digit (or "bit") may be stored by any physical system that can be in either of two stable states, to represent 0 and 1. Such a system is called bistable. This could be an on-off switch, an electrical capacitor that can store or lose a charge, a magnet with its polarity up or down, or a surface that can have a pit or not. Today capacitors and transistors, functioning as tiny electrical switches, are used for temporary storage and either disks or tape with a magnetic coating, or plastic discs with patterns of pits are used for long-term storage.

Computer memory is divided into main (or primary) memory and auxiliary (or secondary) memory. Main memory holds instructions and data when a program is executing, while auxiliary memory holds data and programs not currently in use and provides long-term storage.

Main Memory

The earliest memory devices were electro-mechanical switches, or relays, and electron tubes. In the late 1940s the first stored-program computers used ultrasonic waves in tubes of mercury or charges in special electron tubes as main memory. The latter were the first random-access memory (RAM). RAM contains storage cells that can be accessed directly for read and write operations, as opposed to serial access memory, such as magnetic tape, in which each cell in sequence must be accessed till the required cell is located.

Magnetic Drum Memory

Magnetic drums, which had fixed read/write heads for each of many tracks on the outside surface of a rotating cylinder coated with a ferromagnetic material, were used for both main and auxiliary memory in the 1950s, although their data access was serial.

Magnetic Core Memory

About 1952 the first relatively cheap RAM was developed: magnetic core memory, an arrangement of tiny ferrite cores on a wire grid through which current could be directed to change individual core alignments. Because of the inherent advantage of RAM, core memory was the principal form of main memory until superseded by semiconductor memory in the late 1960s.

Semiconductor Memory

There are two basic kinds of semiconductor memory. Static RAM (SRAM) consists of flip-flops, a bistable circuit composed of four to six transistors. Once a flip-flop stores a bit, it keeps that value until the opposite value is stored in it. SRAM gives fast access to data, but it is physically relatively large. It is used primarily for small amounts of memory called registers in a computer's central processing unit (CPU) and for fast "cache" memory. Dynamic RAM (DRAM) stores each bit in an electrical capacitor rather than in a flip-flop, using a transistor as a switch to charge or discharge the capacitor. Because it has fewer electrical components, a DRAM storage cell is smaller than SRAM. However, access to its value is slower and, because capacitors gradually leak charges, stored values must be recharged approximately 50 times per second. Nonetheless, DRAM is generally used for main memory because the same size chip can hold several times as much DRAM as SRAM.

Storage cells in RAM have addresses. It is common to organize RAM into "words" of 8 to 64 bits, or 1 to 8 bytes (8 bits = 1 byte). The size of a word is generally the number of bits that can be transferred at a time between main memory and the CPU. Every word, and usually every byte, has an address. A memory chip must have additional decoding circuits that select the set of storage cells that are at a particular address and either store a value at that address or fetch what is stored there. The main memory of a modern computer consists of a number of memory chips, each of which might hold many megabytes (millions of bytes), and still further addressing circuitry selects the appropriate chip for each address. In addition, DRAM requires circuits to detect its stored values and refresh them periodically.

Main memories take longer to access data than CPUs take to operate on them. For instance, DRAM memory access typically takes 20 to 80 nanoseconds (billionths of a second), but CPU arithmetic operations may take only a nanosecond or less. There are several ways in which this disparity is handled. CPUs have a small number of registers, very fast SRAM that hold current instructions and the data on which they operate. Cache memory is a larger amount (up to several megabytes) of fast SRAM on the CPU chip. Data and instructions from main memory are transferred to the cache, and since programs frequently exhibit "locality of reference"—that is, they execute the same instruction sequence for a while in a repetitive loop and operate on sets of related data—memory references can be made to the fast cache once values are copied into it from main memory.

Much of the DRAM access time goes into decoding the address to select the appropriate storage cells. The locality of reference property means that a sequence of memory addresses will frequently be used, and fast DRAM is designed to speed access to subsequent addresses after the first one. Synchronous DRAM (SDRAM) and EDO (extended data output) are two such types of fast memory.

Nonvolatile semiconductor memories, unlike SRAM and DRAM, do not lose their contents when power is turned off. Some nonvolatile memories, such as read-only memory (ROM), are not rewritable once manufactured or written. Each memory cell of a ROM chip has either a transistor for a 1 bit or none for a 0 bit. ROMs are used for programs that are essential parts of a computer's operation, such as the bootstrap program that starts a computer and loads its operating system or the BIOS (basic input/output system) that addresses external devices in a personal computer (PC).

EPROM (erasable programmable ROM), EAROM (electrically alterable ROM), and flash memory are types of nonvolatile memories that are rewritable, though the rewriting is far more time-consuming than reading. They are thus used as special-purpose memories where writing is seldom necessary—if used for the BIOS, for example, they may be changed to correct errors or update features.

Auxiliary Memory

Auxiliary memory units are among computer peripheral equipment. They trade slower access rates for greater storage capacity and data stability. Auxiliary memory holds programs and data for future use, and, because it is nonvolatile (like ROM), it is used to store inactive programs and to archive data. Early forms of auxiliary storage included punched paper tape, punched cards, and magnetic drums. Since the 1980s, the most common forms of auxiliary storage have been magnetic disks, magnetic tapes, and optical discs.

Magnetic Disk Drives

Magnetic disks are coated with a magnetic material such as iron oxide. There are two types: hard disks made of rigid aluminum or glass, and removable diskettes made of flexible plastic. In 1956 the first magnetic hard drive (HD) was invented at IBM; consisting of 50 21-inch (53-cm) disks, it had a storage capacity of 5 megabytes. By the 1990s the standard HD diameter for PCs had shrunk to 3.5 inches (about 8.9 cm), with storage capacities in excess of 100 gigabytes (billions of bytes); the standard size HD for portable PCs ("laptops") was 2.5 inches (about 6.4 cm). Since the invention of the floppy disk drive (FDD) at IBM by Alan Shugart in 1967, diskettes have shrunk from 8 inches (about 20 cm) to the current standard of 3.5 inches (about 8.9 cm). FDDs have low capacity—generally less than two megabytes—and have become obsolete since the introduction of optical disc drives in the 1990s.

Hard drives generally have several disks, or platters, with an electromagnetic read/write head for each surface; the entire assembly is called a comb. A microprocessor in the drive controls the motion of the heads and also contains RAM to store data for transfer to and from the disks. The heads move across the disk surface as it spins up to 15,000 revolutions per minute; the drives are hermetically sealed, permitting the heads to float on a thin film of air very close to the disk's surface. A small current is applied to the head to magnetize tiny spots on the disk surface for storage; similarly, magnetized spots on the disk generate currents in the head as it moves by, enabling data to be read. FDDs function similarly, but the removable diskettes spin at only a few hundred revolutions per minute.

Data are stored in close concentric tracks that require very precise control of the read/write heads. Refinements in controlling the heads have enabled smaller and closer packing of tracks—up to 20,000 tracks per inch (8,000 tracks per cm) by the start of the 21st century—which has resulted in the storage capacity of these devices growing nearly 30 percent per year since the 1980s. RAID (redundant array of inexpensive disks) combines multiple disk drives to store data redundantly for greater reliability and faster access. They are used in high-performance computer network servers.

Magnetic Tape

Magnetic tape, similar to the tape used in tape recorders, has also been used for auxiliary storage, primarily for archiving data. Tape is cheap, but access time is far slower than that of a magnetic disk because it is sequential-access memory—i.e., data must be sequentially read and written as a tape is unwound, rather than retrieved directly from the desired point on the tape. Servers may also use large collections of tapes or optical discs, with robotic devices to select and load them, rather like old-fashioned jukeboxes.

Optical Discs

Another form of largely read-only memory is the optical compact disc, developed from videodisc technology during the early 1980s. Data are recorded as tiny pits in a single spiral track on plastic discs that range from 3 to 12 inches (7.6 to 30 cm) in diameter, though a diameter of 4.8 inches (12 cm) is most common. The pits are produced by a laser or by a stamping machine and are read by a low-power laser and a photocell that generates an electrical signal from the varying light reflected from the pattern of pits. Optical discs are removable and have a far greater memory capacity than diskettes; the largest ones can store many gigabytes of information.

A common optical disc is the CD-ROM (compact disc read-only memory). It holds about 700 megabytes of data, recorded with an error-correcting code that can correct bursts of errors caused by dust or imperfections. CD-ROMs are used to distribute software, encyclopaedias, and multimedia text with audio and images. CD-R (CD-recordable), or WORM (write-once read-many), is a variation of CD-ROM on which a user may record information but not subsequently change it. CD-RW (CD-rewritable) disks can be re-recorded. DVDs (digital video, or versatile, discs), developed for recording movies, store data more densely than does CD-ROM, with more powerful error correction. Though the same size as CDs, DVDs typically hold 5 to 17 gigabytes—several hours of video or several million text pages.

Magneto-optical Discs

Magneto-optical discs are hybrid storage medium. In reading, spots with different directions of magnetization give different polarization in the reflected light of a low-power laser beam. In writing, every spot on the disk is first heated by a strong laser beam and then cooled under a magnetic field, magnetizing every spot in one direction, to store all 0s. The writing process then reverses the direction of the magnetic field to store 1s where desired.

Memory Hierarchy

The total memory capacity of a computer can be visualized by hierarchy of components. The memory hierarchy system consists of all storage devices contained in a computer system from the slow Auxiliary Memory to fast Main Memory and to smaller Cache memory.

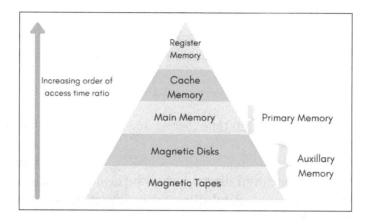

Auxillary memory access time is generally 1000 times that of the main memory, hence it is at the bottom of the hierarchy.

The main memory occupies the central position because it is equipped to communicate directly with the CPU and with auxiliary memory devices through Input/output processor (I/O).

When the program not residing in main memory is needed by the CPU, they are brought in from auxiliary memory. Programs not currently needed in main memory are transferred into auxiliary memory to provide space in main memory for other programs that are currently in use.

The cache memory is used to store program data which is currently being executed in the CPU. Approximate access time ratio between cache memory and main memory is about 1 to 7~10.

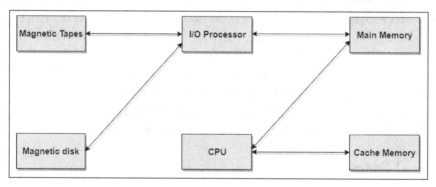

Memory Access Methods

Each memory type is a collection of numerous memory locations. To access data from any memory, first it must be located and then the data is read from the memory location. Following are the methods to access information from memory locations:

1. Random Access: Main memories are random access memories, in which each memory location has a unique address. Using this unique address any memory location can be reached in the same amount of time in any order.

2. Sequential Access: This method allows memory access in a sequence or in order.

3. Direct Access: In this mode, information is stored in tracks, with each track having a separate read/write head.

Characteristics of Memory Hierarchy

The memory hierarchy characteristics mainly include the following:

1. Performance: Previously, the designing of a computer system was done without memory hierarchy, and the speed gap among the main memory as well as the CPU registers enhances because of the huge disparity in access time, which will cause the lower performance of the system. So, the enhancement was mandatory. The enhancement of this was designed in the memory hierarchy model due to the system's performance increase.

2. Ability: The ability of the memory hierarchy is the total amount of data the memory can store. Because whenever we shift from top to bottom inside the memory hierarchy, then the capacity will increase.

3. Access Time: The access time in the memory hierarchy is the interval of the time among the data availability as well as request to read or write. Because whenever we shift from top to bottom inside the memory hierarchy, then the access time will increase.

4. Cost per bit: When we shift from bottom to top inside the memory hierarchy, then the cost for each bit will increase which means an internal Memory is expensive compared with external memory.

Memory Hierarchy Design

The memory hierarchy in computers mainly includes the following:

1. Registers: Usually, the register is a static RAM or SRAM in the processor of the computer which is used for holding the data word which is typically 64 or 128 bits. The program counter register is the most important as well as found in all the processors. Most of the processors use a status word register as well as an accumulator. A status word register is used for decision making, and the accumulator is used to store the data like mathematical operation. Usually, computers like complex instruction set computers have so many registers for accepting main memory, and RISC- reduced instruction set computers have more registers.

2. Cache Memory: Cache memory can also be found in the processor, however rarely it may be another IC (integrated circuit) which is separated into levels. The cache holds the chunk of data which are frequently used from main memory. When the processor has a single core then it will have two (or) more cache levels rarely. Present multi-core processors will be having three, 2-levels for each one core, and one level is shared.

3. Main Memory: The main memory in the computer is nothing but, the memory unit in the CPU that communicates directly. It is the main storage unit of the computer. This memory is fast as well as large memory used for storing the data throughout the operations of the computer. This memory is made up of RAM as well as ROM.

4. Magnetic Disks: The magnetic disks in the computer are circular plates fabricated of plastic otherwise metal by magnetized material. Frequently, two faces of the disk are utilized as well as many disks may be stacked on one spindle by read or write heads obtainable on every plane. All the disks in computer turn jointly at high speed. The tracks in the computer

are nothing but bits which are stored within the magnetized plane in spots next to concentric circles. These are usually separated into sections which are named as sectors.

5. Magnetic Tape: This tape is a normal magnetic recording which is designed with a slender magnetizable covering on an extended, plastic film of the thin strip. This is mainly used to back up huge data. Whenever the computer requires accessing a strip, first it will mount to access the data. Once the data is allowed, then it will be unmounted. The access time of memory will be slower within magnetic strip as well as it will take a few minutes for accessing a strip.

Advantages of Memory Hierarchy

The need for a memory hierarchy includes the following:

1. Memory distributing is simple and economical.
2. Removes external destruction.
3. Data can be spread all over.
4. Permits demand paging & pre-paging.
5. Swapping will be more proficient.

Memory Unit

A computer processor is made up of multiple decisive circuits, each one of which may be either OFF or ON. These two states in terms of memory are represented by a 0 or 1. In order to count higher than 1, such bits (BInary digiTS) are suspended together. A group of eight bits is known as a byte. 1 byte can represent numbers between zero (00000000) and 255 (11111111), or $2^8 = 256$ distinct positions. Of course, these bytes may also be combined together to represent larger numbers. The computer represents all characters and numbers internally in the same fashion. In practical, memory is measured in KiloBytes (KB) or MegaBytes (MB). A kilobyte is not exactly, as one might expect, of 1000 bytes. Rather, the correct amount is 2^{10} i.e. 1024 bytes. Similarly, a megabyte is not 1000^2 i.e. 1, 000, 000 bytes, but instead 1024^2 i.e. 1, 048, 576 bytes. This is a remarkable difference. By the time we reach to a gigabyte (i.e. 1024^3 bytes), the difference between the base two and base ten amounts is almost 71 MegaByte.

Both computer memory and disk space are measured in these units. But it's important not to confuse between these two. "12800 KB RAM" refers to the amount of main memory the computer provides to its CPU whereas "128 MB disk" symbolizes the amount of space that is available for the storage of files, data, and other type of permanent information.

Types of various Units of Memory

Byte

In computer systems, a unit of data that is eight binary digits long is known as a byte. A byte is the unit that computers use to represent a character such as a letter, number or a typographic symbol (for example, "h", "7", or "$"). A byte can also grasp a string of bits that need to be used in some larger units of application processes (e.g., the stream of bits that composes a visual image for a program that represents images or the string of bits that composes the machine code of a computer program).

A byte is abbreviated with a big "B" whereas a bit is abbreviated with a small "b". Computer storage is generally measured in multiples of byte. For example, a 640 MB hard drive holds a nominal 640 million bytes – or megabytes – of data. Byte multiples are made up of exponents of 2 and generally expressed as a "rounded off" decimal number. For example, two megabytes or 2 million bytes are actually 2, 097, 152 (decimal) bytes.

Kilo Byte

The kilobyte is the smallest unit of memory measurement but greater than a byte. A kilobyte is 103 or 1, 000 bytes abbreviated as 'K' or 'KB'. It antecedes the MegaByte, which contains 1, 000, 000 bytes. One kilobyte is technically 1, 000 bytes; therefore, kilobytes are often used synonymously with kibibytes, which contain exactly 1, 024 bytes.

Kilobytes are mostly used to measure the size of small files. For example, a simple text document may contain 10 KB of data and therefore it would have a file size of 10 kilobytes. Graphics of small websites are often between 5 KB and 100 KB in size. Individual files typically take up a minimum of four kilobytes of disk space.

Mega Byte

One megabyte is equal to 1, 000 KBs and antecedes the gigabyte (GB) unit of memory measurement. A megabyte is 106 or 1, 000, 000 bytes and is abbreviated as "MB". 1 MB is technically 1, 000, 000 bytes, therefore, megabytes are often used synonymously with mebibytes, which contain exactly 1, 048, 576 bytes.

Megabytes are mostly used to measure the size of large files. For example, a high resolution JPEG image might range in size from 1-5 megabytes. A 3-minute song saved in a compressed version may be roughly 3MB in size, and the uncompressed version may take upto 30 MB of disk space. Compact Disk's capacity is measured in megabytes (approx 700 to 800 MB), whereas the capacity of most other forms of media drives, such as hard drives and flash drives, is generally measured in gigabytes or terabytes.

Giga Byte

One gigabyte is equal to 1, 000 MBs and precedes the terabyte (TB) unit of memory measurement. A gigabyte is 109 or 1, 000, 000, 000 bytes and is abbreviated as "GB". 1 GB is technically 1, 000, 000, 000 bytes; therefore, gigabytes are used synonymously with gibibytes, which contain exactly 1, 073, 741, 824 bytes.

Gigabytes, are sometimes also abbreviated as "gigs," and are often used to measure storage device's capacity. e.g., a standard DVD drive can hold 4.7 GBs of data. Storage devices that hold 1, 000 GB of data or more are measured in terabytes.

Tera Byte

One terabyte is equal to 1, 000 GBs and precedes the petabyte (PB) unit of memory measurement.A terabyte is 1012 or 1, 000, 000, 000, 000 bytes and is abbreviated as "TB". 1 TB is technically 1 trillion bytes, therefore, terabytes and tebibytes are used synonymously, which contains exactly 1, 099, 511, 627, 776 bytes (1, 024 GB).

Mostly the storage capacity of large storage devices is measured in TeraBytes. Around 2007, consumer hard drives reached a capacity of 1 Tera Byte. Now, HDDs are measured in Terabytes e.g., a typical internal HDD may hold 2 Terabytes of data whereas some servers and high-end workstations that contain multiple hard drives may even have a total storage capacity of over 10 Tera bytes.

Peta Byte

One petabyte is equal to 1, 000 TBs and precedes the exabyte unit of memory measurement. A petabyte is 1015 or 1, 000, 000, 000, 000, 000 bytes and is abbreviated as "PB". A petabyte is lesser in size than a pebibyte, which contains exactly 1, 125, 899, 906, 842, 624 (250) bytes. Most of the storage devices can hold a maximum of a few TBs; therefore, petabytes are rarely used to measure memory capacity of a single device. Instead, PBs is used to measure the total data stored in large networks or server farms. For example, Internet Giants like Google and Facebook store more than over 100 PBs of data on their data servers.

Exa Byte

One exabyte is equal to 1, 000 PBs and precedes the zettabyte unit of memory measurement. An exabyte is 1018 or 1, 000, 000, 000, 000, 000, 000 bytes and is abbreviated as "EB". Exabytes are lesser than exbibytes, which contain exactly 1, 152, 921, 504, 606, 846, 976 (260) bytes. The exabyte unit of memory measurement is so large, that it is not used to measure the capacity of storage devices. Even the data storage capacity of the biggest cloud storage centers is measured in PBs, which is a fraction of 1 EB. Instead, exabytes measure the amount of data over multiple data storage networks or the amount of data that is being transferred over the Internet for a certain amount of time. E.g., several hundred exabytes of data is transferred over the Internet every year.

Zetta Byte

One zettabyte is equal to 1, 000 exabytes or 10^{21} or 1, 000, 000, 000, 000, 000, 000, 000 bytes. Zettabyte is little bit smaller than zebibyte that contain 1, 180, 591, 620, 717, 411, 303, 424 (270) bytes and is abbreviated as "ZB". One zettabyte contains one billion TBs or one sextillion bytes that mean it will take one billion one terabyte hard drives to store one zettabyte of data. Generally, Zettabyte is used to measure the large amounts of data and all the data in the world is just a few zettabytes.

Yotta Byte

One yottabyte is equal to 1, 000 zettabytes. It is the largest SI unit of memory measurement. A yottabyte is 10^{24} ZettaBytes or 1, 000, 000, 000, 000, 000, 000, 000, 000 bytes and is abbreviated as "YB". It is little bit smaller than yobibyte, which contains exactly 1, 208, 925, 819, 614, 629, 174, 706, 176 bytes (280) bytes.

1 yottabyte contains one septillion bytes which is exactly same as one trillion TBs. It is a very large number that human can evaluate. There is no practical use of such a large measurement unit because all the data in the world made of just a few zettabytes.

Tabular Representation of various Memory Sizes

Name	Equal to	Size (in bytes)
Bit	1 bit	1/8
Nibble	4 bits	1/2 (rare)
Byte	8 bits	1
Kilobyte	1024 bytes	1024
Megabyte	1, 024kilobytes	1, 048, 576
Gigabyte	1, 024 megabytes	1, 073, 741, 824
Terrabyte	1, 024 gigabytes	1, 099, 511, 627, 776
Petabyte	1, 024 terrabytes	1, 125, 899, 906, 842, 624
Exabyte	1, 024 petabytes	1, 152, 921, 504, 606, 846, 976
Zettabyte	1, 024 exabytes	1, 180, 591, 620, 717, 411, 303, 424
Yottabyte	1, 024 zettabytes	1, 208, 925, 819, 614, 629, 174, 706, 176

Cache Memory

The Cache Memory is the volatile computer memory which is very nearest to the CPU so also called CPU memory, all the Recent Instructions are Stored into the Cache Memory. It is the fastest memory that provides high-speed data access to a computer microprocessor. Cache meaning is that it is used for storing the input which is given by the user and which is necessary for the computer microprocessor to perform a Task. But the Capacity of the Cache Memory is too low in compare to Mcmory (random access memory (RAM)) and Hard Disk.

Importance of Cache Memory

The cache memory lies in the path between the processor and the memory. The cache memory therefore, has lesser access time than memory and is faster than the main memory. Cache memories have an access time of 100ns, while the main memory may have an access time of 700ns.

The cache memory is very expensive and hence is limited in capacity. Earlier cache memories were available separately but the microprocessors contain the cache memory on the chip itself.

The need for the cache memory is due to the mismatch between the speeds of the main memory and the CPU. The CPU clock is very fast, whereas the main memory access time is comparatively slower. Hence, no matter how fast the processor is, the processing speed depends more on the speed of the main memory (the strength of a chain is the strength of its weakest link). It is because of this reason that a cache memory having access time closer to the processor speed is introduced.

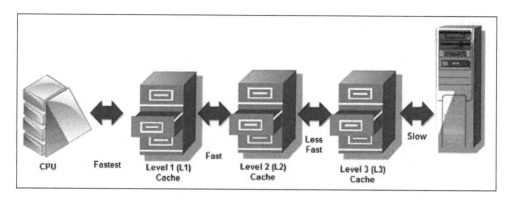

The cache memory stores the program (or its part) currently being executed or which may be executed within a short period of time. The cache memory also stores temporary data that the CPU may frequently require for manipulation.

The cache memory works according to various algorithms, which decide what information it has to store. These algorithms work out the probability to decide which data would be most frequently needed. This probability is worked out on the basis of past observations.

It acts as a high speed buffer between CPU and main memory and is used to temporary store very active data and action during processing since the cache memory is faster than main memory, the processing speed is increased by making the data and instructions needed in current processing available in cache. The cache memory is very expensive and hence is limited in capacity.

Type of Cache Memory

Cache memory improves the speed of the CPU, but it is expensive.Type of Cache Memory is divided into different levels that are L1, L2, L3:

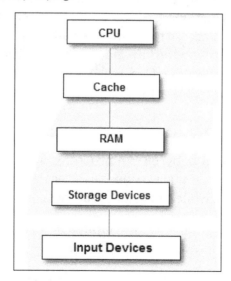

Level 1 (L1) Cache or Primary Cache

L1 is the primary type cache memory. The Size of the L1 cache very small comparison to others that is between 2KB to 64KB, it depent on computer processor. It is a embedded register in the computer microprocessor (CPU). The instructions that are required by the CPU that are firstly searched in L1 Cache. Example of registers are accumulator, address register, program counter etc.

Level 2 (L2) Cache or Secondary Cache

L2 is secondary type cache memory. The Size of the L2 cache is more capacious than L1 that is between 256KB to 512KB.L2 cache is Located on computer microprocessor. After searching the Instructions in L1 Cache, if not found then it searched into L2 cache by computer microprocessor. The high-speed system bus interconnecting the cache to the microprocessor.

Level 3 (L3) Cache or Main Memory

The L3 cache is larger in size but also slower in speed than L1 and L2,its size is between 1MB to 8MB.In Multicore processors, each core may have separate L1 and L2,but all core share a common L3 cache. L3 cache double speed than the RAM.

Cache Performance

When the processor needs to read or write a location in main memory, it first checks for a corresponding entry in the cache.

- If the processor finds that the memory location is in the cache, a cache hit has occurred and data is read from cache.

- If the processor does not find the memory location in the cache, a cache miss has occurred. For a cache miss, the cache allocates a new entry and copies in data from main memory, and then the request is fulfilled from the contents of the cache.

The performance of cache memory is frequently measured in terms of a quantity called Hit ratio.

```
Hit ratio = hit / (hit + miss) =  no. of hits/total accesses
```

We can improve cache performance using higher cache block size, higher associativity, reduce miss rate, reduce miss penalty, and reduce the time to hit in the cache.

Cache Mapping

There are three different types of mapping used for the purpose of cache memory which are as follows: Direct mapping, Associative mapping, and Set-Associative mapping. These are explained as following below:

- Direct Mapping: The simplest technique, known as direct mapping, maps each block of main memory into only one possible cache line. Or In Direct mapping, assigned each memory block to a specific line in the cache. If a line is previously taken up by a memory block when a new block needs to be loaded, the old block is trashed. An address space is split into two parts index field and a tag field. The cache is used to store the tag field whereas the rest is stored in the main memory. Direct mapping`s performance is directly proportional to the Hit ratio.

```
i = j modulo m
```

```
where

i=cache line number

j= main memory block number

m=number of lines in the cache
```

For purposes of cache access, each main memory address can be viewed as consisting of three fields. The least significant w bits identify a unique word or byte within a block of main memory. In most contemporary machines, the address is at the byte level. The remaining s bits specify one of the 2^s blocks of main memory. The cache logic interprets these s bits as a tag of s-r bits (most significant portion) and a line field of r bits. This latter field identifies one of the $m=2^r$ lines of the cache.

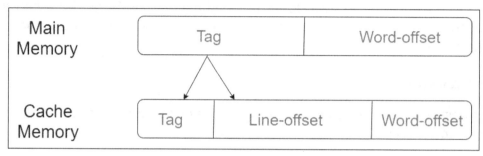

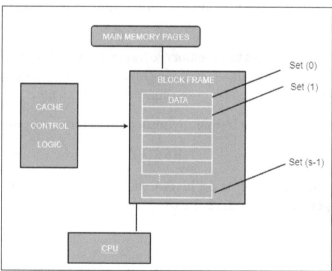

- Associative Mapping: In this type of mapping, the associative memory is used to store content and addresses both of the memory word. Any block can go into any line of the cache. This means that the word id bits are used to identify which word in the block is needed, but the tag becomes all of the remaining bits. This enables the placement of any word at any place in the cache memory. It is considered to be the fastest and the most flexible mapping form.

- Set-associative Mapping: This form of mapping is an enhanced form of direct mapping where the drawbacks of direct mapping are removed. Set associative addresses the problem of possible thrashing in the direct mapping method. It does this by saying that instead of having exactly one line that a block can map to in the cache; we will group a few lines together creating a *set*. Then a block in memory can map to any one of the lines of a specific set. Set-associative mapping allows that each word that is present in the cache can have two or more words in the main memory for the same index address. Set associative cache mapping combines the best of direct and associative cache mapping techniques.

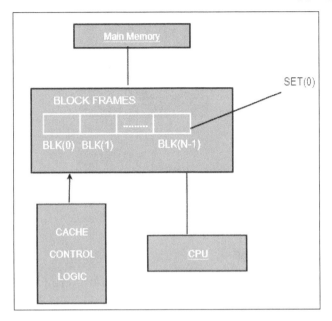

In this case, the cache consists of a number of sets, each of which consists of a number of lines. The relationships are:

```
m = v * k

i= j mod v


where

i=cache set number

j-main memory block number

v=number of sets

m=number of lines in the cache number of sets

k=number of lines in each set
```

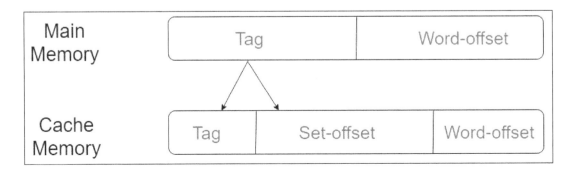

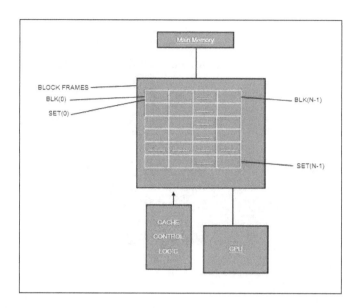

Application of Cache Memory

1. Usually, the cache memory can store a reasonable number of blocks at any given time, but this number is small compared to the total number of blocks in the main memory.

2. The correspondence between the main memory blocks and those in the cache is specified by a mapping function.

Locality of Reference

Since size of cache memory is less as compared to main memory. So to check which part of main memory should be given priority and loaded in cache is decided based on locality of reference.

Types of Locality of Reference

1. Spatial Locality of reference: This says that there is a chance that element will be present in the close proximity to the reference point and next time if again searched then more close proximity to the point of reference.

2. Temporal Locality of reference: In this Least recently used algorithm will be used. Whenever there is page fault occurs within a word will not only load word in main memory but complete page fault will be loaded because spatial locality of reference rule says that if you are referring any word next word will be referred in its register that's why we load complete page table so the complete block will be loaded.

Virtual Memory

A computer can address more memory than the amount physically installed on the system. This extra memory is actually called virtual memory and it is a section of a hard disk that's set up to emulate the computer's RAM.

The main visible advantage of this scheme is that programs can be larger than physical memory. Virtual memory serves two purposes. First, it allows us to extend the use of physical memory by using disk. Second, it allows us to have memory protection, because each virtual address is translated to a physical address.

Following are the situations, when entire program is not required to be loaded fully in main memory:

- User written error handling routines are used only when an error occurred in the data or computation.

- Certain options and features of a program may be used rarely.

- Many tables are assigned a fixed amount of address space even though only a small amount of the table is actually used.

- The ability to execute a program that is only partially in memory would counter many benefits.

- Less number of I/O would be needed to load or swap each user program into memory.

- A program would no longer be constrained by the amount of physical memory that is available.

- Each user program could take less physical memory; more programs could be run the same time, with a corresponding increase in CPU utilization and throughput.

Modern microprocessors intended for general-purpose use, a memory management unit, or MMU, is built into the hardware. The MMU's job is to translate virtual addresses into physical addresses. A basic example is given below:

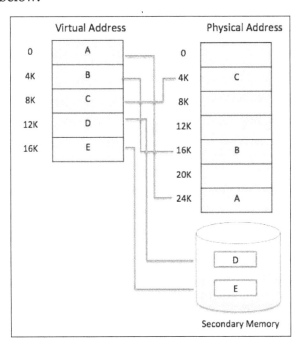

Virtual memory is commonly implemented by demand paging. It can also be implemented in a segmentation system. Demand segmentation can also be used to provide virtual memory.

Demand Paging

A demand paging system is quite similar to a paging system with swapping where processes reside in secondary memory and pages are loaded only on demand, not in advance. When a context switch occurs, the operating system does not copy any of the old program's pages out to the disk or any of the new program's pages into the main memory Instead, it just begins executing the new program after loading the first page and fetches that program's pages as they are referenced.

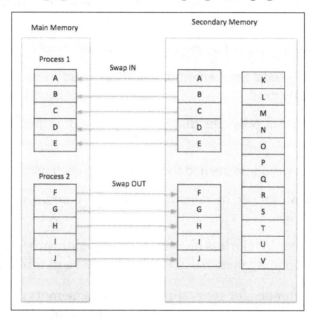

While executing a program, if the program references a page which is not available in the main memory because it was swapped out a little ago, the processor treats this invalid memory reference as a page fault and transfers control from the program to the operating system to demand the page back into the memory.

Advantages

Following are the advantages of Demand Paging:

- Large virtual memory.
- More efficient use of memory.
- There is no limit on degree of multiprogramming.

Disadvantages

- Number of tables and the amount of processor overhead for handling page interrupts are greater than in the case of the simple paged management techniques.

Page Replacement Algorithm

Page replacement algorithms are the techniques using which an Operating System decides which memory pages to swap out, write to disk when a page of memory needs to be allocated. Paging happens whenever a page fault occurs and a free page cannot be used for allocation purpose accounting to reason that pages are not available or the number of free pages is lower than required pages.

When the page that was selected for replacement and was paged out, is referenced again, it has to read in from disk, and this requires for I/O completion. This process determines the quality of the page replacement algorithm: the lesser the time waiting for page-ins, the better is the algorithm.

A page replacement algorithm looks at the limited information about accessing the pages provided by hardware, and tries to select which pages should be replaced to minimize the total number of page misses, while balancing it with the costs of primary storage and processor time of the algorithm itself. There are many different page replacement algorithms. We evaluate an algorithm by running it on a particular string of memory reference and computing the number of page faults.

Reference String

The string of memory references is called reference string. Reference strings are generated artificially or by tracing a given system and recording the address of each memory reference. The latter choice produces a large number of data, where we note two things.

- For a given page size, we need to consider only the page number, not the entire address.

- If we have a reference to a page p, then any immediately following references to page p will never cause a page fault. Page p will be in memory after the first reference; the immediately following references will not fault.

- For example, consider the following sequence of addresses – 123, 215, 600, 1234, 76, 96.

- If page size is 100, then the reference string is 1,2,6,12,0,0.

First In First Out (FIFO) Algorithm

- Oldest page in main memory is the one which will be selected for replacement.

- Easy to implement, keep a list, replace pages from the tail and add new pages at the head.

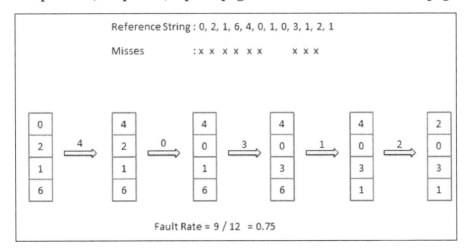

Optimal Page Algorithm

- An optimal page-replacement algorithm has the lowest page-fault rate of all algorithms. An optimal page-replacement algorithm exists, and has been called OPT or MIN.

- Replace the page that will not be used for the longest period of time. Use the time when a page is to be used.

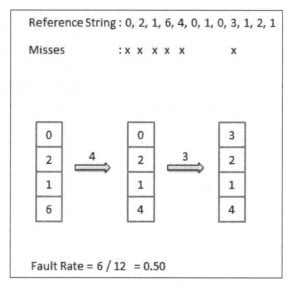

Least Recently used (LRU) Algorithm

- Page which has not been used for the longest time in main memory is the one which will be selected for replacement.

- Easy to implement, keep a list, replace pages by looking back into time.

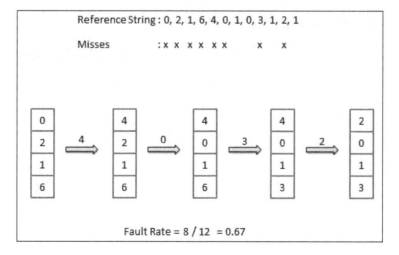

Page Buffering Algorithm

- To get a process start quickly, keep a pool of free frames.

- On page fault, select a page to be replaced.

- Write the new page in the frame of free pool, mark the page table and restart the process.

- Now write the dirty page out of disk and place the frame holding replaced page in free pool.

Least Frequently used (LFU) Algorithm

- The page with the smallest count is the one which will be selected for replacement.

- This algorithm suffers from the situation in which a page is used heavily during the initial phase of a process, but then is never used again.

Most Frequently used (MFU) Algorithm

- This algorithm is based on the argument that the page with the smallest count was probably just brought in and has yet to be used.

Swapping

Swapping a process out means removing all of its pages from memory, or marking them so that they will be removed by the normal page replacement process. Suspending a process ensures that it is not runnable while it is swapped out. At some later time, the system swaps back the process from the secondary storage to main memory. When a process is busy swapping pages in and out then this situation is called thrashing.

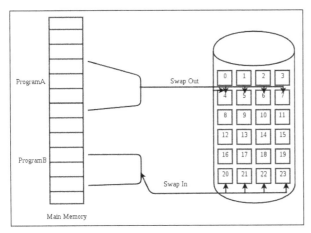

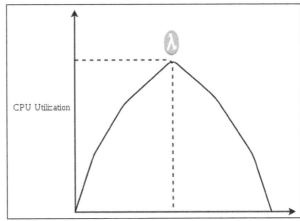

Thrashing   Degree of Multiprogramming.

At any given time, only few pages of any process are in main memory and therefore more processes can be maintained in memory. Furthermore time is saved because unused pages are not swapped in and out of memory. However, the OS must be clever about how it manages this scheme. In the steady state practically, all of main memory will be occupied with process's pages, so that the processor and OS has direct access to as many processes as possible. Thus when the OS brings one page in, it must throw another out. If it throws out a page just before it is used, then it will just have to get that page again almost immediately. Too much of this leads to a condition called Thrashing. The system spends most of its time swapping pages rather than executing instructions. So a good page replacement algorithm is required.

In the given diagram, initial degree of multi programming upto some extent of point (lamda), the CPU utilization is very high and the system resources are utilized 100%. But if we further increase the degree of multi programming the CPU utilization will drastically fall down and the system will spent more time only in the page replacement and the time taken to complete the execution of the process will increase. This situation in the system is called as thrashing.

Causes of Thrashing

1. High degree of multiprogramming: If the number of processes keeps on increasing in the memory than number of frames allocated to each process will be decreased. So, less number of frames will be available to each process. Due to this, page fault will occur more frequently and more CPU time will be wasted in just swapping in and out of pages and the utilization will keep on decreasing.

For example: Let free frames = 400

Case 1: Number of process = 100. Then, each process will get 4 frames.

Case 2: Number of process = 400. Each process will get 1 frame.

Case 2 is a condition of thrashing, as the numbers of processes are increased, frames per process are decreased. Hence CPU time will be consumed in just swapping pages.

2. Lacks of Frames: If a process has less number of frames then less pages of that process will be able to reside in memory and hence more frequent swapping in and out will be required. This may lead to thrashing. Hence sufficient amount of frames must be allocated to each process in order to prevent thrashing.

Recovery of Thrashing

1. Do not allow the system to go into thrashing by instructing the long term scheduler not to bring the processes into memory after the threshold.

2. If the system is already in thrashing then instruct the midterm scheduler to suspend some of the processes so that we can recover the system from thrashing.

ROM

Read-Only Memory (ROM) is the primary memory unit of any computer system along with the Random Access Memory (RAM), but unlike RAM, in ROM, the binary information is stored permanently. Now, this information to be stored is provided by the designer and is then stored inside the ROM. Once, it is stored, it remains within the unit, even when power is turned off and on again.

The information is embedded in the ROM, in the form of bits, by a process known as programming the ROM. Here, programming is used to refer to the hardware procedure which specifies the bits that are going to be inserted in the hardware configuration of the device. And this is what makes ROM a Programmable Logic Device (PLD).

Programmable Logic Device

A Programmable Logic Device (PLD) is an IC (Integrated Circuit) with internal logic gates connected through electronic paths that behave similar to fuses. In the original state, all the fuses are intact, but when we program these devices, we blow away certain fuses along the paths that must be removed to achieve a particular configuration. And this is what happens in ROM, ROM consists of nothing but basic logic gates arranged in such a way that they store the specified bits.

Typically, a PLD can have hundreds to millions of gates interconnected through hundreds to thousands of internal paths. In order to show the internal logic diagram of such a device a special symbology is used, as shown below:

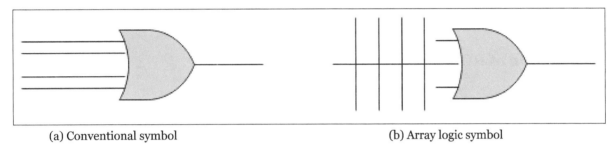

| (a) Conventional symbol | (b) Array logic symbol |

The first image shows the conventional way of representing inputs to a logic gate and the second symbol shows the special way of showing inputs to a logic gate, called as Array Logic Symbol, where each vertical line represents the input to the logic gate.

Structure of ROM

The block diagram for the ROM is as given below:

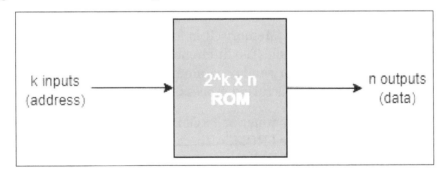

Block Structure

- It consists of k input lines and n output lines.

- The k input lines is used to take the input address from where we want to access the content of the ROM.

- Since each of the k input lines can be either 0 or 1, so there are $2k$ total addresses which can be referred to by these input lines and each of these addresses contains n bit information, which is given out as the output of the ROM.

- Such a ROM is specified as $2k$ x n ROM.

Internal Structure

- It consists of two basic components – Decoder and OR gates.

- A Decoder is a combinational circuit which is used to decode any encoded form (such as binary, BCD) to a more known form (such as decimal form).

- In ROM, the input to a decoder will be in binary form and the output will represent its decimal equivalent.

- The Decoder is represented as $l \times 2^l$, that is, it has l inputs and has 2^l outputs, which implies that it will take l-bit binary number and decode it into one of the 2^l decimal number.

- All the OR gates present in the ROM will have outputs of the decoder as their input.

Classification of ROM

Mask ROM

In this type of ROM, the specification of the ROM (its contents and their location), is taken by the manufacturer from the customer in tabular form in a specified format and then makes corresponding masks for the paths to produce the desired output. This is costly, as the vendor charges special fee from the customer for making a particular ROM (recommended, only if large quantity of the same ROM is required).

Uses: They are used in network operating systems, server operating systems, storing of fonts for laser printers, sound data in electronic musical instruments.

PROM

It stands for Programmable Read-Only Memory. It is first prepared as blank memory, and then it is programmed to store the information. The difference between PROM and Mask ROM is that PROM is manufactured as blank memory and programmed after manufacturing, whereas a Mask ROM is programmed during the manufacturing process.

To program the PROM, a PROM programmer or PROM burner is used. The process of programming the PROM is called as burning the PROM. Also, the data stored in it cannot be modified, so it is called as one – time programmable device.

Uses: They have several different applications, including cell phones, video game consoles, RFID tags, medical devices, and other electronics.

EPROM

It stands for Erasable Programmable Read-Only Memory. It overcomes the disadvantage of PROM that once programmed; the fixed pattern is permanent and cannot be altered. If a bit pattern has been established, the PROM becomes unusable, if the bit pattern has to be changed.

This problem has been overcome by the EPROM, as when the EPROM is placed under a special ultraviolet light for a length of time, the shortwave radiation makes the EPROM return to its initial state, which then can be programmed accordingly. Again for erasing the content, PROM programmer or PROM burner is used.

Uses: Before the advent of EEPROMs, some micro-controllers, like some versions of Intel 8048, the Freescale 68HC11 used EPROM to store their program.

EEPROM

It stands for Electrically Erasable Programmable Read-Only Memory. It is similar to EPROM, except that in this, the EEPROM is returned to its initial state by application of an electrical signal, in place of ultraviolet light. Thus, it provides the ease of erasing, as this can be done, even if the memory is positioned in the computer. It erases or writes one byte of data at a time.

Uses: It is used for storing the computer system BIOS.

Flash ROM

It is an enhanced version of EEPROM. The difference between EEPROM and Flash ROM is that in EEPROM, only 1 byte of data can be deleted or written at a particular time, whereas, in flash memory, blocks of data (usually 512 bytes) can be deleted or written at a particular time. So, Flash ROM is much faster than EEPROM.

Uses: Many modern PCs have their BIOS stored on a flash memory chip, called as flash BIOS and they are also used in modems as well.

Programming the Read-Only Memory (ROM)

To understand how to program a ROM, consider a 4 x 4 ROM, which means that it has total of 4 addresses at which information is stored, and each of those addresses has a 4-bit information, which is permanent and must be given as the output, when we access a particular address. The following steps need to be performed to program the ROM:

1. Construct a truth table, which would decide the content of each address of the ROM and based upon which a particular ROM will be programmed.

   So, the truth table for the specification of the 4 x 4 ROM is described as below:

Input		Outputs			
X	Y	A	B	C	D
0	0	0	0	1	1
0	1	1	1	0	0
1	0	1	1	1	1
1	1	0	1	1	1

   This truth table shows that at location 00, content to be stored is 0011, at location 01; the content should be 1100, and so on, such that whenever a particular address is given as input, the content at that particular address is fetched. Since, with 2 input bits, 4 input combinations are possible and each of these combinations holds a 4-bit information, so this ROM is a 4 X 4 ROM.

2. Now, based upon the total no. of addresses in the ROM and the length of their content, decide the decoder as well as the no. of OR gates to be used. Generally, for a 2^k x n ROM, a k x 2^k decoder is used, and the total no. of OR gates is equal to the total no. of bits stored at each location in the ROM.

So, in this case, for a 4 x 4 ROM, the decoder to be used is a 2 x 4 decoder. The following is a 2 x 4 decoder:

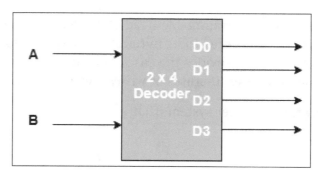

The truth table for a 2 x 4 decoder is as follows:

Input		Outputs			
A	B	Do	D1	D2	D3
0	0	1	0	0	0
0	1	0	1	0	0
1	0	0	0	1	0
1	1	0	0	0	1

When both the inputs are 0, and then only D is 1 and rest are 0, when input is 01, then, only D is high and so on. (Just remember that if the input combination of the decoder resolves to a particular decimal number d, then at the output side the terminal which is at position d + 1 from the top will be 1 and rest will be 0).

Now, since we want each address to store 4 – bits in the 4 x 4 ROM, so, there will be 4 OR gates, with each of the 4 outputs of the decoder being input to each one of the 4 OR gates, whose output will be the output of the ROM, as follows:

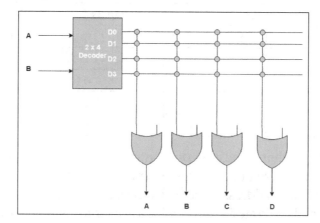

A cross sign in this figure shows connection between the two lines is intact. Now, since there are 4 OR gates and 4 output lines from the decoder, so there are total of 16 intersections, called as crosspoint.

3. Now, program the intersection between the two lines, as per the truth table, so that the output of the ROM (OR gates) is in accordance with the truth table. For programming the crosspoints, initially all the crosspoints are left intact, which means that it is logically equivalent to a closed switch, but these intact connections can be blown by the application of a high – voltage pulse into these fuse, which will disconnect the two interconnected lines, and in this way the output of a ROM can be manipulated.

So, to program a ROM, just look at the truth table specifying the ROM and blow away (if required) a connection. The connection for the 4 x 4 ROM as per the truth table is as shown below:

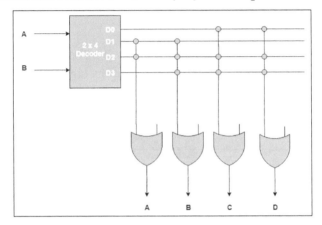

Remember, a cross sign is used to denote that the connection is left intact and if there is no cross this means that there is no connection.

In this figure, since, as can be seen from the truth table specifying the ROM, when the input is 00, then, the output is 0011, so as we know from the truth table of a decoder, that input 00 gives output such that only D is 1 and rest are 0, so to get output 0011 from the OR gates, the connections of with the first two OR gates has been blown away, to get the outputs as 0, while the last two OR gates give the output as 1, which is what is required.

Similarly, when the input is 01, then the output should be 1100, and with input 01, in decoder only D is 1 and rest are 0, so to get the desired output the first two OR gates have their connection intact with D, while last two OR gates have their connection blown away. And for the rest also the same procedure is followed.

So, this is how a ROM is programmed and since, the output of these gates will remain constant every time, so that is how the information is stored permanently in the ROM, and does not get altered even on switching on and off.

RAM

RAM is short for random access memory. There are two basic types of RAM in common use today, static and dynamic random access memory, abbreviated SRAM and DRAM respectively. Both are physically organized as an array of memory cells. Both use a decoder whose input is a set of address lines to select one or more memory cells for the memory operation. Both can store data as long as power is applied. However, even when powered, a DRAM loses data if it is not periodically refreshed, whereas in a SRAM the data can be stored without any kind of extra processing or refreshing. As a result, SRAMs are fewer complexes than DRAMs, and because of this we study them before DRAMs, but only after we have defined how the performance of a memory system in general will be measured.

The performance of a memory is measured in two ways: by its access time and cycle time. The access time is the time required to select a word and read it. The cycle time is the time required to complete a write operation.

SRAM

SRAM is an acronym for Static Random Access Memory. The basic architecture of SRAM includes one or more rectangular arrays of memory cells with support circuitry to decode addresses and implement the required read and write operations. Additional support circuitry for special features such as burst operation or pipelined reads may be present on the memory chip. Figure contains a block diagram of a SRAM.

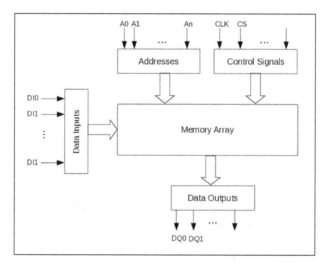

The inputs to SRAM include:

- Address line (log of height bits) also called a word line;
- Chip select signal;
- Output enable signal;
- Write enable signal;
- Data input signal (w bits, where w = width of the SRAM).

The output is an output line of w bits, where w is the width of the SRAM.

The individual memory cells in an SRAM are built out of circuits that resemble D-flip-flops. A single cell typically requires from four to eight transistors, depending upon the design (four-transistor cells are not as stable as eight-transistor cells.) The core of the cell is a pair of inverting gates, which store the state of the cell. Figure illustrates how the cross-coupled inverting gates store state. The figure shows that, in addition to the inverting gates, the cell uses a pair of transistors to connect it to the word and bit lines of the SRAM. The word line is the address line for that particular cell. The bit line is the line for the particular bit of that address. Conceptually the word lines are the rows of the SRAM, and the bit lines are the columns. Each unique word address corresponds to a single row.

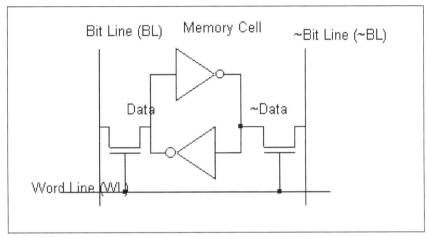

An SRAM cell represented by a pair of inverting gates
is a circuit diagram for a six-transistor memory cell

SRAMs may be synchronous or asynchronous. Asynchronous SRAMs respond to changes at the device's address pins by generating a signal that drives the internal circuitry to perform a read or write as requested. They are not clocked, and are limited in their performance. Synchronous SRAMs (SSRAMs) are faster. They are driven by one or more external clock signals that control the SRAM operations, which allow them to synchronize with the fastest processors. Asynchronous SRAMs come in two flavors, fast and slow. The fast variety has access times under 25 ns, whereas the slow ones have access times greater than 45 ns. In contrast, SSRAMs can have access times under 1 ns. As of this writing, there are many different types of SSRAM, including:

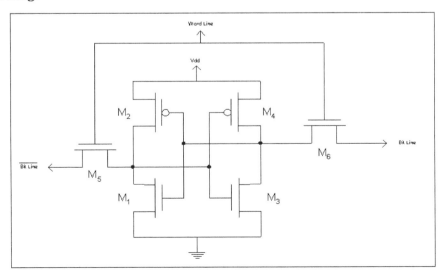

A six-transistor SRAM cell.

- Single Data Rate SRAM.

  o Pipelined vs. Flow through SRAMs.

  o Burst SRAMs.

  o Network SRAMs - NoBL/ZBT SRAMs.

- Double Data Rate SRAMs – Standard DDR SRAMs – QDR SRAMs.

- NetRAM.

Storage capacities for a single SRAM chip have reached 72 Mbits. Synchronous SRAM tends to have greater storage capacity than asynchronous SRAM. SRAM chips are specified by their height h and width w, e.g., a 256K x 1 SRAM has height 256K and width 1. This means it has 256K addresses, each 1 bit wide. Common shapes are x1, x4, x8, x16, x18, and x36. Figure shows a 4 by 2 SRAM module, with a single 2-to-4 decoder.

Decoding is usually two-dimensional for better performance. For example, if the height is 1M (2^{20}), a single decoder would be 20 x 2^{20} and require 2^{20} 20-input AND-gates. If instead, we break the address into a 10-bit upper and a 10-bit lower part, then we can use two 10 x 1024 decoders, requiring only 2048 AND-gates instead of more than one million.

Another design for smaller memories uses a combination of a decoder and multiplexers. Figure illustrates this idea. The high order bits are input to a decoder, which selects a row that is enabled in all of the SRAM modules. The low-order bits are the input signal to a series of multiplexers, each of which selects a single bit from each array.

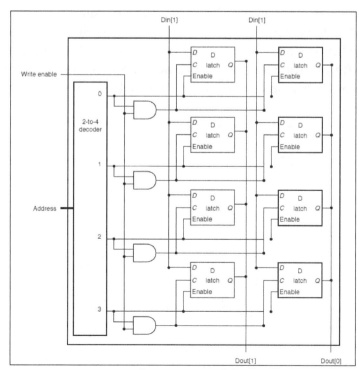

A 4 by 2 SRAM module

It is impractical to use a multiplexer exclusively to select the output of an SRAM cell. It would be on the order of 64K-to-1 or worse. The technology to build SRAMs uses a combination of decoders and multiplexers, and is based on tri-state buffers.

Tri-state buffers can be connected to form an efficient multiplexer. A tri-state buffer is a buffer with a data input, an output-enable input, and a single output. If the output-enable is asserted, the value of the data input is placed on the output line. If the output-enable is de-asserted, the output line is in a high impedance state. This means, in essence, that the output line is neither low nor high voltage, but is neutral voltage, and that another tri-state buffer can put a value on the line.

In practice many SRAMs are built with three-state buffers incorporated into the flip-flops themselves and these share an output line.

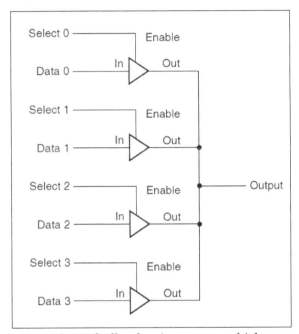

Four tri-state buffers forming a 4 to 1 multiplexor

A 4M by 8 SRAM can be organized into 4096 rows with 1024 x 8 bits per row. Therefore, eight 4K x 1024 SRAM chips can be used as shown in figure.

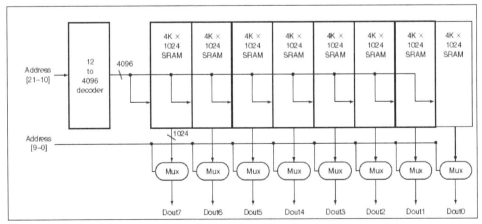

Eight 4096 by 1024 SRAM chips forming a 4MB memory

DRAM

A DRAM (Dynamic Random Access Memory) stores a cell's state in a capacitor rather than in a set of inverting gates, and it changes the state with a transistor. This uses less than one-fourth to one-sixth of the space used by a SRAM with equal capacity, since each cell uses a single transistor and a single capacitor. However, because the capacitor cannot hold the state indefinitely, it must be refreshed periodically, hence the term "dynamic". Refreshing can be done by a separate controller, and can use 1% to 2% of the active memory cycles.

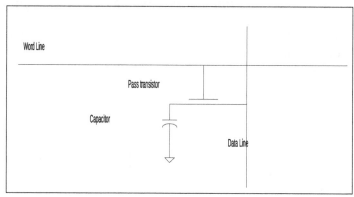

A DRAM cell

To write data into a DRAM cell, a voltage signal is placed on the data line and a signal is applied to the address line. This switches on the transistor, which allows a high voltage to charge the capacitor. If there is a 0 signal, the capacitor receives no charge. To read the cell the address line is activated, and any charge in the capacitor is transferred onto the data line. This is a destructive read. Therefore, the data read out must be amplified and written back to the cell. This rewrite is often combined with the periodic refresh cycle that is necessary in DRAM chips.

DRAM cells store a very small charge, saving on power consumption. The read out requires that the data line be charged to a voltage about halfway between the voltages representing 0 and 1. The small change in voltage is detected on the data line.

DRAMs use a two level decoder. The address is split into a row and a column, and the row is sent followed by the column. The row number is usually formed from the high order bits, and the column, from the low order bits. The address path is only wide enough for one of these.

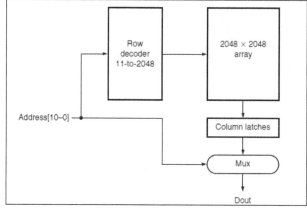

DRAM module

The row address is placed on the address line and the Row Access Strobe (RAS) is sent to the DRAM to indicate that the address is a row address. The row decoder decodes it and a single row is activated. All of the bits in that row are sent to the column latches. The column address is placed on the address line and the Column Access Strobe (CAS) is activated. The bits of the individual columns are chosen by the output side multiplexor and placed on the Data Out line.

The two-level access and the more complex circuitry make DRAMs about 5 to 10 times slower than SRAMs, although their cost is much less. DRAMs are used for main memories; SRAMs for caches.

Synchronous DRAM

DRAM was originally an asynchronous type of RAM. Synchronous DRAM (SDRAM), like synchronous SRAM, uses an external clock signal to respond to its input signals. This makes it possible to synchronize with the bus and therefore, to improve its performance. Basically, it allows for an internal pipelined type of operation: after an initial setup, a sequence of addresses can be accessed partly in parallel.

In asynchronous DRAM, if a sequence of consecutive rows needs to be transferred to or from the memory, each address is decoded separately, one after the other. In SDRAM, a single address and a burst length are supplied to the memory. Additional circuitry within the SDRAM allows one row to be latched while the next row is accessed. The external clock signal is used to coordinate the transfer of successive rows. This obviates the need to decode multiple addresses, speeding up the transfer.

Segmentation

Segmentation is the process in which the main memory of the computer is logically divided into different segments and each segment has its own base address. It is basically used to enhance the speed of execution of the computer system, so that the processor is able to fetch and execute the data from the memory easily and fast.

Need for Segmentation

The Bus Interface Unit (BIU) contains four 16 bit special purpose registers called as Segment Registers.

- Code segment register (CS): is used for addressing memory location in the code segment of the memory, where the executable program is stored.

- Data segment register (DS): points to the data segment of the memory where the data is stored.

- Extra Segment Register (ES): also refers to a segment in the memory which is another data segment in the memory.

- Stack Segment Register (SS): is used for addressing stack segment of the memory. The stack segment is that segment of memory which is used to store stack data.

The number of address lines in 8086 is 20, 8086 BIU will send 20bit address, so as to access one of the 1MB memory locations. The four segment registers actually contain the upper 16 bits of the starting addresses of the four memory segments of 64 KB each with which the 8086 is working at that instant of time. A segment is a logical unit of memory that may be up to 64 kilobytes long. Each segment is made up of contiguous memory locations. It is an independent, separately addressable unit. Starting address will always be changing. It will not be fixed.

Note that the 8086 does not work the whole 1MB memory at any given time. However, it works only with four 64KB segments within the whole 1MB memory.

Below is the one way of positioning four 64 kilobyte segments within the 1M byte memory space of an 8086.

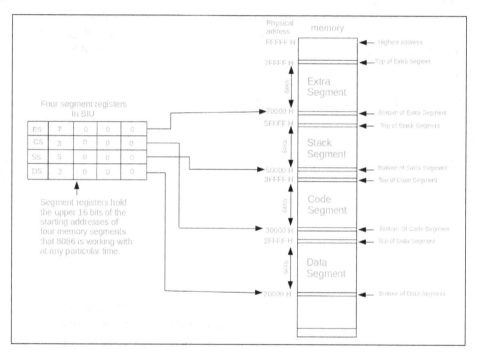

Types of Segmentation

- Overlapping Segment: A segment starts at a particular address and its maximum size can go up to 64kilobytes. But if another segment starts along with this 64kilobytes location of the first segment, then the two are said to be *Overlapping Segment*.

- Non-Overlapped Segment: A segment starts at a particular address and its maximum size can go up to 64kilobytes. But if another segment starts before this 64kilobytes location of the first segment, then the two segments are said to be *Non-Overlapped Segment*.

Rules of Segmentation

Segmentation process follows some rules as follows:

- The starting address of a segment should be such that it can be evenly divided by 16.

- Minimum size of a segment can be 16 bytes and the maximum can be 64 kB.

Segment	Offset Registers	Function
CS	IP	Address of the next instruction
DS	BX,DI,SI	Address of data
SS	SP,BP	Address in the stack
ES	BX,DI,SI	Address of destination data (for string operations)

Advantages of the Segmentation

The main advantages of segmentation are as follows:

- It provides a powerful memory management mechanism.
- Data related or stack related operations can be performed in different segments.
- Code related operation can be done in separate code segments.
- It allows to processes to easily share data.
- It allows extending the address ability of the processor, i.e. segmentation allows the use of 16 bit registers to give an addressing capability of 1 Megabytes. Without segmentation, it would require 20 bit registers.
- It is possible to enhance the memory size of code data or stack segments beyond 64 KB by allotting more than one segment for each area.

Paging

Paging is a memory management scheme that eliminates the need for contiguous allocation of physical memory. This scheme permits the physical address space of a process to be non – contiguous.

- Logical Address or Virtual Address (represented in bits): An address generated by the CPU.
- Logical Address Space or Virtual Address Space (represented in words or bytes): The set of all logical addresses generated by a program.
- Physical Address (represented in bits): An address actually available on memory unit.
- Physical Address Space (represented in words or bytes): The set of all physical addresses corresponding to the logical addresses.

Example:

- If Logical Address = 31 bit, then Logical Address Space = 2^{31} words = 2 G words (1 G = 2^{30}).
- If Logical Address Space = 128 M words = $2^7 * 2^{20}$ words, then Logical Address = $\log_2 2^{27}$ = 27 bits.
- If Physical Address = 22 bit, then Physical Address Space = 2^{22} words = 4 M words (1 M = 2^{20}).

- If Physical Address Space = 16 M words = $2^4 * 2^{20}$ words, then Physical Address = $\log_2 2^{24}$ = 24 bits.

The mapping from virtual to physical address is done by the memory management unit (MMU) which is a hardware device and this mapping is known as paging technique.

- The Physical Address Space is conceptually divided into a number of fixed-size blocks, called frames.

- The Logical address Space is also splitted into fixed-size blocks, called pages.

- Page Size = Frame Size.

Let us consider an example:

- Physical Address = 12 bits, then Physical Address Space = 4 K words.

- Logical Address = 13 bits, then Logical Address Space = 8 K words.

- Page size = frame size = 1 K words (assumption).

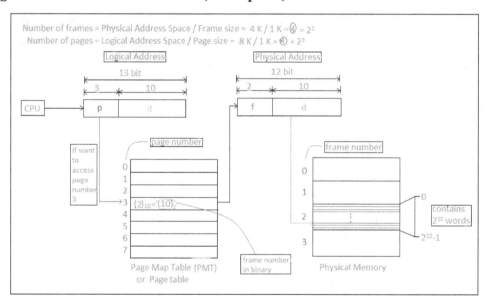

Address generated by CPU is divided into:

- Page number (p): Number of bits required to represent the pages in Logical Address Space or Page number.

- Page offset (d): Number of bits required to represent particular word in a page or page size of Logical Address Space or word number of a page or page offset.

Physical Address is divided into:

- Frame number (f): Number of bits required to represent the frame of Physical Address Space or Frame number.

- Frame offset (d): Number of bits required to represent particular word in a frame or frame size of Physical Address Space or word number of a frame or frame offset.

The hardware implementation of page table can be done by using dedicated registers. But the usage of register for the page table is satisfactory only if page table is small. If page table contain large number of entries then we can use TLB (translation Look-aside buffer), a special, small, fast look up hardware cache.

- The TLB is associative, high speed memory.

- Each entry in TLB consists of two parts: a tag and a value.

- When this memory is used, then an item is compared with all tags simultaneously. If the item is found, then corresponding value is returned.

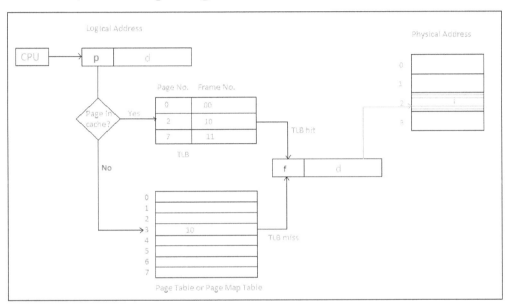

Main memory access time = m

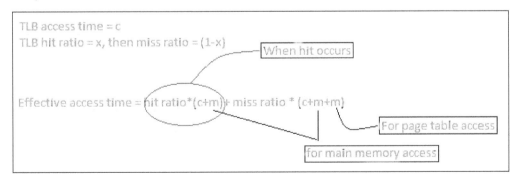

If page table are kept in main memory, Effective access time = m (for page table) + m (for particular page in page table).

References

- Computer-memory, technology: britannica.com, retrieved 5 february, 2019

- Memory-organization, computer-architecture: studytonight.com, retrieved 19 april, 2019

- Memory-hierarchy-in-computer-architecture: elprocus.com, retrieved 17 may, 2019

- Understanding-file-sizes-bytes-kb-mb-gb-tb-pb-eb-zb-yb: geeksforgeeks.org, retrieved 14 july, 2019
- What-is-cache-memory, disk-operating-system, fundamental: ecomputernotes.com, retrieved 19 may, 2019
- Cache-memory-in-computer-organization: geeksforgeeks.org, retrieved 28 april, 2019
- Os-virtual-memory, operating-system: tutorialspoint.com, retrieved 21 july, 2019
- Virtual-memory-in-operating-system: geeksforgeeks.org, retrieved 7 may, 2019
- Memory-segmentation-8086-microprocessor: geeksforgeeks.org, retrieved 15 january, 2019

Input and Output Systems

The signals or data which are received by the computer are termed as input signals and the data or signals which are sent from it to a human user or another information processing system is termed as an output system. All the diverse components of input and output systems such as the various input and output devices have been carefully analyzed in this chapter.

Input/Output Architecture

The computer system's I/O architecture is its interface to the outside world. This architecture is designed to provide a systematic means of controlling interaction with the outside world and to provide the operating system with the information it needs to manage I/O activity effectively.

There are three principal I/O techniques: programmed I/O, in which I/O occurs under the direct and continuous control of the program requesting the I/O operation; interrupt-driven I/O, in which a program issues an I/O command and then continues to execute, until it is interrupted by the I/O hardware to signal the end of the I/O operations; and direct memory access (DMA), in which a specialized I/O processor takes over control of an I/O operation to move a large block of data.

Two important examples of external I/O interfaces are FireWire and Infiniband.

Peripherals and the System Bus

- There are a wide variety of peripherals each with varying methods of operation.
  - Impractical to for the processor to accommodate all.
- Data transfer rates are often slower than the processor and memory.
  - Impractical to use the high-speed system bus to communicate directly.
- Data transfer rates may be faster than that of the processor and memory.
  - This mismatch may lead to inefficiencies if improperly managed.
- Peripheral often use different data formats and word lengths.

Purpose of I/O Modules

- Interface to the processor and memory via the system bus or control switch.
- Interface to one or more peripheral devices.

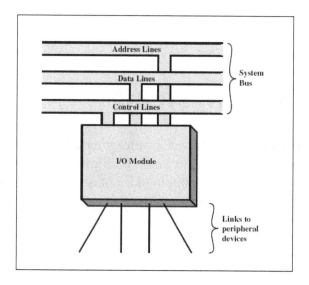

Input/Output Devices

The computer will be of no use unless it is able to communicate with the outside world. Input/Output devices are required for users to communicate with the computer. In simple terms, input devices bring information INTO the computer and output devices bring information OUT of a computer system. These input/output devices are also known as peripherals since they surround the CPU and memory of a computer system.

Some commonly used Input/Output devices are listed in table below:

Input Devices	Output Devices
Keyboard	Monitor
Mouse	LCD
Joystick	Printer
Scanner	Plotter
Light Pen	Plotter
Touch Screen	

Input Devices

Some of the important input devices used in a computer are:

Keyboard

Keyboard is the most common and very popular input device which helps to input data to the computer. The layout of the keyboard is like that of traditional typewriter, although there are some additional keys provided for performing additional functions.

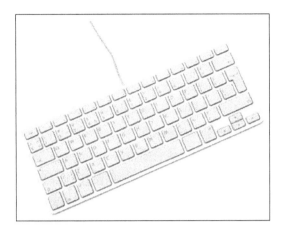

Keyboards are of two sizes 84 keys or 101/102 keys, but now keyboards with 104 keys or 108 keys are also available for Windows and Internet.

The keys on the keyboard are as follows:

Keys	Description
Typing Keys	These keys include the letter keys (A-Z) and digit keys (09) which generally give the same layout as that of typewriters.
Numeric Keypad	It is used to enter the numeric data or cursor movement. Generally, it consists of a set of 17 keys that are laid out in the same configuration used by most adding machines and calculators.
Function Keys	The twelve function keys are present on the keyboards which are arranged in a row at the top of the keyboard. Each function key has a unique meaning and is used for some specific purpose.
Control keys	These keys provide cursor and screen control. It includes four directional arrow keys. Control keys also include Home, End, Insert, Delete, Page Up, Page Down, Control(Ctrl), Alternate(Alt), Escape(Esc).
Special Purpose Keys	Keyboard also contains some special purpose keys such as Enter, Shift, Caps Lock, Num Lock, Space bar, Tab, and Print Screen.

Mouse

Mouse is the most popular pointing device. It is a very famous cursor-control device having a small palm size box with a ground ball at its base, which senses the movement of the mouse and sends corresponding signals to the CPU when the mouse buttons are pressed.

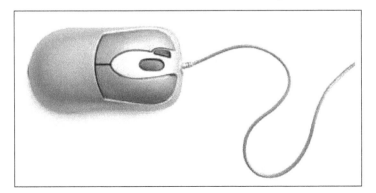

Generally, it has two buttons called the left and the right button and a wheel is present between the buttons. A mouse can be used to control the position of the cursor on the screen, but it cannot be used to enter text into the computer.

Advantages

- Easy to use.

- Not very expensive.

- Moves the cursor faster than the arrow keys of the keyboard.

Joystick

Joystick is also a pointing device, which is used to move the cursor position on a monitor screen. It is a stick having a spherical ball at its both lower and upper ends. The lower spherical ball moves in a socket. The joystick can be moved in all four directions.

The function of the joystick is similar to that of a mouse. It is mainly used in Computer Aided Designing (CAD) and playing computer games.

Light Pen

Light pen is a pointing device similar to a pen. It is used to select a displayed menu item or draw pictures on the monitor screen. It consists of a photocell and an optical system placed in a small tube.

When the tip of a light pen is moved over the monitor screen and the pen button is pressed, its photocell sensing element detects the screen location and sends the corresponding signal to the CPU.

Track Ball

Track ball is an input device that is mostly used in notebook or laptop computer, instead of a mouse. This is a ball which is half inserted and by moving fingers on the ball, the pointer can be moved.

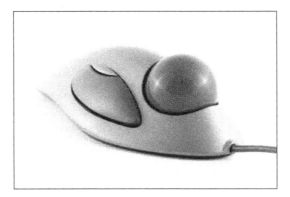

Since the whole device is not moved, a track ball requires less space than a mouse. A track ball comes in various shapes like a ball, a button, or a square.

Scanner

Scanner is an input device, which works more like a photocopy machine. It is used when some information is available on paper and it is to be transferred to the hard disk of the computer for further manipulation.

Scanner captures images from the source which are then converted into a digital form that can be stored on the disk. These images can be edited before they are printed.

Digitizer

Digitizer is an input device which converts analog information into digital form. Digitizer can convert a signal from the television or camera into a series of numbers that could be stored in a computer. They can be used by the computer to create a picture of whatever the camera had been pointed at.

Digitizer is also known as Tablet or Graphics Tablet as it converts graphics and pictorial data into binary inputs. A graphic tablet as digitizer is used for fine works of drawing and image manipulation applications.

Microphone

Microphone is an input device to input sound that is then stored in a digital form.

The microphone is used for various applications such as adding sound to a multimedia presentation or for mixing music.

Magnetic Ink Card Reader (MICR)

MICR input device is generally used in banks as there are large number of cheques to be processed every day. The bank's code number and cheque number are printed on the cheques with a special type of ink that contains particles of magnetic material that are machine readable.

This reading process is called Magnetic Ink Character Recognition (MICR). The main advantage of MICR is that it is fast and less error prone.

Optical Character Reader (OCR)

OCR is an input device used to read a printed text.

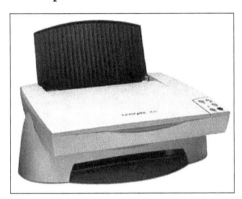

OCR scans the text optically, character by character, converts them into a machine readable code, and stores the text on the system memory.

Bar Code Readers

Bar Code Reader is a device used for reading bar coded data (data in the form of light and dark lines). Bar coded data is generally used in labeling goods, numbering the books, etc. It may be a handheld scanner or may be embedded in a stationary scanner.

Bar Code Reader scans a bar code image, converts it into an alphanumeric value, which is then fed to the computer that the bar code reader is connected to.

Optical Mark Reader (OMR)

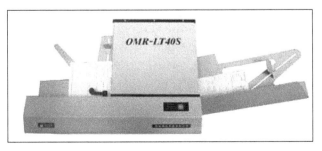

OMR is a special type of optical scanner used to recognize the type of mark made by pen or pencil. It is used where one out of a few alternatives is to be selected and marked.

It is specially used for checking the answer sheets of examinations having multiple choice questions.

Output Devices

Some of the important output devices used in a computer are:

Monitors

Monitors, commonly called as Visual Display Unit (VDU), are the main output device of a computer. It forms images from tiny dots, called pixels that are arranged in a rectangular form. The sharpness of the image depends upon the number of pixels.

There are two kinds of viewing screen used for monitors:

- Cathode-Ray Tube (CRT).

- Flat-Panel Display.

Cathode-Ray Tube (CRT) Monitor

The CRT display is made up of small picture elements called pixels. The smaller the pixels, the better the image clarity or resolution. It takes more than one illuminated pixel to form a whole character, such as the letter 'e' in the word help.

A finite number of characters can be displayed on a screen at once. The screen can be divided into a series of character boxes - fixed location on the screen where a standard character can be placed. Most screens are capable of displaying 80 characters of data horizontally and 25 lines vertically.

There are some disadvantages of CRT:

- Large in Size.

- High power consumption.

Flat-Panel Display Monitor

The flat-panel display refers to a class of video devices that have reduced volume, weight and power requirement in comparison to the CRT. You can hang them on walls or wear them on your wrists. Current uses of flat-panel displays include calculators, video games, monitors, laptop computer, and graphics display.

The flat-panel display is divided into two categories:

- Emissive Displays; Emissive displays are devices that convert electrical energy into light. For example, plasma panel and LED (Light-Emitting Diodes).

- Non-Emissive Displays: Non-emissive displays use optical effects to convert sunlight or light from some other source into graphics patterns. For example, LCD (Liquid-Crystal Device).

Printers

Printer is an output device, which is used to print information on paper.

There are two types of printers:

- Impact Printers.
- Non-Impact Printers.

Impact Printers

Impact printers print the characters by striking them on the ribbon, which is then pressed on the paper.

Characteristics of Impact Printers are the following:

- Very low consumable costs;
- Very noisy;
- Useful for bulk printing due to low cost;
- There is physical contact with the paper to produce an image.

These printers are of two types:

- Character printers.
- Line printers.

Character Printers

Character printers are the printers which print one character at a time.

These are further divided into two types:

- Dot Matrix Printer(DMP).
- Daisy Wheel.

Dot Matrix Printer

In the market, one of the most popular printers is Dot Matrix Printer. These printers are popular because of their ease of printing and economical price. Each character printed is in the form of pattern of dots and head consists of a Matrix of Pins of size (5*7, 7*9, 9*7 or 9*9) which comes out to form a character which is why it is called Dot Matrix Printer.

Advantages

- Inexpensive.
- Widely Used.
- Other language characters can be printed.

Disadvantages

- Slow Speed.
- Poor Quality.

Daisy Wheel

Head is lying on a wheel and pins corresponding to characters are like petals of Daisy (flower) which is why it is called Daisy Wheel Printer. These printers are generally used for word-processing in offices that require a few letters to be sent here and there with very nice quality.

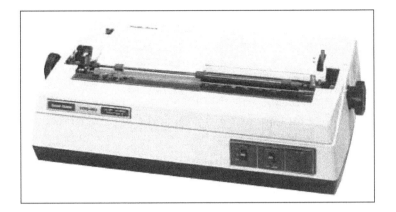

Advantages

- More reliable than DMP.

- Better quality.

- Fonts of character can be easily changed.

Disadvantages

- Slower than DMP.

- Noisy.

- More expensive than DMP.

Line Printers

Line printers are the printers which print one line at a time.

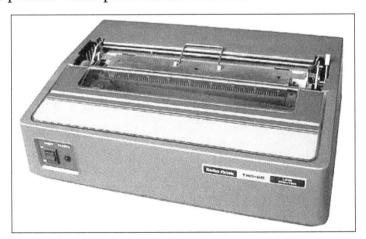

These are of two types:

- Drum Printer.

- Chain Printer.

Drum Printer

This printer is like a drum in shape hence it is called drum printer. The surface of the drum is divided into a number of tracks. Total tracks are equal to the size of the paper, i.e. for a paper width of 132 characters, drum will have 132 tracks. A character set is embossed on the track. Different character sets available in the market are 48 character set, 64 and 96 characters set. One rotation of drum prints one line. Drum printers are fast in speed and can print 300 to 2000 lines per minute.

Advantages

- Very high speed.

Disadvantages

- Very expensive.
- Characters fonts cannot be changed.

Chain Printer

In this printer, a chain of character sets is used; hence it is called Chain Printer. A standard character set may have 48, 64, or 96 characters.

Advantages

- Character fonts can easily be changed.
- Different languages can be used with the same printer.

Disadvantages

- Noisy.

Non-impact Printers

Non-impact printers print the characters without using the ribbon. These printers print a complete page at a time, thus they are also called as Page Printers.

These printers are of two types:

- Laser Printers.
- Inkjet Printers.

Characteristics of Non-impact Printers

- Faster than impact printers;
- They are not noisy;
- High quality;
- Supports many fonts and different character size.

Laser Printers

These are non-impact page printers. They use laser lights to produce the dots needed to form the characters to be printed on a page.

Advantages

- Very high speed;
- Very high quality output;
- Good graphics quality;
- Supports many fonts and different character size.

Disadvantages

- Expensive;
- Cannot be used to produce multiple copies of a document in a single printing.

Inkjet Printers

Inkjet printers are non-impact character printers based on a relatively new technology. They print characters by spraying small drops of ink onto paper. Inkjet printers produce high quality output with presentable features.

They make less noise because no hammering is done and these have many styles of printing modes available. Color printing is also possible. Some models of Inkjet printers can produce multiple copies of printing also.

Advantages

- High quality printing.

- More reliable.

Disadvantages

- Expensive as the cost per page is high.

- Slow as compared to laser printer.

Bus Architecture

A bus is a common pathway to connect various subsystems in a computer system. A bus consists of the connection media like wires and connectors, and a bus protocol. Buses can be serial or parallel, synchronous or asynchronous. Depending on these and other features, several bus architectures have been devised in the past. The Universal Serial Bus (USB) and IEEE 1394 are examples of serial buses while the ISA and PCI buses are examples of popular parallel buses.

A typical computer system is composed of several components such as the Central Processing Unit (CPU), memory chips, and Input/Output (I/O) devices. A bus is a common pathway or a set of wires that interconnect these various subsystems. The bus thus allows the different components to communicate with each other. The concept of a bus is illustrated in figure.

A bus, in computer language, is a channel over which information flows between units or devices. It typically has access points, or places into which a device can tap to become part of the channel. Most buses are bidirectional and devices can send or receive information. A bus is a shared communication link between the different devices. It allows adding new devices easily and facilitates portability of peripheral devices between different computer systems. However, if too many devices are connected to the same bus, the bandwidth of the bus can become a bottleneck. Typically more than two devices or subsystems are involved in a bus, and channels connecting only two components are sometimes referred to as ports instead of buses.

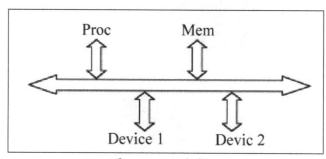

The concept of a bus

Buses often include wires to carry signals for addresses, data, control, status, clock, power and ground as illustrated in figure. The address lines indicate the source or destination of the data on the data lines. Control lines are used to implement the bus protocol. Often there are lines to request bus control, to handle interrupts, etc. Status lines indicate the progress of the current transaction. Clock signals are used in synchronous bus systems to synchronize bus operations.

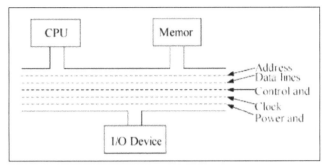

Different kinds of wires in a bus

The communications needs of the different devices in a computer system vary. For instance, fast high bandwidth communication is needed between processors and memory whereas bandwidth requirements are not so high on buses to I/O devices. This has led to the creation of different kinds of buses differing in their width, latency and bandwidth capabilities. Typically there are two kinds of buses, CPU-memory buses and I/O buses. CPU-memory buses are fast and short, and I/O buses are typically long and slow. I/O buses also have many devices connected to them. Some refer to this arrangement as a bus hierarchy with fast buses closer to the processor and slow buses farther away from the processor. Figure illustrates the bus hierarchy in a typical computer that uses the Pentium II processor.

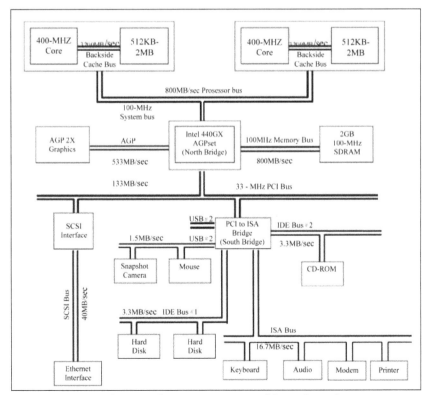

Buses in a typical personal computer system with Intel Pentium Processor

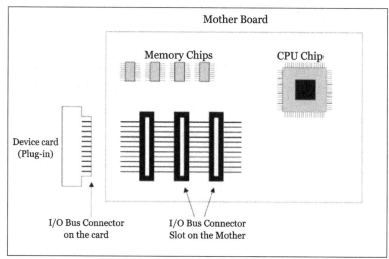

Simplified sketch of I/O device slots on a motherboard

The I/O buses in a personal computer are often etched on to a printed circuit board, which has connector slots to insert the peripheral device card. The I/O device cards have tabs that will fit into the connector, as illustrated in figure The tab on the I/O card has metallic strips on each side to make electrical contact with the bus.

Bus Protocols

A bus is a communication channel shared by many devices and hence rules need to be established in order for the communication to happen correctly. These rules are called bus protocols. Design of bus architecture involves several tradeoffs related to the width of the data bus, data transfer size, bus protocols, clocking, etc. Depending on whether the bus transactions are controlled by a clock or not, buses are classified into synchronous and asynchronous buses. Depending on whether the data bits are sent on parallel wires or multiplexed onto one single wire, there are parallel and serial buses. Control of the bus communication in the presence of multiple devices necessitates defined procedures called arbitration schemes.

Synchronous and Asynchronous Buses

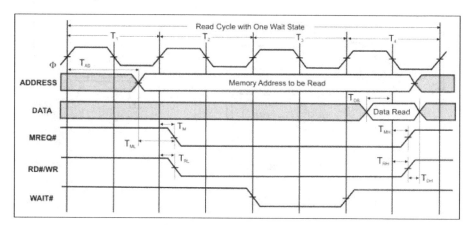

Read Operation on a Synchronous Bus

In a synchronous bus, bus operations are synchronized with reference to a clock signal. The bus clock is generally derived from the computer system clock; however, often it is slower than the master clock. For instance, 66MHz buses are used in systems with a processor clock of over 500MHz. Buses were traditionally slower than processors because memory access times are typically longer than processor clock cycles. A bus transaction often takes several clock cycles, although the cycles are collectively referred to by many as a bus cycle.

A memory read transaction on the synchronous bus typically proceeds as illustrated in figure. During the first clock cycle the CPU places the address of the location it wants to read, on the address lines of the bus. Later during the same clock cycle, once the address lines have stabilized, the READ request is asserted by the CPU. Many times, some of these control signals are active low and asserting the signal means that they are pulled low. A few clock cycles are needed for the memory to perform accessing of the requested location. In a simple non-pipelined bus, these appear as wait states and the data is placed on the bus by the memory after the two or three wait cycles. The CPU then releases the bus by de-asserting the READ control signal. The write transaction is similar except that the processor is the data source and the WRITE signal is the one that is asserted. Different bus architectures synchronize bus operations with respect to the rising edge or falling edge or level of the clock signal.

An asynchronous bus has no system clock. Handshaking is done to properly conduct the transmission of data between the sender and the receiver. The process is illustrated in figure. For example, in an asynchronous read operation, the bus master puts the address and control signals on the bus and then asserts a synchronization signal. The synchronization signal from the master prompts the slave to get synchronized and once it has accessed the data, it asserts its own synchronization signal. The slave's synchronization signal indicates to the processor that there is valid data on the bus, and it reads the data. The master then de-asserts its synchronization signal, which indicates to the slave that the master has read the data. The slave then de-asserts its synchronization signal. This method of synchronization is referred to as a full handshake. Note that there is no clock and that starting and ending of the data transfer are indicated by special synchronization signals. An asynchronous communication protocol can be considered as a pair of Finite State machines (FSMs) that operate in such a way that one FSM does not proceed until the other FSM has reached a certain state.

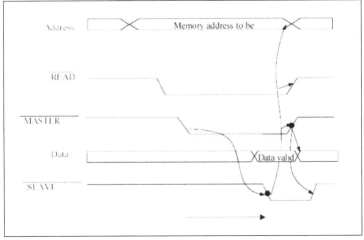

Read Operations on an Asynchronous Bus

Synchronous buses are typically faster than asynchronous buses because there is no overhead to establish a time reference for each transaction. Another reason that helps the synchronous bus to operate fast is that the bus protocol is predetermined and very little logic is involved in implementing the Finite State machine. However, synchronous buses are affected by clock skew and they cannot be very long. But asynchronous buses work well even when they are long because clock skew problems do not affect them. Thus asynchronous buses can handle longer physical distances and higher number of devices. Processor-memory buses are typically synchronous because the devices connected to the bus are fast, are small in number and are located in close proximity. I/O buses are typically asynchronous because many peripherals need only slow data rates and are physically situated far away.

Serial and Parallel Buses

Buses that transfer several data bits at the same are called parallel buses. It is desirable to have wide buses because large chunks of data can be transferred quickly when multiple lines can be used. Parallel buses typically have 8, 16, 32 or 64 data lines. The ISA, PCI, VESA, and EISA buses are examples of parallel buses. Serial buses use the same line to transfer different data bits of the same byte/word. Typically they have only one data line and the bits are sent one after the other, as a packet. The Universal Standard Bus (USB) and IEEE 1394 bus architecture are examples of serial buses. Serial buses are less expensive than parallel buses, however, parallel buses have higher throughput.

Functions of Buses in Computers

1. Data sharing: All types of buses found in a computer transfer data between the computer peripherals connected to it.

   The buses transfer or send data either in the serial or parallel method of data transfer. This allows for the exchange of 1, 2, 4 or even 8 bytes of data at a time. (A byte is a group of 8 bits). Buses are classified depending on how many bits they can move at the same time, which means that we have 8-bit, 16-bit, 32-bit or even 64-bit buses.

2. Addressing: A bus has address lines, which match those of the processor. This allows data to be sent to or from specific memory locations.

3. Power: A bus supplies power to various peripherals connected to it.

4. Timing: The bus provides a system clock signal to synchronize the peripherals attached to it with the rest of the system.

   The expansion bus facilitates easy connection of more or additional components and devices on a computer such as a TV card or sound card.

Types of Buses

Computers have two major types of buses:

1. System bus: This is the bus that connects the CPU to the main memory on the motherboard. The system bus is also called the front-side bus, memory bus, local bus, or host bus.

2. A number of I/O Buses: These buses connect various peripheral devices to the CPU. These devices connect to the system bus via a 'bridge' implemented in the processors' chipset. Other names for the I/O bus include "expansion bus", "external bus" or "host bus".

Expansion Bus Types

These are some of the common expansion bus types that have ever been used in computers:

1. ISA - Industry Standard Architecture;

2. EISA - Extended Industry Standard Architecture;

3. MCA - Micro Channel Architecture;

4. VESA - Video Electronics Standards Association;

5. PCI - Peripheral Component Interconnect;

6. PCI Express (PCI-X);

7. PCMCIA - Personal Computer Memory Card Industry Association (Also called PC bus);

8. AGP - Accelerated Graphics Port;

9. SCSI - Small Computer Systems Interface.

The 8 Bit and 16 Bit ISA Buses

8 Bit and 16 Bit ISA Buses

ISA Bus

This is the most common type of early expansion bus, which was designed for use in the original IBM PC. The IBM PC-XT used an 8-bit bus design. This means that the data transfers take place in 8-bit chunks (i.e. one byte at a time) across the bus. The ISA bus ran at a clock speed of 4.77 MHz.

For the 80286-based IBM PC-AT, an improved bus design, which could transfer 16-bits of data at a time, was announced. The 16-bit version of the ISA bus is sometimes known as the AT bus (AT-Advanced Technology).

The improved AT bus also provided a total of 24 address lines, which allowed 16MB of memory to be addressed. The AT bus was backward compatible with its 8-bit predecessor and allowed 8-bit cards to be used in 16-bit expansion slots.

When it first appeared the 8-bit ISA bus ran at a speed of 4.77MHZ – the same speed as the processor. Improvements done over the years eventually made the AT bus ran at a clock speed of 8MHz.

Table: Comparison Between 8 and 16 Bit ISA Bus.

8-Bit ISA card (XT-Bus)	16-Bit ISA (AT –Bus card)
8-bit data interface	16-bit data interface
4.77 MHZ bus	8-MHZ bus
62-pin connector	62-pin connector
	36-pin AT extension connection

MCA (Micro Channel Architecture)

IBM developed this bus as a replacement for ISA when they designed the PS/2 PC launched in 1987.

The bus offered a number of technical improvements over the ISA bus. For instance, the MCA ran at a faster speed of 10MHz and supported either 16-bit or 32-bit data. It also supported bus mastering - a technology that placed a mini-processor on each expansion card. These mini-processors controlled much of the data transfer allowing the CPU to do other tasks.

One advantage of MCA was that the plug-in cards were software configurable; this means that they required minimal intervention by the user when configuring.

The MCA expansion bus did not support ISA cards and IBM decided to charge other manufacturers royalties for use of the technology. This made it unpopular and it is now obsolete technology.

The EISA Bus

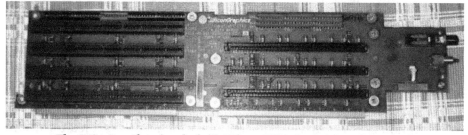

The EISA Bus Slots (on the left): Where EISA Cards Were Connected

EISA (Extended Industry Standard Architecture)

This is a bus technology developed by a group of manufactures as an alternative to MCA. The bus architecture was designed to use a 32-bit data path and provided 32 address lines giving access to 4GB of memory.

Like the MCA, EISA offered a disk-based setup for the cards, but it still ran at 8MHz in order for it to be compatible with ISA.

The EISA expansion slots are twice as deep as an ISA slot. If an ISA card is placed in an EISA slot it will use only the top row of connectors, however, a full EISA card uses both rows. It offered bus mastering.

EISA cards were relatively expensive and were normally found on high-end workstations and network servers.

VESA Bus

It was also known as the Local bus or the VESA-Local bus. VESA (Video Electronics Standards Association) was invented to help standardize PCs video specifications, thus solving the problem of proprietary technology where different manufacturers were attempting to develop their own buses.

The VL Bus provided 32-bit data path and ran at 25 or 33 MHZ. It ran at the same clock frequency as the host CPU. But this became a problem as processor speeds increased because, the faster the peripherals are required to run, the more expensive they are to manufacture.

It was difficult to implement the VL-Bus on newer chips such as the 486s and the new Pentiums and so eventually the VL-Bus was superseded by PCI.

VESA slots had an extra set of connectors and thus the cards were larger. The VESA design was backward compatible with the older ISA cards.

Features of the VESA local bus card:

- 32-bit interface.

- 62/36-pin connector.

- 90+20 pin VESA local bus extension.

Peripheral Component Interconnect

Peripheral Component Interconnect (PCI) is one of the latest developments in bus architecture and is the current standard for PC expansion cards. Intel developed and launched it as the expansion bus for the Pentium processor in 1993. It is a local bus like VESA, that is, it connects the CPU, memory, and peripherals to a wider, faster data pathway.

PCI supports both 32-bit and 64-bit data width; it is compatible with 486s and Pentiums. The bus data width is equal to the processor, such as a 32-bit processor would have a 32 bit PCI bus, and operates at 33MHz.

PCI was used in developing Plug and Play (PnP) and all PCI cards support PnP. This means a user can plug a new card into the computer, power it on and it will "self-identify" and "self-specify" and start working without manual configuration using jumpers.

Unlike VESA, PCI supports bus mastering that is, the bus has some processing capability and thus the CPU spends less time processing data. Most PCI cards are designed for 5v, but there are also 3v and dual-voltage cards. Keying slots used help to differentiate 3v and 5v cards and also to make sure that a 3v card is not slotted into a 5v socket and vice versa.

The PCI Slots

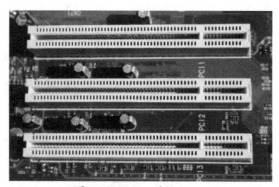

The PCI Bus Architecture

Accelerated Graphics Port

The need for high quality and very fast performance of video on computers led to the development of the Accelerated Graphics Port (AGP). The AGP Port connects to the CPU and operates at the speed of the processor bus. This means that video information is sent more quickly to the card for processing.

The AGP uses the main PC memory to hold 3D images. In effect, this gives the AGP video card an unlimited amount of video memory. To speed up the data transfer, Intel designed the port as a direct path to the PC's main memory.

Data transfer rate ranges from 264 Mbps to 528mbps, 800 Mbps up to 1.5 Gbps. AGP connector is identified by its brown colour.

Personal Computer Memory Card Industry Association (PC Card)

The Personal Computer Memory Card Industry Association was founded to give a standard bus for laptop computers. So it is basically used in the small computers.

Small Computer System Interface

Short for Small Computer System Interface, a parallel interface standard used by Apple Macintosh computers, PCs and Unix systems for attaching peripheral devices to a computer.

The SCSI Port

Mac LC SCSI Port

Universal Serial Bus (USB)

This is an external bus standard that supports data transfer rates of 12 Mbps. A single USB port connects up to 127 peripheral devices, such as mice, modems, and keyboards. The USB also supports hot plugging or insertion (ability to connect a device without turning the PC off) and plug and play (You connect a device and start using it without configuration).

We have two versions of USB:

- USB 1x: First released in 1996, the original USB 1.0 standard offered data rates of 1.5 Mbps. The USB 1.1 standard followed with two data rates: 12 Mbps for devices such as disk drives that need high-speed throughput and 1.5 Mbps for devices such as joysticks that need much less bandwidth.

- USB 2x: In 2002 a newer specification USB 2.0, also called Hi-Speed USB 2.0, was introduced. It increased the data transfer rate for PC to a USB device to 480 Mbps, which is 40 times faster than the USB 1.1 specification. With the increased bandwidth, high throughput peripherals such as digital cameras, CD burners, and video equipment could now be connected with USB.

IEEE 1394

The IEEE 1394 is a very fast external serial bus interface standard that supports data transfer rates of up to 400Mbps (in 1394a) and 800Mbps (in 1394b). This makes it ideal for devices that need to transfer high levels of data in real-time, such as video devices. It was developed by Apple with the name fire wire.

A single 1394 port can connect up 63 external devices:

- It supports Plug and play,
- Supports hot plugging, and
- Provides power to peripheral devices.

Input/Output Interface

The method that is used to transfer information between internal storage and external I/O devices is known as I/O interface.

Input Output Interface provides a method for transferring information between internal storage and external I/O devices.

Peripherals connected to a computer need special communication links for interfacing them with the central processing unit.

The purpose of communication link is to resolve the differences that exist between the central computer and each peripheral.

The Major Differences are:

- Peripherals are electro-mechanical and electromagnetic devices and CPU and memory are electronic devices. Therefore, a conversion of signal values may be needed.

- The data transfer rate of peripherals is usually slower than the transfer rate of CPU and consequently, a synchronization mechanism may be needed.

- Data codes and formats in the peripherals differ from the word format in the CPU and memory.

- The operating modes of peripherals are different from each other and must be controlled so as not to disturb the operation of other peripherals connected to the CPU.

To resolve these differences, computer systems include special hardware components between the CPU and Peripherals to supervises and synchronizes all input and out transfers:

- These components are called Interface Units because they interface between the processor bus and the peripheral devices.

I/O BUS and Interface Module

It defines the typical link between the processor and several peripherals. The I/O Bus consists of data lines, address lines and control lines. The I/O bus from the processor is attached to all peripherals interface.

To communicate with a particular device, the processor places a device address on address lines. Each Interface decodes the address and control received from the I/O bus, interprets them for peripherals and provides signals for the peripheral controller.

It is also synchronizes the data flow and supervises the transfer between peripheral and processor. Each peripheral has its own controller.

For example, the printer controller controls the paper motion, the print timing. The control lines are referred as I/O command. The commands are as following:

- Control command: A control command is issued to activate the peripheral and to inform it what to do.

- Status command: A status command is used to test various status conditions in the interface and the peripheral.

- Data Output command: A data output command causes the interface to respond by transferring data from the bus into one of its registers.

- Data Input command: The data input command is the opposite of the data output.

In this case the interface receives on item of data from the peripheral and places it in its buffer register. I/O Versus Memory Bus.

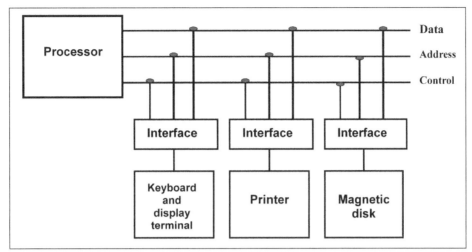

Connection of I/O bus to input-output devices

To communicate with I/O, the processor must communicate with the memory unit. Like the I/O bus, the memory bus contains data, address and read/write control lines. There are 3 ways that computer buses can be used to communicate with memory and I/O:

- Use two Separate buses, one for memory and other for I/O.

- Use one common bus for both memory and I/O but separate control lines for each.

- Use one common bus for memory and I/O with common control lines.

I/O Processor

In the first method, the computer has independent sets of data, address and control buses one for accessing memory and other for I/O. This is done in computers that provide a separate I/O processor (IOP). The purpose of IOP is to provide an independent pathway for the transfer of information between external device and internal memory.

Asynchronous Data Transfer

This Scheme is used when speed of I/O devices does not match with microprocessor, and timing characteristics of I/O devices is not predictable. In this method, process initiates the device and checks its status. As a result, CPU has to wait till I/O device is ready to transfer data. When device is ready CPU issues instruction for I/O transfer. In this method two types of techniques are used based on signals before data transfer:

- Strobe Control

- Handshaking.

Strobe Signal

The strobe control method of Asynchronous data transfer employs a single control line to time each transfer. The strobe may be activated by either the source or the destination unit.

Data Transfer Initiated by Source Unit:

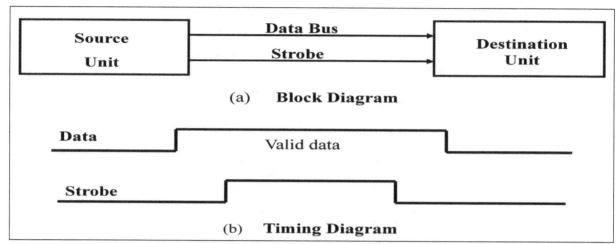

Sources-Initiated strobe for Data Transfer

In the block diagram figure (a), the data bus carries the binary information from source to destination unit. Typically, the bus has multiple lines to transfer an entire byte or word. The strobe is a single line that informs the destination unit when a valid data word is available.

The timing diagram figure (b) the source unit first places the data on the data bus. The information on the data bus and strobe signal remains in the active state to allow the destination unit to receive the data.

Data Transfer Initiated by Destination Unit

In this method, the destination unit activates the strobe pulse, to informing the source to provide the data. The source will respond by placing the requested binary information on the data bus.

The data must be valid and remain in the bus long enough for the destination unit to accept it. When accepted the destination unit then disables the strobe and the source unit removes the data from the bus.

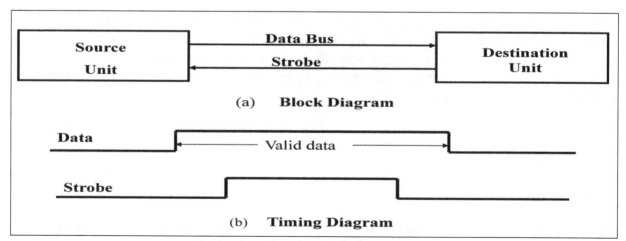

Destination-Initiated strobe for Data Transfer

Disadvantage of Strobe Signal

The disadvantage of the strobe method is that, the source unit initiates the transfer has no way of knowing whether the destination unit has actually received the data item that was places in the bus. Similarly, a destination unit that initiates the transfer has no way of knowing whether the source unit has actually placed the data on bus. The Handshaking method solves this problem.

Handshaking

The handshaking method solves the problem of strobe method by introducing a second control signal that provides a reply to the unit that initiates the transfer.

Principle of Handshaking

The basic principle of the two-wire handshaking method of data transfer is as follow:

One control line is in the same direction as the data flows in the bus from the source to destination. It is used by source unit to inform the destination unit whether there a valid data in the bus. The other control line is in the other direction from the destination to the source. It is used by the destination unit to inform the source whether it can accept the data. The sequence of control during the transfer depends on the unit that initiates the transfer.

Source Initiated Transfer using Handshaking

The sequence of events shows four possible states that the system can be at any given time. The source unit initiates the transfer by placing the data on the bus and enabling its data valid signal. The data accepted signal is activated by the destination unit after it accepts the data from the bus. The source unit then disables its data accepted signal and the system goes into its initial state.

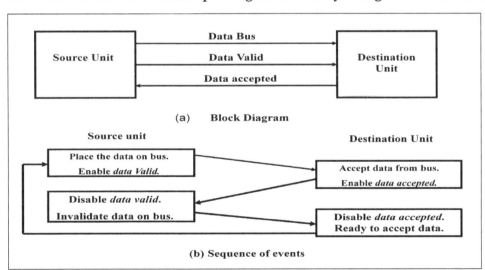

Destination Initiated Transfer using Handshaking

The name of the signal generated by the destination unit has been changed to ready for data to reflects its new meaning. The source unit in this case does not place data on the bus until after it receives the ready for data signal from the destination unit. From there on, the handshaking procedure follows the same pattern as in the source initiated case.

The only difference between the Source Initiated and the Destination Initiated transfer is in their choice of Initial sate.

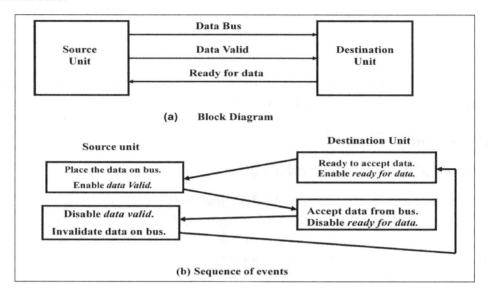

Destination-Initiated transfer using Handshaking.

Advantage of the Handshaking method

- The Handshaking scheme provides degree of flexibility and reliability because the successful completion of data transfer relies on active participation by both units.

- If any of one unit is faulty, the data transfer will not be completed. Such an error can be detected by means of a Timeout mechanism which provides an alarm if the data is not completed within time.

Asynchronous Serial Transmission

The transfer of data between two units is serial or parallel. In parallel data transmission, n bit in the message must be transmitted through n separate conductor path. In serial transmission, each bit in the message is sent in sequence one at a time.

Parallel transmission is faster but it requires many wires. It is used for short distances and where speed is important. Serial transmission is slower but is less expensive.

In Asynchronous serial transfer, each bit of message is sent a sequence at a time, and binary information is transferred only when it is available. When there is no information to be transferred, line remains idle.

In this technique each character consists of three points:

- Start Bit: First bit, called start bit is always zero and used to indicate the beginning character.

- Stop Bit: Last bit, called stop bit is always one and used to indicate end of characters. Stop bit is always in the 1- state and frame the end of the characters to signify the idle or wait state.

- Character Bit: Bits in between the start bit and the stop bit are known as character bits. The character bits always follow the start bit.

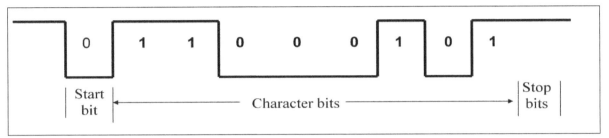

Asynchronous Serial Transmission

Serial Transmission of Asynchronous is done by two ways:

- Asynchronous Communication Interface.

- First In First out Buffer.

Asynchronous Communication Interface

It works as both a receiver and a transmitter. Its operation is initialized by CPU by sending a byte to the control register.

The transmitter register accepts a data byte from CPU through the data bus and transferred to a shift register for serial transmission.

The receive portion receives information into another shift register, and when a complete data byte is received it is transferred to receiver register.

CPU can select the receiver register to read the byte through the data bus. Data in the status register is used for input and output flags.

First In First Out Buffer (FIFO)

A First In First Out (FIFO) Buffer is a memory unit that stores information in such a manner that the first item is in the item first out. A FIFO buffer comes with separate input and output terminals. The important feature of this buffer is that it can input data and output data at two different rates.

When placed between two units, the FIFO can accept data from the source unit at one rate, rate of transfer and deliver the data to the destination unit at another rate.

If the source is faster than the destination, the FIFO is useful for source data arrive in bursts that fills out the buffer. FIFO is useful in some applications when data are transferred asynchronously.

Data Transfer Modes

Transfer of data is required between CPU and peripherals or memory or sometimes between any two devices or units of your computer system. To transfer a data from one unit to another one should be sure that both units have proper connection and at the time of data transfer the receiving unit is not busy. This data transfer with the computer is Internal Operation.

All the internal operations in a digital system are synchronized by means of clock pulses supplied by a common clock pulse Generator. The data transfer can be:

- Synchronous.

- Asynchronous.

When both the transmitting and receiving units use same clock pulse then such a data transfer is called Synchronous process. On the other hand, if the three is not concept of clock pulses and the sender operates at different moment than the receiver then such a data transfer is called Asynchronous data transfer.

The data transfer can be handled by various modes. Some of the modes use CPU as an intermediate path, others transfer the data directly to and from the memory unit and this can be handled by 3 following ways:

- Programmed I/O.

- Interrupt-Initiated I/O.

- Direct Memory Access (DMA).

Programmed I/O Mode

In this mode of data transfer the operations are the results in I/O instructions which are a part of computer program. Each data transfer is initiated by an instruction in the program. Normally the transfer is from a CPU register to peripheral device or vice-versa.

The processor issues an I/O command, on behalf of a process, to an I/O module; that process then busy waits for the operation to be completed before proceeding.

When the processor is executing a program and encounters an instruction relating to input/output, it executes that instruction by issuing a command to the appropriate input/output module. With the programmed input/output, the input/output module will perform the required action and then set the appropriate bits in the input/output status register. The input/output module takes no further action to alert the processor. In particular it doesn't interrupt the processor. Thus, it is the responsibility of the processor to check the status of the input/output module periodically, until it finds that the operation is complete.

It is simplest to illustrate programmed I/O by means of an example. Consider a process that wants to print the eight character string ABCDEFGH.

- It first assembles the string in a buffer in user space as shown in figure.

- The user process then acquires the printer for writing by making system call to open it.

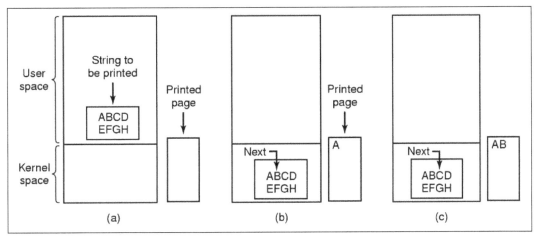

Steps in printing a string

- If printer is in use by other the call will fail and enter an error code or will block until printer is available, depending on OS and the parameters of the call.

- Once it has printer the user process makes a system call to print it.

- OS then usually copies the buffer with the string to an array; say P in the kernel space where it is more easily accessed since the kernel may have to change the memory map to get to user space.

- As the printer is available the OS copies the first character to the printer data register, in this example using memory mapped I/O. This action activates the printer. The character may not appear yet because some printers buffer a line or a page before printing.

- As soon as it has copied the first character to the printer the OS checks to see if the printer is ready to accept another one.

- Generally printer has a second register which gives its status.

The actions followed by the OS are summarized in figure below. First data are copied to the kernel, and then the OS enters a tight loop outputting the characters one at a time. The essentials aspects of programmed I/O is after outputting a character, the CPU continuously polls the device to see if it is ready to accept one. This behavior is often called polling or busy waiting.

```
copy_from_user(buffer,p,count); /*P is the kernel buffer*/

for(i=0;i<count;i++) { /* loop on every characters*/

while(*printer_status_reg!=READY); /*loop until ready*/

printer_data_register=P[i]; /*output one character */

}

return_to_user();
```

Programmed I/O is simple but has disadvantages of tying up the CPU full time until all the I/O is done.

Interrupt-Initiated I/O

Data transfer between the CPU and the peripherals is initiated by the CPU. But the CPU cannot start the transfer unless the peripheral is ready to communicate with the CPU. When a device is ready to communicate with the CPU, it generates an interrupt signal. A number of input-output devices are attached to the computer and each device is able to generate an interrupt request.

The main job of the interrupt system is to identify the source of the interrupt. There is also a possibility that several devices will request simultaneously for CPU communication. Then, the interrupt system has to decide which device is to be serviced first.

Priority Interrupt

A priority interrupt is a system which decides the priority at which various devices, which generates the interrupt signal at the same time, will be serviced by the CPU. The system has authority to decide which conditions are allowed to interrupt the CPU, while some other interrupt is being serviced. Generally, devices with high speed transfer such as *magnetic disks* are given high priority and slow devices such as *keyboards* are given low priority.

When two or more devices interrupt the computer simultaneously, the computer services the device with the higher priority first.

Types of Interrupts

Following are some different types of interrupts:

Hardware Interrupts

When the signal for the processor is from an external device or hardware then this interrupts is known as hardware interrupt.

Let us consider an example: when we press any key on our keyboard to do some action, then this pressing of the key will generate an interrupt signal for the processor to perform certain action. Such an interrupt can be of two types:

- Maskable Interrupt: The hardware interrupts which can be delayed when a much high priority interrupt has occurred at the same time.

- Non Maskable Interrupt: The hardware interrupts which cannot be delayed and should be processed by the processor immediately.

Software Interrupts

The interrupt that is caused by any internal system of the computer system is known as a software interrupt. It can also be of two types:

- Normal Interrupt: The interrupts that are caused by software instructions are called normal software interrupts.

- Exception: Unplanned interrupts which are produced during the execution of some program are called exceptions, such as division by zero.

Daisy Chaining Priority

This way of deciding the interrupt priority consists of serial connection of all the devices which generates an interrupt signal. The device with the highest priority is placed at the first position followed by lower priority devices and the device which has lowest priority among all is placed at the last in the chain.

In daisy chaining system all the devices are connected in a serial form. The interrupt line request is common to all devices. If any device has interrupt signal in low level state then interrupt line goes to low level state and enables the interrupt input in the CPU. When there is no interrupt the interrupt line stays in high level state. The CPU respond to the interrupt by enabling the interrupt acknowledge line. This signal is received by the device 1 at its PI input. The acknowledge signal passes to next device through PO output only if device 1 is not requesting an interrupt.

The following figure shows the block diagram for daisy chaining priority system.

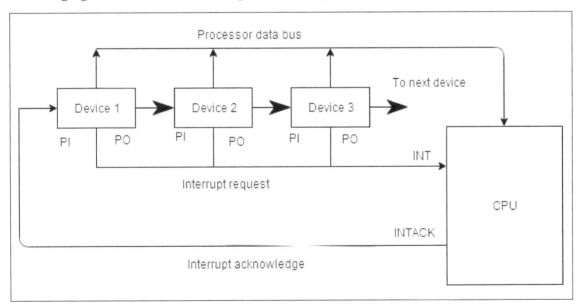

Direct Memory Access

In the Direct Memory Access (DMA) the interface transfer the data into and out of the memory unit through the memory bus. The transfer of data between a fast storage device such as magnetic disk and memory is often limited by the speed of the CPU. Removing the CPU from the path and letting the peripheral device manage the memory buses directly would improve the speed of transfer. This transfer technique is called Direct Memory Access (DMA).

During the DMA transfer, the CPU is idle and has no control of the memory buses. A DMA Controller takes over the buses to manage the transfer directly between the I/O device and memory.

The CPU may be placed in an idle state in a variety of ways. One common method extensively used in microprocessor is to disable the buses through special control signals such as:

- Bus Request (BR).

- Bus Grant (BG).

These two control signals in the CPU that facilitates the DMA transfer. The Bus Request (BR) input is used by the DMA controller to request the CPU. When this input is active, the CPU terminates the execution of the current instruction and places the address bus; data bus and read write lines into a high Impedance state. High Impedance state means that the output is disconnected.

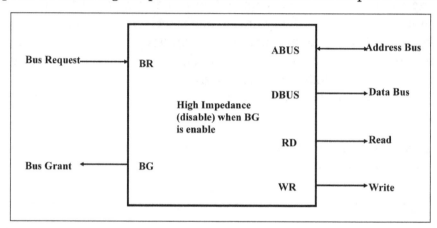

CPU Bus Signals for DMA Transfer

The CPU activates the Bus Grant (BG) output to inform the external DMA that the Bus Request (BR) can now take control of the buses to conduct memory transfer without processor.

When the DMA terminates the transfer, it disables the Bus Request (BR) line. The CPU disables the Bus Grant (BG), takes control of the buses and return to its normal operation.

The transfer can be made in several ways that are:

- DMA Burst: In DMA Burst transfer, a block sequence consisting of a number of memory words is transferred in continuous burst while the DMA controller is master of the memory buses.

- Cycle Stealing: Cycle stealing allows the DMA controller to transfer one data word at a time, after which it must returns control of the buses to the CPU.

DMA Controller

The hardware device used for direct memory access is called the DMA controller. DMA controller is a control unit, part of I/O device's interface circuit, which can transfer blocks of data between I/O devices and main memory with minimal intervention from the processor.

DMA Controller Diagram in Computer Architecture

DMA controller provides an interface between the bus and the input-output devices. Although it transfers data without intervention of processor, it is controlled by the processor. The processor initiates the DMA controller by sending the starting address, Number of words in the data block and direction of transfer of data. i.e. from I/O devices to the memory or from main memory to I/O devices. More than one external device can be connected to the DMA controller.

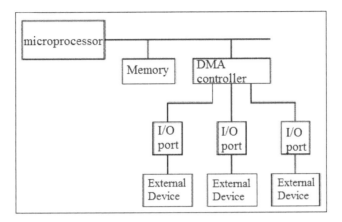

DMA controller contains an address unit, for generating addresses and selecting I/O device for transfer. It also contains the control unit and data count for keeping counts of the number of blocks transferred and indicating the direction of transfer of data. When the transfer is completed, DMA informs the processor by raising an interrupt. The typical block diagram of the DMA controller is shown in the figure.

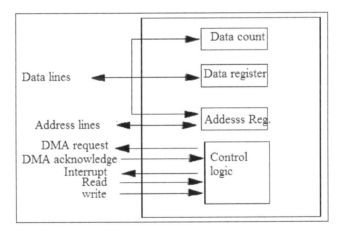

Working of DMA Controller

DMA controller has to share the bus with the processor to make the data transfer. The device that holds the bus at a given time is called bus master. When a transfer from I/O device to the memory or vice versa has to be made, the processor stops the execution of the current program, increments the program counter, moves data over stack then sends a DMA select signal to DMA controller over the address bus.

If the DMA controller is free, it requests the control of bus from the processor by raising the bus request signal. Processor grants the bus to the controller by raising the bus grant signal, now DMA controller is the bus master. The processor initiates the DMA controller by sending the memory addresses, number of blocks of data to be transferred and direction of data transfer. After assigning the data transfer task to the DMA controller, instead of waiting ideally till completion of data transfer, the processor resumes the execution of the program after retrieving instructions from the stack.

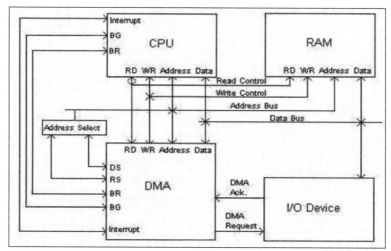

Transfer of Data in Computer By DMA Controller

DMA controller now has the full control of buses and can interact directly with memory and I/O devices independent of CPU. It makes the data transfer according to the control instructions received by the processor. After completion of data transfer, it disables the bus request signal and CPU disables the bus grant signal thereby moving control of buses to the CPU.

When an I/O device wants to initiate the transfer then it sends a DMA request signal to the DMA controller, for which the controller acknowledges if it is free. Then the controller requests the processor for the bus, raising the bus request signal. After receiving the bus grant signal it transfers the data from the device. For n channeled DMA controller n number of external devices can be connected.

The DMA transfers the data in three modes which include the following:

- Burst Mode: In this mode DMA handover the buses to CPU only after completion of whole data transfer. Meanwhile, if the CPU requires the bus it has to stay ideal and wait for data transfer.

- Cycle Stealing Mode: In this mode, DMA gives control of buses to CPU after transfer of every byte. It continuously issues a request for bus control, makes the transfer of one byte and returns the bus. By this CPU doesn't have to wait for a long time if it needs a bus for higher priority task.

- Transparent Mode: Here, DMA transfers data only when CPU is executing the instruction which does not require the use of buses.

Advantages and Disadvantages of DMA Controller

The advantages and disadvantages of DMA controller include the following:

Advantages

- DMA speedups the memory operations by bypassing the involvement of the CPU.

- The work overload on the CPU decreases.

- For each transfer, only a few numbers of clock cycles are required.

Disadvantages

- Cache coherence problem can be seen when DMA is used for data transfer.

- Increases the price of the system.

References

- Computer-input-devices, computer-fundamentals: tutorialspoint.com, retrieved 1 august , 2019

- Computer-outpu-devices, computer-fundamentals: tutorialspoint.com, retrieved 9 may, 2019

- Buses, computers: turbofuture.com, retrieved 13 july, 2019

- Priority-interrupt, computer-architecture: studytonight.com, retrieved 12 april, 2019

- Direct-memory-access-dma-in-computer-architecture: elprocus.com, retrieved 3 june, 2019

Parallel Computing and Pipelining

A type of computing where multiple processes are executed simultaneously is known as parallel computing. Pipelining refers to a process by which instruction are accumulated from the processor through a pipeline. This chapter has been carefully written to provide an easy understanding of the varied facets of parallel computing and pipelining.

Parallel Computing

Parallel Computing is the use of multiple processing elements simultaneously for solving any problem. Problems are broken down into instructions and are solved concurrently as each resource which has been applied to work is working at the same time.

Advantages of Parallel Computing over Serial Computing are as follows:

1. It saves time and money as many resources working together will reduce the time and cut potential costs.

2. It can be impractical to solve larger problems on Serial Computing.

3. It can take advantage of non-local resources when the local resources are finite.

4. Serial Computing 'wastes' the potential computing power, thus Parallel Computing makes better work of hardware.

Types of Parallelism

1. Bit-level parallelism: It is the form of parallel computing which is based on the increasing processor's size. It reduces the number of instructions that the system must execute in order to perform a task on large-sized data.

    Example: Consider a scenario where an 8-bit processor must compute the sum of two 16-bit integers. It must first sum up the 8 lower-order bits, then add the 8 higher-order bits, thus requiring two instructions to perform the operation. A 16-bit processor can perform the operation with just one instruction.

2. Instruction-level parallelism: A processor can only address less than one instruction for each clock cycle phase. These instructions can be re-ordered and grouped which are later on executed concurrently without affecting the result of the program. This is called instruction-level parallelism.

3. Task Parallelism: Task parallelism employs the decomposition of a task into subtasks and then allocating each of the subtasks for execution. The processors perform execution of sub tasks concurrently.

Convergence of Parallel Architectures

Parallel machines have been developed with several distinct architecture.

Communication Architecture

Parallel architecture enhances the conventional concepts of computer architecture with communication architecture. Computer architecture defines critical abstractions (like user-system boundary and hardware-software boundary) and organizational structure, whereas communication architecture defines the basic communication and synchronization operations. It also addresses the organizational structure.

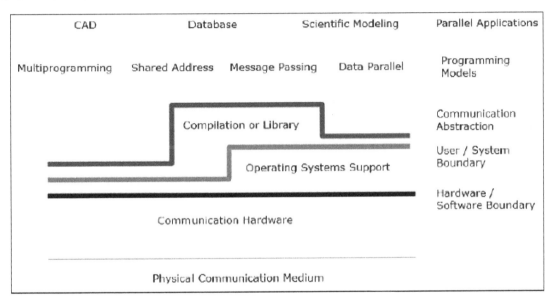

Programming model is the top layer. Applications are written in programming model. Parallel programming models include:

- Shared address space: Shared address programming is just like using a bulletin board, where one can communicate with one or many individuals by posting information at a particular location, which is shared by all other individuals. Individual activity is coordinated by noting who is doing what task.

- Message passing: Message passing is like a telephone call or letters where a specific receiver receives information from a specific sender.

- Data parallel programming: Data parallel programming is an organized form of cooperation. Here, several individuals perform an action on separate elements of a data set concurrently and share information globally.

Shared Memory

Shared memory multiprocessors are one of the most important classes of parallel machines. It gives better throughput on multiprogramming workloads and supports parallel programs.

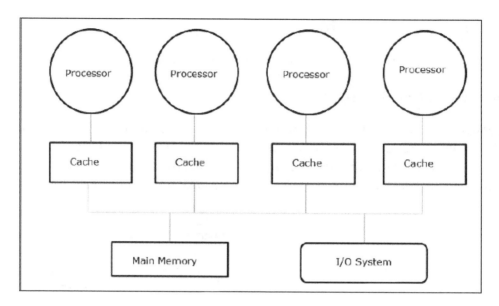

In this case, all the computer systems allow a processor and a set of I/O controller to access a collection of memory modules by some hardware interconnection. The memory capacity is increased by adding memory modules and I/O capacity is increased by adding devices to I/O controller or by adding additional I/O controller. Processing capacity can be increased by waiting for a faster processor to be available or by adding more processors.

All the resources are organized around a central memory bus. Through the bus access mechanism, any processor can access any physical address in the system. As all the processors are equidistant from all the memory locations, the access time or latency of all the processors is same on a memory location. This is called symmetric multiprocessor.

Message-passing Architecture

Message passing architecture is also an important class of parallel machines. It provides communication among processors as explicit I/O operations. In this case, the communication is combined at the I/O level, instead of the memory system.

In message passing architecture, user communication executed by using operating system or library calls that perform many lower level actions, which includes the actual communication operation. As a result, there is a distance between the programming model and the communication operations at the physical hardware level.

Send and receive is the most common user level communication operations in message passing system. Send specifies a local data buffer (which is to be transmitted) and a receiving remote processor. Receive specifies a sending process and a local data buffer in which the transmitted data will be placed. In send operation, an identifier or a tag is attached to the message and the receiving operation specifies the matching rule like a specific tag from a specific processor or any tag from any processor.

The combination of a send and a matching receive completes a memory-to-memory copy. Each end specifies its local data address and a pair wise synchronization event.

Convergence

Development of the hardware and software has faded the clear boundary between the shared memory and message passing camps. Message passing and a shared address space represents two distinct programming models; each gives a transparent paradigm for sharing, synchronization and communication. However, the basic machine structures have converged towards a common organization.

Data Parallel Processing

Another important class of parallel machine is variously called – processor arrays, data parallel architecture and single-instruction-multiple-data machines. The main feature of the programming model is that operations can be executed in parallel on each element of a large regular data structure (like array or matrix).

Data parallel programming languages are usually enforced by viewing the local address space of a group of processes, one per processor, forming an explicit global space. As all the processors communicate together and there is a global view of all the operations, so either a shared address space or message passing can be used.

Fundamental Design Issues

Development of programming model only cannot increase the efficiency of the computer nor can the development of hardware alone do it. However, development in computer architecture can make the difference in the performance of the computer. We can understand the design problem by focusing on how programs use a machine and which basic technologies are provided.

Communication Abstraction

Communication abstraction is the main interface between the programming model and the system implementation. It is like the instruction set that provides a platform so that the same program can run correctly on many implementations. Operations at this level must be simple. Communication abstraction is like a contract between the hardware and software, which allows each other the flexibility to improve without affecting the work.

Programming Model Requirements

A parallel program has one or more threads operating on data. A parallel programming model defines what data the threads can name, which operations can be performed on the named data, and which order is followed by the operations. To confirm that the dependencies between the programs are enforced, a parallel program must coordinate the activity of its threads.

Parallel Computer Architecture - Models

Parallel processing has been developed as an effective technology in modern computers to meet the demand for higher performance, lower cost and accurate results in real-life applications. Concurrent events are common in today's computers due to the practice of multiprogramming, multiprocessing, or multi-computing.

Modern computers have powerful and extensive software packages. To analyze the development of the performance of computers, first we have to understand the basic development of hardware and software.

- Computer Development Milestones: There is two major stages of development of computer - mechanical or electromechanical parts. Modern computers evolved after the introduction of electronic components. High mobility electrons in electronic computers replaced the operational parts in mechanical computers. For information transmission, electric signal which travels almost at the speed of a light replaced mechanical gears or levers.

- Elements of Modern computers: A modern computer system consists of computer hardware, instruction sets, application programs, system software and user interface.

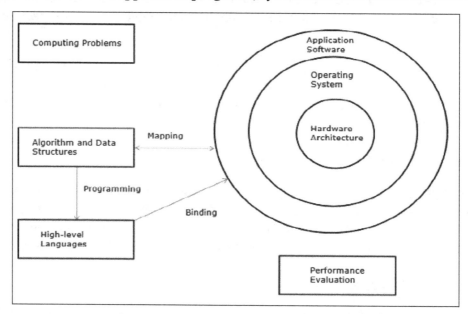

The computing problems are categorized as numerical computing, logical reasoning, and transaction processing. Some complex problems may need the combination of all the three processing modes.

- Evolution of Computer Architecture: In last four decades, computer architecture has gone through revolutionary changes. We started with Von Neumann architecture and now we have multicomputers and multiprocessors.

- Performance of a computer system: Performance of a computer system depends both on machine capability and program behavior. Machine capability can be improved with better hardware technology, advanced architectural features and efficient resource management. Program behavior is unpredictable as it is dependent on application and run-time conditions.

Shared-memory Multicomputers

Three most common shared memory multiprocessors models are:

Uniform Memory Access (UMA)

In this model, all the processors share the physical memory uniformly. All the processors have equal access time to all the memory words. Each processor may have a private cache memory. Same rule is followed for peripheral devices.

When all the processors have equal access to all the peripheral devices, the system is called a symmetric multiprocessor. When only one or a few processors can access the peripheral devices, the system is called an asymmetric multiprocessor.

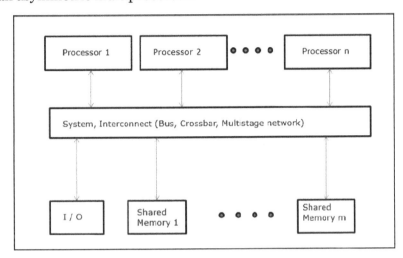

Non-uniform Memory Access (NUMA)

In NUMA multiprocessor model, the access time varies with the location of the memory word. Here, the shared memory is physically distributed among all the processors, called local memories. The collection of all local memories forms a global address space which can be accessed by all the processors.

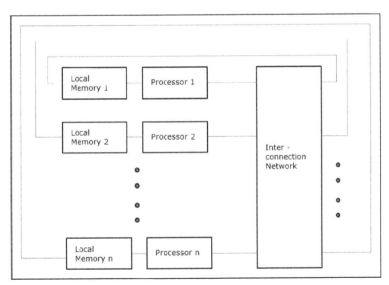

Cache Only Memory Architecture (COMA)

The COMA model is a special case of the NUMA model. Here, all the distributed main memories are converted to cache memories.

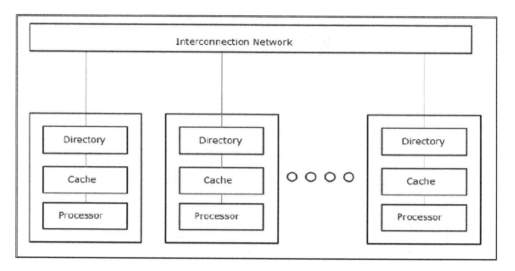

- Distributed - Memory Multicomputers: A distributed memory multicomputer system consists of multiple computers, known as nodes, inter-connected by message passing network. Each node acts as an autonomous computer having a processor, a local memory and sometimes I/O devices. In this case, all local memories are private and are accessible only to the local processors. This is why; the traditional machines are called no-remote-memory-access (NORMA) machines.

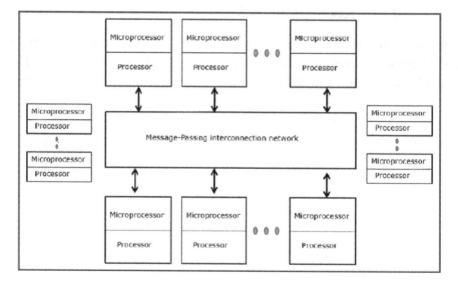

Multivector and SIMD Computers

Vector Supercomputers

In a vector computer, a vector processor is attached to the scalar processor as an optional feature. The host computer first loads program and data to the main memory. Then the scalar control unit decodes all the instructions. If the decoded instructions are scalar operations or program operations, the scalar processor executes those operations using scalar functional pipelines.

On the other hand, if the decoded instructions are vector operations then the instructions will be sent to vector control unit.

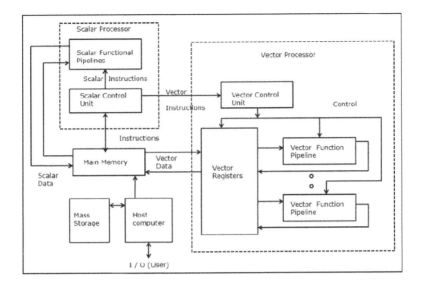

SIMD Supercomputers

In SIMD computers, 'N' number of processors are connected to a control unit and all the processors have their individual memory units. All the processors are connected by an interconnection network.

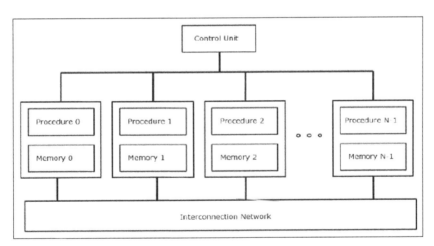

PRAM and VLSI Models

The ideal model gives a suitable framework for developing parallel algorithms without considering the physical constraints or implementation details.

The models can be enforced to obtain theoretical performance bounds on parallel computers or to evaluate VLSI complexity on chip area and operational time before the chip is fabricated.

Parallel Random-Access Machines

Sheperdson and Sturgis modeled the conventional Uniprocessor computers as random-access-machines (RAM). Fortune and Wyllie developed a parallel random-access-machine (PRAM) model for modeling an idealized parallel computer with zero memory access overhead and synchronization.

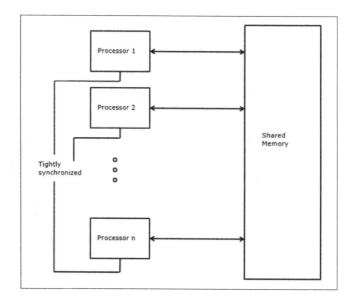

An N-processor PRAM has a shared memory unit. This shared memory can be centralized or distrib-uted among the processors. These processors operate on a synchronized read-memory, write-memo-ry and compute cycle. So, these models specify how concurrent read and write operations are handled.

Following are the possible memory update operations:

- Exclusive read (ER): In this method, in each cycle only one processor is allowed to read from any memory location.

- Exclusive write (EW): In this method, at least one processor is allowed to write into a mem-ory location at a time.

- Concurrent read (CR): It allows multiple processors to read the same information from the same memory location in the same cycle.

- Concurrent write (CW): It allows simultaneous write operations to the same memory loca-tion. To avoid write conflict some policies are set up.

VLSI Complexity Model

Parallel computers use VLSI chips to fabricate processor arrays, memory arrays and large-scale switching networks.

Nowadays, VLSI technologies are 2-dimensional. The size of a VLSI chip is proportional to the amount of storage (memory) space available in that chip.

We can calculate the space complexity of an algorithm by the chip area (A) of the VLSI chip imple-mentation of that algorithm. If T is the time (latency) needed to execute the algorithm, then A.T gives an upper bound on the total number of bits processed through the chip (or I/O). For certain computing, there exists a lower bound, f(s), such that

$$A.T^2 >= O\ (f(s))$$

Where, A=chip area and T=time.

Architectural Development Tracks

The evolution of parallel computers I spread along the following tracks:

- Multiple Processor Tracks
  - Multiprocessor track
  - Multicomputer track
- Multiple data track
  - Vector track
  - SIMD track
- Multiple threads track
  - Multithreaded track
  - Dataflow track

In multiple processor track, it is assumed that different threads execute concurrently on different processors and communicate through shared memory (multiprocessor track) or message passing (multicomputer track) system.

In multiple data track, it is assumed that the same code is executed on the massive amount of data. It is done by executing same instructions on a sequence of data elements (vector track) or through the execution of same sequence of instructions on a similar set of data (SIMD track).

In multiple threads track, it is assumed that the interleaved execution of various threads on the same processor to hide synchronization delays among threads executing on different processors. Thread interleaving can be coarse (multithreaded track) or fine (dataflow track).

Processor in Parallel Systems

In the 80's, a special purpose processor was popular for making multicomputers called Transputer. A transputer consisted of one core processor, a small SRAM memory, a DRAM main memory interface and four communication channels, all on a single chip. To make a parallel computer communication, channels were connected to form a network of Transputers. But it has a lack of computational power and hence couldn't meet the increasing demand of parallel applications. This problem was solved by the development of RISC processors and it was cheap also.

Modern parallel computer uses microprocessors which use parallelism at several levels like instruction-level parallelism and data level parallelism.

High Performance Processors

RISC and RISCy processors dominate today's parallel computers market.

Characteristics of traditional RISC are:

- Has few addressing modes.

- Has a fixed format for instructions, usually 32 or 64 bits.

- Has dedicated load/store instructions to load data from memory to register and store data from register to memory.

- Arithmetic operations are always performed on registers.

- Uses pipelining.

Most of the microprocessors these days are superscalar, i.e. in a parallel computer multiple instruction pipelines are used. Therefore, superscalar processors can execute more than one instruction at the same time. Effectiveness of superscalar processors is dependent on the amount of instruction-level parallelism (ILP) available in the applications. To keep the pipelines filled, the instructions at the hardware level are executed in a different order than the program order.

Many modern microprocessors use *super pipelining* approach. In *super pipelining*, to increase the clock frequency, the work done within a pipeline stage is reduced and the number of pipeline stages is increased.

Very Large Instruction Word (VLIW) Processors

These are derived from horizontal microprogramming and superscalar processing. Instructions in VLIW processors are very large. The operations within a single instruction are executed in parallel and are forwarded to the appropriate functional units for execution. So, after fetching a VLIW instruction, its operations are decoded. Then the operations are dispatched to the functional units in which they are executed in parallel.

Vector Processors

Vector processors are co-processor to general-purpose microprocessor. Vector processors are generally register-register or memory-memory. A vector instruction is fetched and decoded and then a certain operation is performed for each element of the operand vectors, whereas in a normal processor a vector operation needs a loop structure in the code. To make it more efficient, vector processors chain several vector operations together, i.e., the result from one vector operation are forwarded to another as operand.

Caching

Caches are important element of high-performance microprocessors. After every 18 months, speed of microprocessors become twice, but DRAM chips for main memory cannot compete with this speed. So, caches are introduced to bridge the speed gap between the processor and memory. A cache is a fast and small SRAM memory. Many more caches are applied in modern processors like Translation Look-aside Buffers (TLBs) caches, instruction and data caches, etc.

Direct Mapped Cache

In direct mapped caches, a 'modulo' function is used for one-to-one mapping of addresses in the main memory to cache locations. As same cache entry can have multiple main memory blocks mapped to it, the processor must be able to determine whether a data block in the cache is the data block that is actually needed. This identification is done by storing a tag together with a cache block.

Fully Associative Cache

A fully associative mapping allows for placing a cache block anywhere in the cache. By using some replacement policy, the cache determines a cache entry in which it stores a cache block. Fully associative caches have flexible mapping, which minimizes the number of cache-entry conflicts. Since a fully associative implementation is expensive, these are never used large scale.

Set-associative Cache

A set-associative mapping is a combination of a direct mapping and a fully associative mapping. In this case, the cache entries are subdivided into cache sets. As in direct mapping, there is a fixed mapping of memory blocks to a set in the cache. But inside a cache set, a memory block is mapped in a fully associative manner.

Cache Strategies

Other than mapping mechanism, caches also need a range of strategies that specify what should happen in the case of certain events. In case of (set-) associative caches, the cache must determine which cache block is to be replaced by a new block entering the cache.

Some well-known replacement strategies are:

- First-In First Out (FIFO)
- Least Recently Used (LRU).

Multiprocessors and Multicomputers

Multiprocessor System Interconnects

Parallel processing needs the use of efficient system interconnects for fast communication among the Input/Output and peripheral devices, multiprocessors and shared memory.

Hierarchical Bus Systems

A hierarchical bus system consists of a hierarchy of buses connecting various systems and sub-systems/components in a computer. Each bus is made up of a number of signal, control, and power lines. Different buses like local buses, backplane buses and I/O buses are used to perform different interconnection functions.

Local buses are the buses implemented on the printed-circuit boards. A backplane bus is a printed circuit on which many connectors are used to plug in functional boards. Buses which connect input/output devices to a computer system are known as I/O buses.

Crossbar Switch and Multiport Memory

Switched networks give dynamic interconnections among the inputs and outputs. Small or medium size systems mostly use crossbar networks. Multistage networks can be expanded to the larger systems, if the increased latency problem can be solved.

Both crossbar switch and multiport memory organization is a single-stage network. Though a single stage network is cheaper to build, but multiple passes may be needed to establish certain connections. A multistage network has more than one stage of switch boxes. These networks should be able to connect any input to any output.

Multistage and Combining Networks

Multistage networks or multistage interconnection networks are a class of high-speed computer networks which is mainly composed of processing elements on one end of the network and memory elements on the other end, connected by switching elements.

These networks are applied to build larger multiprocessor systems. This includes Omega Network, Butterfly Network and many more.

Multicomputers

Multicomputers are distributed memory MIMD architectures. The following diagram shows a conceptual model of a multicomputer.

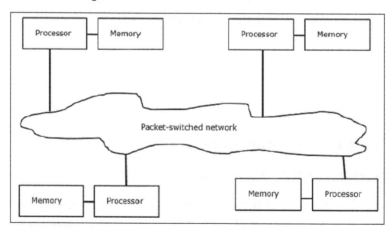

Multicomputers are message-passing machines which apply packet switching method to exchange data. Here, each processor has a private memory, but no global address space as a processor can access only its own local memory. So, communication is not transparent: here programmers have to explicitly put communication primitives in their code.

Having no globally accessible memory is a drawback of multicomputers. This can be solved by using the following two schemes:

- Virtual Shared Memory (VSM)

- Shared Virtual Memory (SVM)

In these schemes, the application programmer assumes a big shared memory which is globally addressable. If required, the memory references made by applications are translated into the message-passing paradigm.

Virtual Shared Memory (VSM)

VSM is a hardware implementation. So, the virtual memory system of the Operating System is transparently implemented on top of VSM. So, the operating system thinks it is running on a machine with a shared memory.

Shared Virtual Memory (SVM)

SVM is a software implementation at the Operating System level with hardware support from the Memory Management Unit (MMU) of the processor. Here, the unit of sharing is Operating System memory pages.

If a processor addresses a particular memory location, the MMU determines whether the memory page associated with the memory access is in the local memory or not. If the page is not in the memory, in a normal computer system it is swapped in from the disk by the Operating System. But, in SVM, the Operating System fetches the page from the remote node which owns that particular page.

Message Passing Mechanisms

Message passing mechanisms in a multicomputer network needs special hardware and software support.

Message-Routing Schemes

In multicomputer with store and forward routing scheme, packets are the smallest unit of information transmission. In wormhole–routed networks, packets are further divided into flits. Packet length is determined by the routing scheme and network implementation, whereas the flit length is affected by the network size.

In Store and forward routing, packets are the basic unit of information transmission. In this case, each node uses a packet buffer. A packet is transmitted from a source node to a destination node through a sequence of intermediate nodes. Latency is directly proportional to the distance between the source and the destination.

In wormhole routing, the transmission from the source node to the destination node is done through a sequence of routers. All the flits of the same packet are transmitted in an inseparable sequence in a pipelined fashion. In this case, only the header flit knows where the packet is going.

Deadlock and Virtual Channels

A virtual channel is a logical link between two nodes. It is formed by flit buffer in source node and receiver node, and a physical channel between them. When a physical channel is allocated for a pair, one source buffer is paired with one receiver buffer to form a virtual channel.

When all the channels are occupied by messages and none of the channel in the cycle is freed, a deadlock situation will occur. To avoid this deadlock avoidance scheme has to be followed.

Cache Coherence and Synchronization

The Cache Coherence Problem

In a multiprocessor system, data inconsistency may occur among adjacent levels or within the same level of the memory hierarchy. For example, the cache and the main memory may have inconsistent copies of the same object.

As multiple processors operate in parallel, and independently multiple caches may possess different copies of the same memory block, this creates cache coherence problem. Cache coherence schemes help to avoid this problem by maintaining a uniform state for each cached block of data.

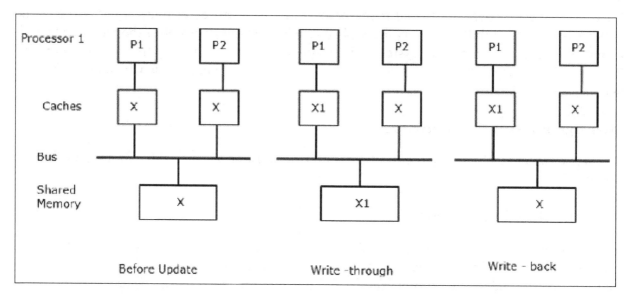

Let X be an element of shared data which has been referenced by two processors, P1 and P2. In the beginning, three copies of X are consistent. If the processor P1 writes a new data X1 into the cache, by using write-through policy, the same copy will be written immediately into the shared memory. In this case, inconsistency occurs between cache memory and the main memory. When a write-back policy is used, the main memory will be updated when the modified data in the cache is replaced or invalidated.

In general, there are three sources of inconsistency problem:

- Sharing of writable data.

- Process migration.

- I/O activity.

Snoopy Bus Protocols

Snoopy protocols achieve data consistency between the cache memory and the shared memory through a bus-based memory system. Write-invalidate and write-update policies are used for maintaining cache consistency.

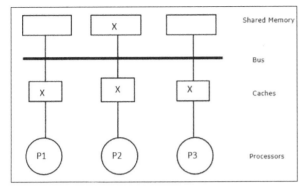 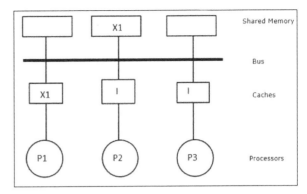

Consistent copies of block X are in shared memory
and three processor caches

After a write invalidate operation by P1

In this case, we have three processors P1, P2, and P3 having a consistent copy of data element 'X' in their local cache memory and in the shared memory. Processor P1 writes X1 in its cache memory using write-invalidate protocol. So, all other copies are invalidated via the bus. It is denoted by 'I'. Invalidated blocks are also known as dirty, i.e. they should not be used. The write-update protocol updates all the cache copies via the bus. By using write back cache, the memory copy is also updated.

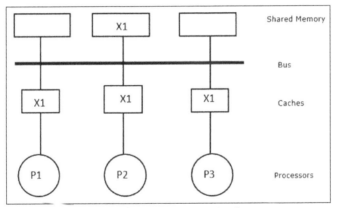

After a write Update operation by P1

Cache Events and Actions

Following events and actions occur on the execution of memory-access and invalidation commands:

- Read-miss: When a processor wants to read a block and it is not in the cache, a read-miss occurs. This initiates a bus-read operation. If no dirty copy exists, then the main memory that has a consistent copy, supplies a copy to the requesting cache memory. If a dirty copy exists in a remote cache memory, that cache will restrain the main memory and send a copy to the requesting cache memory. In both the cases, the cache copy will enter the valid state after a read miss.

- Write-hit: If the copy is in dirty or reserved state, write is done locally and the new state is dirty. If the new state is valid, write-invalidate command is broadcasted to all the caches, invalidating their copies. When the shared memory is written through, the resulting state is reserved after this first write.

- Write-miss: If a processor fails to write in the local cache memory, the copy must come either from the main memory or from a remote cache memory with a dirty block. This is done by sending a read-invalidate command, which will invalidate all cache copies. Then the local copy is updated with dirty state.

- Read-hit: Read-hit is always performed in local cache memory without causing a transition of state or using the snoopy bus for invalidation.

- Block replacement: When a copy is dirty, it is to be written back to the main memory by block replacement method. However, when the copy is either in valid or reserved or invalid state, no replacement will take place.

Directory-based Protocols

By using a multistage network for building a large multiprocessor with hundreds of processors, the snoopy cache protocols need to be modified to suit the network capabilities. Broadcasting being very expensive to perform in a multistage network, the consistency commands is sent only to those caches that keep a copy of the block. This is the reason for development of directory-based protocols for network-connected multiprocessors.

In a directory-based protocols system, data to be shared are placed in a common directory that maintains the coherence among the caches. Here, the directory acts as a filter where the processors ask permission to load an entry from the primary memory to its cache memory. If an entry is changed the directory either updates it or invalidates the other caches with that entry.

Hardware Synchronization Mechanisms

Synchronization is a special form of communication where instead of data control, information is exchanged between communicating processes residing in the same or different processors.

Multiprocessor systems use hardware mechanisms to implement low-level synchronization operations. Most multiprocessors have hardware mechanisms to impose atomic operations such as memory read, write or read-modify-write operations to implement some synchronization primitives. Other than atomic memory operations, some inter-processor interrupts are also used for synchronization purposes.

Cache Coherency in Shared Memory Machines

Maintaining cache coherency is a problem in multiprocessor system when the processors contain local cache memory. Data inconsistency between different caches easily occurs in this system.

The major concern areas are:

- Sharing of writable data.

- Process migration.

- I/O activity.

Sharing of Writable Data

When two processors (P1 and P2) have same data element (X) in their local caches and one process (P1) writes to the data element (X), as the caches are write-through local cache of P1, the main memory is also updated. Now when P2 tries to read data element (X), it does not find X because the data element in the cache of P2 has become outdated.

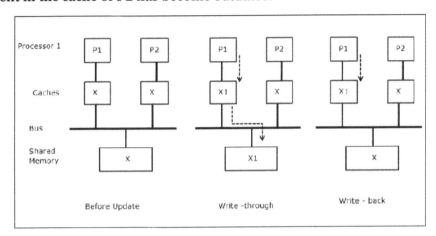

Process Migration

In the first stage, cache of P1 has data element X, whereas P2 does not have anything. A process on P2 first writes on X and then migrates to P1. Now, the process starts reading data element X, but as the processor P1 has outdated data the process cannot read it. So, a process on P1 writes to the data element X and then migrates to P2. After migration, a process on P2 starts reading the data element X but it finds an outdated version of X in the main memory.

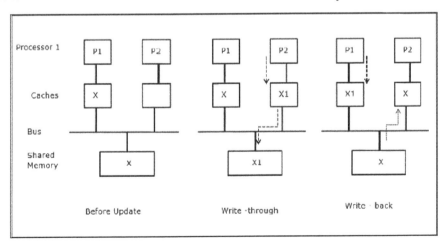

I/O Activity

As illustrated in the figure, an I/O device is added to the bus in a two-processor multiprocessor architecture. In the beginning, both the caches contain the data element X. When the I/O device receives a new element X, it stores the new element directly in the main memory. Now, when either P1 or P2 (assume P1) tries to read element X it gets an outdated copy. So, P1 writes to element X. Now, if I/O device tries to transmit X it gets an outdated copy.

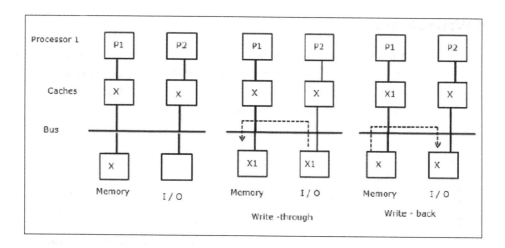

Uniform Memory Access (UMA)

Uniform Memory Access (UMA) architecture means the shared memory is the same for all processors in the system. Popular classes of UMA machines, which are commonly used for (file-) servers, are the so-called Symmetric Multiprocessors (SMPs). In an SMP, all system resources like memory, disks, other I/O devices, etc. are accessible by the processors in a uniform manner.

Non-Uniform Memory Access (NUMA)

In NUMA architecture, there are multiple SMP clusters having an internal indirect/shared network, which are connected in scalable message-passing network. So, NUMA architecture is logically shared physically distributed memory architecture.

In a NUMA machine, the cache-controller of a processor determines whether a memory reference is local to the SMP's memory or it is remote. To reduce the number of remote memory accesses, NUMA architectures usually apply caching processors that can cache the remote data. But when caches are involved, cache coherency needs to be maintained. So these systems are also known as CC-NUMA (Cache Coherent NUMA).

Cache Only Memory Architecture (COMA)

COMA machines are similar to NUMA machines, with the only difference that the main memories of COMA machines act as direct-mapped or set-associative caches. The data blocks are hashed to a location in the DRAM cache according to their addresses. Data that is fetched remotely is actually stored in the local main memory. Moreover, data blocks do not have a fixed home location, they can freely move throughout the system.

COMA architectures mostly have a hierarchical message-passing network. A switch in such a tree contains a directory with data elements as its sub-tree. Since data has no home location, it must be explicitly searched for. This means that a remote access requires a traversal along the switches in the tree to search their directories for the required data. So, if a switch in the network receives multiple requests from its subtree for the same data, it combines them into a single request which is sent to the parent of the switch. When the requested data returns, the switch sends multiple copies of it down its subtree.

COMA versus CC-NUMA

Following are the differences between COMA and CC-NUMA:

- COMA tends to be more flexible than CC-NUMA because COMA transparently supports the migration and replication of data without the need of the OS.

- COMA machines are expensive and complex to build because they need non-standard memory management hardware and the coherency protocol is harder to implement.

- Remote accesses in COMA are often slower than those in CC-NUMA since the tree network needs to be traversed to find the data.

Hardware Software Tradeoffs

There are many methods to reduce hardware cost. One method is to integrate the communication assist and network less tightly into the processing node and increasing communication latency and occupancy.

Another method is to provide automatic replication and coherence in software rather than hardware. The latter method provides replication and coherence in the main memory, and can execute at a variety of granularities. It allows the use of off-the-shelf commodity parts for the nodes and interconnects, minimizing hardware cost. This puts pressure on the programmer to achieve good performance.

Relaxed Memory Consistency Models

The memory consistency model for a shared address space defines the constraints in the order in which the memory operations in the same or different locations seem to be executing with respect to one another. Actually, any system layer that supports a shared address space naming model must have a memory consistency model which includes the programmer's interface, user-system interface, and the hardware-software interface. Software that interacts with that layer must be aware of its own memory consistency model.

System Specifications

The system specification of architecture specifies the ordering and reordering of the memory operations and how much performance can actually be gained from it.

Following are the few specification models using the relaxations in program order:

- Relaxing the Write-to-Read Program Order: This class of models allows the hardware to suppress the latency of write operations that was missed in the first-level cache memory. When the write miss is in the write buffer and not visible to other processors, the processor can complete reads which hit in its cache memory or even a single read that misses in its cache memory.

- Relaxing the Write-to-Read and Write-to-Write Program Orders: Allowing writes to bypass previous outstanding writes to various locations lets multiple writes to be merged in the write buffer before updating the main memory. Thus multiple write misses to be overlapped and becomes visible out of order. The motivation is to further minimize the impact of write latency on processor break time, and to raise communication efficiency among the processors by making new data values visible to other processors.

- Relaxing All Program Orders: No program orders are assured by default except data and control dependences within a process. Thus, the benefit is that the multiple read requests can be outstanding at the same time, and in program order can be bypassed by later writes, and can they complete out of order, allowing us to hide read latency. These types of models are particularly useful for dynamically scheduled processors, which can continue past read misses to other memory references. They allow many of the re-orderings, even elimination of accesses that are done by compiler optimizations.

The Programming Interface

The programming interfaces assume that program orders do not have to be maintained at all among synchronization operations. It is ensured that all synchronization operations are explicitly labeled or identified as such. Runtime library or the compiler translates these synchronization operations into the suitable order-preserving operations called for by the system specification.

The system then assures sequentially consistent executions even though it may reorder operations among the synchronization operations in any way it desires without disrupting dependences to a location within a process. This allows the compiler sufficient flexibility among synchronization points for the reordering it desires, and also grants the processor to perform as many reordering as allowed by its memory model. At the programmer's interface, the consistency model should be at least as weak as that of the hardware interface, but need not be the same.

Translation Mechanisms

In most microprocessors, translating labels to order maintaining mechanisms amounts to inserting a suitable memory barrier instruction before and after each operation labeled as synchronization. It would save instructions with individual loads/stores indicating what orderings to enforce and avoiding extra instructions. However, since the operations are usually infrequent, this is not the way that most microprocessors have taken so far.

Overcoming Capacity Limitations

We have discussed the systems which provide automatic replication and coherence in hardware only in the processor cache memory. A processor cache, without it being replicated in the local main memory first, replicates remotely allocated data directly upon reference.

A problem with these systems is that the scope for local replication is limited to the hardware cache. If a block is replaced from the cache memory, it has to be fetched from remote memory when it is needed again. The main purpose of the systems is to solve the replication capacity problem but still providing coherence in hardware and at fine granularity of cache blocks for efficiency.

Tertiary Caches

To solve the replication capacity problem, one method is to use a large but slower remote access cache. This is needed for functionality, when the nodes of the machine are themselves small-scale multiprocessors and can simply be made larger for performance. It will also hold replicated remote blocks that have been replaced from local processor cache memory.

Cache-only Memory Architectures (COMA)

In COMA machines, every memory block in the entire main memory has a hardware tag linked with it. There is no fixed node where there is always assurance to be space allocated for a memory block. Data dynamically migrates to or is replicated in the main memories of the nodes that access/attract them. When a remote block is accessed, it is replicated in attraction memory and brought into the cache, and is kept consistent in both the places by the hardware. A data block may reside in any attraction memory and may move easily from one to the other.

Reducing Hardware Cost

Reducing cost means moving some functionality of specialized hardware to software running on the existing hardware. It is much easier for software to manage replication and coherence in the main memory than in the hardware cache. The low-cost methods tend to provide replication and coherence in the main memory. For coherence to be controlled efficiently, each of the other functional components of the assist can be benefited from hardware specialization and integration.

Research efforts aim to lower the cost with different approaches, like by performing access control in specialized hardware, but assigning other activities to software and commodity hardware. Another approach is by performing access control in software, and is designed to allot a coherent shared address space abstraction on commodity nodes and networks with no specialized hardware support.

Implications for Parallel Software

Relaxed memory consistency model needs that parallel programs label the desired conflicting accesses as synchronization points. A programming language provides support to label some variables as synchronization, which will then be translated by the compiler to the suitable order-preserving instruction. To restrict compilers own reordering of accesses to shared memory, the compiler can use labels by itself.

Interconnection Network Design

An interconnection network in a parallel machine transfers information from any source node to any desired destination node. This task should be completed with as small latency as possible. It should allow a large number of such transfers to take place concurrently. Moreover, it should be inexpensive as compared to the cost of the rest of the machine.

The network is composed of links and switches, which helps to send the information from the source node to the destination node. A network is specified by its topology, routing algorithm, switching strategy, and flow control mechanism.

Organizational Structure

Interconnection networks are composed of following three basic components:

- Links: A link is a cable of one or more optical fibers or electrical wires with a connector at each end attached to a switch or network interface port. Through this, an analog signal is transmitted from one end, received at the other to obtain the original digital information stream.

- Switches: A switch is composed of a set of input and output ports, an internal "cross-bar" connecting all input to all output, internal buffering, and control logic to effect the input-output connection at each point in time. Generally, the number of input ports is equal to the number of output ports.

- Network Interfaces: The network interface behaves quite differently than switch nodes and may be connected via special links. The network interface formats the packets and constructs the routing and control information. It may have input and output buffering, compared to a switch. It may perform end-to-end error checking and flow control. Hence, its cost is influenced by its processing complexity, storage capacity, and number of ports.

Interconnection Network

Interconnection networks are composed of switching elements. Topology is the pattern to connect the individual switches to other elements, like processors, memories and other switches. A network allows exchange of data between processors in the parallel system.

- Direct connection networks: Direct networks have point-to-point connections between neighboring nodes. These networks are static, which means that the point-to-point connections are fixed. Some examples of direct networks are rings, meshes and cubes.

- Indirect connection networks: Indirect networks have no fixed neighbors. The communication topology can be changed dynamically based on the application demands. Indirect networks can be subdivided into three parts: bus networks, multistage networks and crossbar switches.

  ○ Bus networks: A bus network is composed of a number of bit lines onto which a number of resources are attached. When busses use the same physical lines for data and addresses, the data and the address lines are time multiplexed. When there are multiple bus-masters attached to the bus, an arbiter is required.

  ○ Multistage networks: A multistage network consists of multiple stages of switches. It is composed of 'axb' switches which are connected using a particular inter-stage connection pattern (ISC). Small 2x2 switch elements are a common choice for many multistage networks. The number of stages determines the delay of the network. By choosing different inter-stage connection patterns, various types of multistage network can be created.

  ○ Crossbar switches: A crossbar switch contains a matrix of simple switch elements that can switch on and off to create or break a connection. Turning on a switch element in the matrix, a connection between a processor and a memory can be made. Crossbar switches are non-blocking, that is all communication permutations can be performed without blocking.

Evaluating Design Trade-offs in Network Topology

If the main concern is the routing distance, then the dimension has to be maximized and a hyper-cube made. In store-and-forward routing, assuming that the degree of the switch and the number of links were not a significant cost factor, and the numbers of links or the switch degree are the main costs, the dimension has to be minimized and a mesh built.

In worst case traffic pattern for each network, it is preferred to have high dimensional networks where all the paths are short. In patterns where each node is communicating with only one or two nearby neighbors, it is preferred to have low dimensional networks, since only a few of the dimensions are actually used.

Routing

The routing algorithm of a network determines which of the possible paths from source to destination is used as routes and how the route followed by each particular packet is determined. Dimension order routing limits the set of legal paths so that there is exactly one route from each source to each destination. The one obtained by first traveling the correct distance in the high-order dimension, then the next dimension and so on.

Routing Mechanisms

Arithmetic, source-based port select, and table look-up are three mechanisms that high-speed switches use to determine the output channel from information in the packet header. All of these mechanisms are simpler than the kind of general routing computations implemented in traditional LAN and WAN routers. In parallel computer networks, the switch needs to make the routing decision for all its inputs in every cycle, so the mechanism needs to be simple and fast.

Deterministic Routing

A routing algorithm is deterministic if the route taken by a message is determined exclusively by its source and destination, and not by other traffic in the network. If a routing algorithm only selects shortest paths toward the destination, it is minimal, otherwise it is non-minimal.

Deadlock Freedom

Deadlock can occur in a various situations. When two nodes attempt to send data to each other and each begins sending before either receives, a 'head-on' deadlock may occur. Another case of deadlock occurs, when there are multiple messages competing for resources within the network.

The basic technique for proving a network is deadlock free is to clear the dependencies that can occur between channels as a result of messages moving through the networks and to show that there are no cycles in the overall channel dependency graph; hence there is no traffic patterns that can lead to a deadlock. The common way of doing this is to number the channel resources such that all routes follow a particular increasing or decreasing sequences, so that no dependency cycles arise.

Switch Design

Design of a network depends on the design of the switch and how the switches are wired together. The degree of the switch, its internal routing mechanisms, and its internal buffering decides what topologies can be supported and what routing algorithms can be implemented. Like any other hardware component of a computer system, a network switch contains data path, control, and storage.

Ports

The total number of pins is actually the total number of input and output ports times the channel width. As the perimeter of the chip grows slowly compared to the area, switches tend to be pin limited.

Internal Datapath

The datapath is the connectivity between each of the set of input ports and every output port. It is generally referred to as the internal cross-bar. A non-blocking cross-bar is one where each input port can be connected to a distinct output in any permutation simultaneously.

Channel Buffers

The organization of the buffer storage within the switch has an important impact on the switch performance. Traditional routers and switches tend to have large SRAM or DRAM buffers external to the switch fabric, while in VLSI switches the buffering is internal to the switch and comes out of the same silicon budget as the datapath and the control section. As the chip size and density increases, more buffering is available and the network designer has more options, but still the buffer real-estate comes at a prime choice and its organization is important.

Flow Control

When multiple data flows in the network attempt to use the same shared network resources at the same time, some action must be taken to control these flows. If we don't want to lose any data, some of the flows must be blocked while others proceed.

The problem of flow control arises in all networks and at many levels. But it is qualitatively different in parallel computer networks than in local and wide area networks. In parallel computers, the network traffic needs to be delivered about as accurately as traffic across a bus and there are a very large number of parallel flows on very small-time scale.

Latency Tolerance

The speed of microprocessors has increased by more than a factor of ten per decade, but the speed of commodity memories (DRAMs) has only doubled, i.e., access time is halved. Therefore, the latency of memory access in terms of processor clock cycles grow by a factor of six in 10 years. Multiprocessors intensified the problem.

In bus-based systems, the establishment of a high-bandwidth bus between the processor and the memory tends to increase the latency of obtaining the data from the memory. When the memory is physically distributed, the latency of the network and the network interface is added to that of the accessing the local memory on the node.

Latency usually grows with the size of the machine, as more nodes imply more communication relative to computation, more jump in the network for general communication, and likely more contention. The main goal of hardware design is to reduce the latency of the data access while maintaining high, scalable bandwidth.

How latency tolerance is handled is best understood by looking at the resources in the machine and how they are utilized. From the processor point of view, the communication architecture from one node to another can be viewed as a pipeline. The stages of the pipeline include network interfaces at the source and destination, as well as in the network links and switches along the way. There are also stages in the communication assist, the local memory/cache system, and the main processor, depending on how the architecture manages communication.

The utilization problem in the baseline communication structure is either the processor or the communication architecture is busy at a given time, and in the communication pipeline only one stage is busy at a time as the single word being transmitted makes its way from source to destination. The aim in latency tolerance is to overlap the use of these resources as much as possible.

Latency Tolerance in Explicit Message Passing

The actual transfer of data in message-passing is typically sender-initiated, using a send operation. A receive operation does not in itself motivate data to be communicated, but rather copies data from an incoming buffer into the application address space. Receiver-initiated communication is done by issuing a request message to the process that is the source of the data. The process then sends the data back via another send.

A synchronous send operation has communication latency equal to the time it takes to communicate all the data in the message to the destination, and the time for receive processing, and the time for an acknowledgment to be returned. The latency of a synchronous receive operation is its processing overhead; which includes copying the data into the application, and the additional latency if the data has not yet arrived. We would like to hide these latencies, including overheads if possible, at both ends.

Latency Tolerance in a Shared Address Space

The baseline communication is through reads and writes in a shared address space. For convenience, it is called read-write communication. Receiver-initiated communication is done with read operations that result in data from another processor's memory or cache being accessed. If there is no caching of shared data, sender-initiated communication may be done through writes to data that are allocated in remote memories.

With cache coherence, the effect of writes is more complex: either writes leads to sender or receiver-initiated communication depends on the cache coherence protocol. Either receiver-initiated or sender-initiated, the communication in a hardware-supported read writes shared address space is naturally fine-grained, which makes tolerance latency very important.

Block Data Transfer in a Shared Address Space

In a shared address space, either by hardware or software the coalescing of data and the initiation of block transfers can be done explicitly in the user program or transparently by the system. Explicit block transfers are initiated by executing a command similar to a send in the user program. The send command is explained by the communication assist, which transfers the data in a pipelined manner from the source node to the destination. At the destination, the communication assist pulls the data words in from the network interface and stores them in the specified locations.

There are two prime differences from send-receive message passing, both of which arise from the fact that the sending process can directly specify the program data structures where the data is to be placed at the destination, since these locations are in the shared address space.

Proceeding Past Long-latency Events in a Shared Address Space

If the memory operation is made non-blocking, a processor can proceed past a memory operation to other instructions. For writes, this is usually quite simple to implement if the write is put in a write buffer, and the processor goes on while the buffer takes care of issuing the write to the memory system and tracking its completion as required. The difference is that unlike a write, a read is generally followed very soon by an instruction that needs the value returned by the read.

Pre-communication in a Shared Address Space

Pre-communication is a technique that has already been widely adopted in commercial microprocessors, and its importance is likely to increase in the future. A pre-fetch instruction does not replace the actual read of the data item, and the pre-fetch instruction itself must be non-blocking, if it is to achieve its goal of hiding latency through overlap.

In this case, as shared data is not cached, the pre-fetched data is brought into a special hardware structure called a pre-fetch buffer. When the word is actually read into a register in the next iteration, it is read from the head of the pre-fetch buffer rather than from memory. If the latency to hide were much bigger than the time to compute single loop iteration, we would pre-fetch several iterations ahead and there would potentially be several words in the pre-fetch buffer at a time.

Multithreading in a Shared Address Space

In terms of hiding different types of latency, hardware-supported multithreading is perhaps the versatile technique. It has the following conceptual advantages over other approaches:

- It requires no special software analysis or support.

- As it is invoked dynamically, it can handle unpredictable situations, like cache conflicts, etc. just as well as predictable ones.

- Like prefetching, it does not change the memory consistency model since it does not reorder accesses within a thread.

- While the previous techniques are targeted at hiding memory access latency, multithreading can potentially hide the latency of any long-latency event just as easily, as long as the event can be detected at runtime. This includes synchronization and instruction latency as well.

This trend may change in future, as latencies are becoming increasingly longer as compared to processor speeds. Also with more sophisticated microprocessors that already provide methods that can be extended for multithreading, and with new multithreading techniques being developed to combine multithreading with instruction-level parallelism, this trend certainly seems to be undergoing some change in future.

Pipelining

Pipelining is one way of improving the overall processing performance of a processor. This architectural approach allows the simultaneous execution of several instructions. Pipelining is transparent to the programmer; it exploits parallelism at the instruction level by overlapping the execution process of instructions. It is analogous to an assembly line where workers perform a specific task and pass the partially completed product to the next worker.

Pipeline Structure

The pipeline design technique decomposes a sequential process into several sub-processes, called stages or segments. A *stage* performs a particular function and produces an intermediate result. It consists of an input latch, also called a register or buffer, followed by a processing circuit. (A processing circuit can be a combinational or sequential circuit.) The processing circuit of a given stage is connected to the input latch of the next stage. A clock signal is connected to each input latch. At each clock pulse, every stage transfers its intermediate result to the input latch of the next stage. In this way, the final result is produced after the input data have passed through the entire pipeline, completing one stage per clock pulse. The period of the clock pulse should be large enough to provide sufficient time for a signal to traverse through the slowest stage, which is called the *bottleneck* (i.e., the stage needing the longest amount of time to complete). In addition, there should be enough time for a latch to store its input signals. If the clock's period, P, is expressed as $P = t_b + t_l$, then t_b should be greater than the maximum delay of the bottleneck stage, and t_l should be sufficient for storing data into a latch.

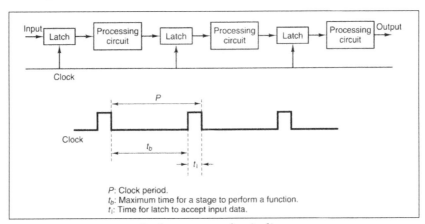

P: Clock period.
t_b: Maximum time for a stage to perform a function.
t_l: Time for latch to accept input data.

Basic structure of a pipeline.

Pipeline Performance Measures

The ability to overlap stages of a sequential process for different input tasks (data or operations) results in an overall theoretical completion time of:

$$T_{pipe} = m_* P + (n-1)_* P,$$

where, n is the number of input tasks, m is the number of stages in the pipeline, and P is the clock period. The term $m_* P$ is the time required for the first input task to get through the pipeline, and the term $(n-1)_* P$ is the time required for the remaining tasks. After the pipeline has been filled, it generates an output on each clock cycle. In other words, after the pipeline is loaded, it will generate output only as fast as its slowest stage. Even with this limitation, the pipeline will greatly outperform non-pipelined techniques, which require each task to complete before another task's execution sequence begins. To be more specific, when n is large, a pipelined processor can produce output approximately m times faster than a non-pipelined processor. On the other hand, in a non-pipelined processor, the above sequential process requires a completion time of:

$$T_{seq} = n * \sum_{i=1}^{m} \tau_i$$

Where τ_i is the delay of each stage. For the ideal case when all stages have equal delay $\tau_i = \tau$ for i = 1 to m, T_{seq} can be rewritten as:

$$T_{seq} = n_* m_* \tau.$$

If we ignore the small storing time t_l that is required for latch storage (i.e., $t_1 = 0$), then:

$$T_{seq} = n_* m_* P.$$

Now, speedup (S) may be represented as:

$$S = T_{seq} / T_{pipe} = n_* m / (m + n - 1).$$

The value S approaches m when n → ∞. That is, the maximum speed up, also called ideal speedup, of a pipeline processor with m stages over an equivalent non-pipelined processor is m. In other words, the ideal speedup is equal to the number of pipeline stages. That is, when n is very large, a pipelined processor can produce output approximately m times faster than a non-pipelined processor. When n is small, the speedup decreases; in fact, for n=1 the pipeline has the minimum speedup of 1.

In addition to speedup, two other factors are often used for determining the performance of a pipeline; they are efficiency and throughput. The efficiency E of a pipeline with m stages is defined as:

$$E = S / m = \left[n_* m / (m + n - 1) \right] / m = n / (m + n - 1).$$

The efficiency E, which represents the speedup per stage, approaches its maximum value of 1 when $n \to \infty$. When n=1, E will have the value $1/m$, which is the lowest obtainable value.

The throughput H, also called bandwidth, of a pipeline is defined as the number of input tasks it can process per unit of time. When the pipeline has m stages, H is defined as:

$$H = n / T_{pipe} = n / \left[m_* P + (n-1)_* P \right] = E / P = S / (mP).$$

When $n \to \infty$, the throughput H approaches the maximum value of one task per clock cycle.

The number of stages in a pipeline often depends on the tradeoff between performance and cost. The optimal choice for such a number can be determined by obtaining the peak value of a performance/cost ratio (PCR). Larson [LAR 73, HWA 93] has defined PCR as follows:

$$PCR \quad \frac{\text{maximum throughput}}{\text{pipeline cost}}$$

To illustrate, assume that a non-pipelined processor requires a completion time of t_{seq} for processing an input task. For a pipeline with m stages to process the same task, a clock period of $P = (t_{seq}/m) + t_l$ is needed. (The time t_l is the latch delay.) Thus the maximum throughput that can be obtained with such a pipeline is:

$$1 / P = 1 / \left[(t_{seq} / m) + t_l \right].$$

The maximum throughput $1/P$ is also called the pipeline frequency. The actual throughput may be less than $1/P$ depending on the rate of consecutive tasks entering the pipeline.

The pipeline cost c_p can be expressed as the total cost of logic gates and latches used in all stages. That is, $c_p = c_g + mcl$ where cg is the cost of all logic stages and c_1 is the cost of each latch. Note that the cost of gates and latches may be interpreted in different ways; for example, the cost may refer to the actual dollar cost, design complexity, or the area required on the chip or circuit board. By substituting the values for maximum throughput and pipeline cost in the PCR equation, the following formula can be obtained:

$$PCR = 1 / \left\{ \left[(t_{seq} / m) + t_l \right] (cg + mc_l) \right\}.$$

This equation has a maximum value m_0, where,

$$m_0 = \sqrt{\frac{(t_{seq} * c_g)}{(t_l * c_l)}}.$$

Since the value m_0 maximizes PCR, this value can be used as an optimal choice for the number of stages.

Pipeline Types

Pipelines are usually divided into two classes: instruction pipelines and arithmetic pipelines. A pipeline in each of these classes can be designed in two ways: static or dynamic. A static pipeline can perform only one operation (such as addition or multiplication) at a time. The operation of a static pipeline can only be changed after the pipeline has been drained. (A pipeline is said to be drained when the last input data leave the pipeline.) For example, consider a static pipeline that is able to perform addition and multiplication. Each time that the pipeline switches from a multiplication operation to an addition operation, it must be drained and set for the new operation. The performance of static pipelines is severely degraded when the operations change often, since this requires the pipeline to be drained and refilled each time. A dynamic pipeline can perform more than one operation at a time. To perform a particular operation on an input data, the data must go through a certain sequence of stages. For example, figure shows a three-stage dynamic pipeline that performs addition and multiplication on different data at the same time. To perform multiplication, the input data must go through stages 1, 2, and 3; to perform addition, the data only need to go through stages 1 and 3. Therefore, the first stage of the addition process can be performed on an input data D_1 at stage 1, while at the same time the last stage of the multiplication process is performed at stage 3 on a different input data D_2. Note that the time interval between the initiation of the inputs D_1 and D_2 to the pipeline should be such that they do not reach stage 3 at the same time; otherwise, there is a collision. In general, in dynamic pipelines the mechanism that controls when data should be fed to the pipeline is much more complex than in static pipelines.

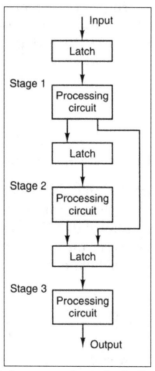

A three-stage dynamic pipeline

Instruction Pipeline

In von Neumann architecture, the process of executing an instruction involves several steps. First, the control unit of a processor fetches the instruction from the cache (or from memory). Then the control unit decodes the instruction to determine the type of operation to be performed. When the operation requires operands, the control unit also determines the address of each operand and fetches them from cache (or memory). Next, the operation is performed on the operands and, finally, the result is stored in the specified location.

An instruction pipeline increases the performance of a processor by overlapping the processing of several different instructions. Often, this is done by dividing the instruction execution process into several stages. As shown in figure, an instruction pipeline often consists of five stages, as follows:

1. Instruction fetch (IF): Retrieval of instructions from cache (or main memory).

2. Instruction decoding (ID): Identification of the operation to be performed.

3. Operand fetch (OF): Decoding and retrieval of any required operands.

4. Execution (EX): Performing the operation on the operands.

5. Write-back (WB): Updating the destination operands.

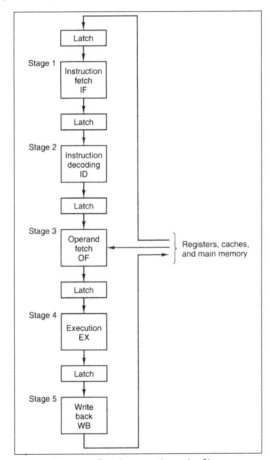

Stages of an instruction pipeline

An instruction pipeline overlaps the process of the preceding stages for different instructions to achieve a much lower total completion time, on average, for a series of instructions. As an example, consider figure, which shows the execution of four instructions in an instruction pipeline. During the first cycle, or clock pulse, instruction i_1 is fetched from memory. Within the second cycle, instruction i1 is decoded while instruction i_2 is fetched. This process continues until all the instructions are executed. The last instruction finishes the write-back stage after the eighth clock cycle. Therefore, it takes 80 nanoseconds (ns) to complete execution of all the four instructions when assuming the clock period to be 10 ns. The total completion time can also be obtained using equation $T_{pipe} = m_* P + (n-1)_* P$, that is,

$$T_{pipe} = m_*P + (n-1)_* P,$$
$$= 5.10 + (4-1)_* 10 = 80 \, \text{ns}.$$

Note that in a non-pipelined design the completion time will be much higher. Using equation $T_{seq} = n_* m_* P$,

$$T_{seq} = n_* m_* P = 4_* 5_* 10 = 200 \, \text{ns}.$$

It is worth noting that a similar execution path will occur for an instruction whether a pipelined architecture is used or not; a pipeline simply takes advantage of these naturally occurring stages to improve processing efficiency. Henry Ford made the same connection when he realized that all cars were built in stages and invented the assembly line in the early 1900s. Some ideas have an enduring quality and can be applied in many different ways.

Even though pipelining speeds up the execution of instructions, it does pose potential problems.

Instruction				Cycles				
	1	2	3	4	5	6	7	8
i_1	IF	ID	OF	EX	WB			
i_2		IF	ID	OF	EX	WB		
i_3			IF	ID	OF	EX	WB	
i_4				IF	ID	OF	EX	WB

Execution cycles of four consecutive instructions in an instruction pipeline

Improving the Throughput of an Instruction Pipeline

Three sources of architectural problems may affect the throughput of an instruction pipeline. They are fetching, bottleneck, and issuing problems. Some solutions are given for each.

1. The fetching problem: In general, supplying instructions rapidly through a pipeline is costly in terms of chip area. Buffering the data to be sent to the pipeline is one simple way of improving the overall utilization of a pipeline. The utilization of a pipeline is defined as the percentage of time that the stages of the pipeline are used over a sufficiently long period of time. A pipeline is utilized 100% of the time when every stage is used (utilized) during each clock cycle.

Occasionally, the pipeline has to be drained and refilled, for example, whenever an interrupt or a branch occurs. The time spent refilling the pipeline can be minimized by having instructions and data loaded ahead of time into various geographically close buffers (like on-chip caches) for immediate transfer into the pipeline. If instructions and data for normal execution can be fetched before they are needed and stored in buffers, the pipeline will have a continuous source of information with which to work. Pre-fetch algorithms are used to make sure potentially needed instructions are available most of the time. Delays from memory access conflicts can thereby be reduced if these algorithms are used, since the time required to transfer data from main memory is far greater than the time required to transfer data from a buffer.

2. The bottleneck problem: The bottleneck problem relates to the amount of load (work) assigned to a stage in the pipeline. If too much work is applied to one stage, the time taken to complete an operation at that stage can become unacceptably long. This relatively long time spent by the instruction at one stage will inevitably create a bottleneck in the pipeline system. In such a system, it is better to remove the bottleneck that is the source of congestion. One solution to this problem is to further subdivide the stage. Another solution is to build multiple copies of this stage into the pipeline.

3. The issuing problem: If an instruction is available, but cannot be executed for some reason, a hazard exists for that instruction. These hazards create issuing problems; they prevent issuing an instruction for execution. Three types of hazard are discussed here. They are called structural hazard, data hazard, and control hazard. A structural hazard refers to a situation in which a required resource is not available (or is busy) for executing an instruction. A data hazard refers to a situation in which there exists a data dependency (operand conflict) with a prior instruction. A control hazard refers to a situation in which an instruction, such as branch, causes a change in the program flow.

4. Structural Hazard: A structural hazard occurs as a result of resource conflicts between instructions. One type of structural hazard that may occur is due to the design of execution units. If an execution unit that requires more than one clock cycle (such as multiply) is not fully pipelined or is not replicated, then a sequence of instructions that uses the unit cannot be subsequently (one per clock cycle) issued for execution. A replicating and pipelining execution unit increases the number of instructions that can be issued simultaneously. Another type of structural hazard that may occur is due to the design of register files. If a register file does not have multiple write (read) ports, multiple writes (reads) to (from) registers cannot be performed simultaneously. For example, under certain situations the instruction pipeline might want to perform two register writes in a clock cycle. This may not be possible when the register file has only one write port.

The effect of a structural hazard can be reduced fairly simply by implementing multiple execution units and using register files with multiple input/output ports.

5. Data Hazard: In a non-pipelined processor, the instructions are executed one by one, and the execution of an instruction is completed before the next instruction is started. In this way, the instructions are executed in the same order as the program. However, this may not be true in a pipelined processor, where instruction executions are overlapped. An instruction may be started and completed before the previous instruction is completed. The data hazard, which is also referred to as the data dependency problem, comes about as a result of overlapping (or changing the order of) the execution of data-dependent instructions. For example, in figure instruction i_2 has a data dependency on i_1 because it uses the result of i_1 (i.e., the contents of register R_2) as input data. If the instructions were sent to a pipeline in the normal manner, i_2 would be in the OF stage before i1 passed through the WB stage. This would result in using the old contents of R_2 for computing a new value for R_5, leading to an invalid result. To have a valid result, i_2 must not enter the OF stage until i1 has passed through the WB stage. In this way, as is shown in figure, the execution of i_2 will be delayed for two clock cycles. In other words, instruction i_2 is said to be stalled for two clock cycles. Often, when an instruction is stalled, the instructions that are positioned after the stalled instruction will also be stalled. However, the instructions before the stalled instruction can continue execution.

i_1	Add	R_2,	R_3,	R_4	-- $R_2 = R_3 + R_4$
i_2	Add	R_5,	R_2,	R_1	-- $R_5 = R_2 + R_1$

	Cycles					
	1	2	3	4	5	6
i_1	IF	ID	OF	EX	WB	
i_2		IF	ID	OF	EX	WB

Instruction i_2 has data dependency on i_1

	Cycles						
	1	2	3	4	5	6	7	8
i_1	IF	ID	OF	EX	WB			
i_2		IF	ID	—	—	OF	EX	WB

	Cycles						
	1	2	3	4	5	6	7	8
i_1	IF	ID	OF	EX	WB			
i_2	—	—	IF	ID	OF	EX	WB	

Two ways of executing data dependent instructions

The delaying of execution can be accomplished in two ways. One way is to delay the OF or IF stages of i_2 for two clock cycles. To insert a delay, an extra hardware component called a pipeline interlock can be added to the pipeline. A pipeline interlock detects the dependency and delays the dependent instructions until the conflict is resolved. Another way is to let the compiler solve the dependency problem. During compilation, the compiler detects the dependency between data and instructions. It then rearranges these instructions so that the dependency is not hazardous to the system. If it is not possible to rearrange the instructions, NOP (no operation) instructions are inserted to create delays. For example, consider the four instructions in figure. These instructions may be reordered so that i_3 and i_4, which are not dependent on i_1 and i_2, are inserted between i_1 and i_2.

i_1	Add	R_2,	R_3,	R_4	-- $R_2 = R_3 + R_4$
i_2	Add	R_5,	R_2,	R_1	-- $R_5 = R_2 + R_1$
i_3	Add	R_6,	R_6,	R_7	-- $R_6 = R_6 + R_7$
i_4	Add	R_8,	R_8,	R_7	-- $R_8 = R_8 + R_7$

	Cycles						
	1	2	3	4	5	6	7	8
i_1	IF	ID	OF	EX	WB			
i_3		IF	ID	OF	EX	WB		
i_4			IF	ID	OF	EX	WB	
i_2				IF	ID	OF	EX	WB

Rearranging the order of instruction execution

In the previous type of data hazard, an instruction uses the result of a previous instruction as input data. In addition to this type of data hazard, other types may occur in designs that allow concurrent execution of instructions. Note that the type of pipeline design considered so far preserves the execution order of instructions in the program.

There are three primary types of data hazards: RAW (read after write), WAR (write after read), and WAW (write after write). The hazard names denote the execution ordering of the instructions that must be maintained to produce a valid result; otherwise, an invalid result might occur. In each explanation, it is assumed that there are two instructions i_1 and i_2, and i_2 should be executed after i_1.

1. RAW: It refers to the situation in which i_2 reads a data source before i_1 writes to it. This may produce an invalid result since the read must be performed after the write in order to obtain a valid result. For example, in the sequence an invalid result may be produced if i_2 reads R_2 before i_1 writes to it.

i_1	Add	R_2,	R_3,	R_4	$-\!-R_2 = R_3 + R_4$
i_2	Add	R_5,	R_2,	R_1	$-\!-R_5 = R_2 + R_1$

2. WAR: This refers to the situation in which i_2 writes to a location before i1 reads it. For example, in the sequence an invalid result may be produced if i_2 writes to R_4 before i_1 reads it; that is, the instruction i_1 might use the wrong value of R_4.

i_1	Add	R_2,	R_3,	R_4	$-\!-R_2 = R_3 + R_4$
i_2	Add	R_4,	R_5,	R_6	$-\!-R_4 = R_5 + R_6$

3. WAW: This refers to the situation in which i_2 writes to a location before i1 writes to it. For example, in the sequence, the value of R_2 is recomputed by i_2.

If the order of execution were reversed, that is, i_2 writes to R_2 before i_1 writes to it, an invalid value for R_2 might be produced.

i_1	Add	R_2,	R_3,	R_4	$-\!-R_2 = R_3 + R_4$
i_2	Add	R_2,	R_5,	R_6	$-\!-R_2 = R_5 + R_6$

Note that the WAR and WAW types of hazards cannot happen when the order of completion of instructions execution in the program is preserved. However, one way to enhance the architecture of an instruction pipeline is to increase concurrent execution of the instructions by dispatching several independent instructions to different functional units, such as adders/subtractors, multipliers, and dividers. That is, the instructions can be executed out of order, and so their execution may be completed out of order too. Hence, in such architectures all types of data hazards are possible.

In today's architectures, the dependencies between instructions are checked statically by the compiler and dynamically by the hardware at run time. This preserves the execution order for dependent instructions, which ensures valid results. Many different static dependency checking techniques have been developed to exploit parallelism in a loop. These techniques have the advantage of being able to look ahead at the entire program and are able to detect most dependencies.

Unfortunately, certain dependencies cannot be detected at compile time. For example, it is not always possible to determine the actual memory addresses of load and store instructions in order to resolve a possible dependency between them. However, during the run time the actual memory addresses are known, and thereby dependencies between instructions can be determined by dynamically checking the dependency. In general, dynamic dependency checking has the advantage of being able to determine dependencies that are either impossible or hard to detect at compile time. However, it may not be able to exploit all the parallelism available in a loop because of the limited look ahead ability that can be supported by the hardware. In practice, a combined static-dynamic dependency checking is often used to take advantage of both approaches.

Two of the most commonly used techniques are called Tomasulo's method and the scoreboard method. The basic concept behind these methods is to use a mechanism for identifying the availability of operands and functional units in successive computations.

Tomasulo's Method

Tomasulo's method was developed by R. Tomasulo to overcome the long memory access delays in the IBM 360/91 processor. Tomasulo's method increases concurrent execution of the instructions with minimal (or no) effort by the compiler or the programmer. In this method, a busy bit and a tag register are associated with registers. The busy bit of a particular register is set when an issued instruction designates that register as a destination. (The destination register, or sink register, is the register that the result of the instruction will be written to.) The busy bit is cleared when the result of the execution is written back to the register. The tag of a register identifies the unit whose result will be sent to the register.

Each functional unit may have more than one set (source_1 and source_2) of input registers. Each such set is called a reservation station and is used to keep the operands of an issued instruction. A tag register is also associated with each register of a reservation station. In addition, a common data bus (CDB) connects the output of the functional units to their inputs and the registers. Such a common data bus structure, called a forwarding technique (also referred to as feed-forwarding), plays a very important role in organizing the order in which various instructions are presented to the pipeline for execution. The CDB makes it possible for the result of an operation to become available to all functional units without first going through a register. It allows a direct copy of the result of an operation to be given to all the functional units waiting for that result. In other words, a currently executing instruction can have access to the result of a previous instruction before the result of the previous instruction has actually been written to an output register.

Figure represents a simple architecture for such a method. In this architecture there are nine units communicating through a common data bus. The units include five registers, two add reservation stations called A_1 and A_2 (virtually two adders), and two multiply reservation stations called M_1 and M_2 (virtually two multipliers). The binary-coded tags 1 to 5 are associated with registers in the register file, 6 and 7 are associated to add stations, and 8 and 9 are associated with multiply stations. The tags are used to direct the result of an instruction to the next instruction through the CDB. For example, consider the execution of the following two instructions.

| i_1 | Add | R_2 | R_3 | R_4 | -- $R_2=R_3+R_4$ |
| i_2 | Add | R_2 | R_2 | R_1 | -- $R_2=R_2+R_1$ |

After issuing the instruction i_1 to the add station A_1, the busy bit of the register R_2 is set to 1, the contents of the registers R_3 and R_4 are sent to source_1 and source_2 of the add station A_1, respectively, and the tag of R_2 is set to 6 (i.e., 110), which is the tag of A_1. Then the adder unit starts execution of i_1. In the meantime, during the process of operand fetch for the instruction i_2, it becomes known that the register R_2 is busy. This means that instruction i2 depends on the result of instruction i_1. To let the execution of i_2 start as soon as possible, the contents of tag of R_2 (i.e., 110) are sent to the tag of the source_1 of the add station A_2; therefore, tag of source_1 of A_2 is set to 6. At this time the tag of R_2 is changed to 7, which means that the result of A_2 must be transferred to R_2. Also, the contents of R1 are sent to source_2 of A_2. Right before the adder finishes the execution of i_1 and produces the result, it sends a request signal to the CDB for sending the result. (Since CDB is shared with many units, its time sharing can be controlled by a central priority circuit.) When the CDB acknowledges the request, the adder A_1 sends the result to the CDB. The CDB broadcasts the result together with the tag of A_1 (i.e., 6) to all the units. Each reservation station, while waiting for data, compares its source register tags with the tag on the CDB. If they match, the data are copied to the proper register(s). Similarly, at the same time, each register whose busy bit is set to 1 compares its tag with the tag on the CDB. If they match, the register updates its data and clears the busy bit. In this case the data are copied to source_1 of A_2. Next, A_2 starts execution and the result is sent to R_2.

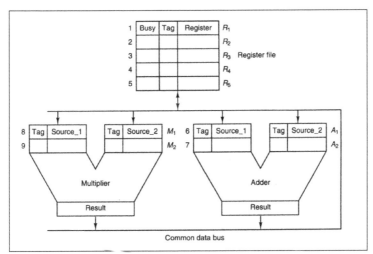

Common data bus architecture

As demonstrated in the preceding example, the main concepts in Tomasulo's method are the addition of reservation stations, the innovation of the CDB, and the development of a simple tagging scheme. The reservation stations do the waiting for operands and hence free up the functional units from such a task. The CDB utilizes the reservation stations by providing them the result of an operation directly from the output of the functional unit. The tagging scheme preserves dependencies between successive operations while encouraging concurrency.

Load	R_1,	A		
Load	R_2,	B		
Load	R_3,	C		
Load	R_4,	D		
Mul	R_5,	R_1,	R_2	-- $R_5 = R_1{}^*R_2$
Add	R_5,	R_5,	R_3	-- $R_5 = R_5 + R_3$
Add	R_4,	R_5,	R_4	-- $R_4 = R_5 + R_4$

Although the extra hardware suggested by the Tomasulo's method encourages concurrent execution of instructions, the programmer and/or compiler still has substantial influence on the degree of concurrency. The following two programs for computing $(A_*B)+(C+D)$ illustrate this.

An alternative to this program that allows more concurrency is:

Load	R_1	A		
Load	R_2	B		
Load	R_3	C		
Load	R_4	D		
Mul	R_5	R_1	R_2	-- $R_5 = R_1 * R_2$
Add	R_4	R_3	R_4	-- $R_4 = R_3 + R_4$
Add	R_4	R_4	R_5	-- $R_4 = R_4 + R_5$

In the second set of instructions, the multiply instruction and the first add instruction can be executed simultaneously, an impossibility in the first set of instructions. Often, in practice, a combination of hardware and software techniques is used to increase concurrency.

Scoreboard Method

The scoreboard method was first used in the high-performance CDC 6600 computer, in which multiple functional units allow instructions to be completed out of the original program order. This scheme maintains information about the status of each issued instruction, each register, and each functional unit in some buffers (or hardware mechanism) known as the scoreboard. When a new instruction is issued for execution, its influence on the registers and the functional units is added to the scoreboard. By considering a snapshot of the scoreboard, it can be determined if waiting is required for the new instruction. If no waiting is required, the proper functional unit immediately starts the execution of the instruction. If waiting is required (for example, one of the input operands is not yet available), execution of the new instruction is delayed until the waiting conditions are removed.

A scoreboard may consist of three tables: instruction status, functional unit status, and destination register status. Figure represents a snapshot of the contents of these tables for the following program:

Load	R_1	A		
Load	R_2	B		
Load	R_3	C		
Load	R_4	D		
Mul	R_5	R_1	R_2	-- $R_5 = R_1 * R_2$
Add	R_2	R_3	R_4	-- $R_2 = R_3 + R_4$
Add	R_2	R_2	R_5	-- $R_2 = R_2 + R_5$

The instruction status table indicates whether or not an instruction is issued for execution. If the instruction is issued, the table shows which stage the instruction is in. After an instruction is brought in and decoded, the scoreboard will attempt to issue an instruction to the proper functional unit.

An instruction will be issued if the functional unit is free and there is no other active instruction using the same destination register; otherwise, the issuing is delayed. In other words, an instruction is issued when WAW hazards and structural hazards do not exist. When such hazards exist, the issuing of the instruction and the instructions following are delayed until the hazards are removed. In this way the instructions are issued in order, while independent instructions are allowed to be executed out of order.

The functional unit status table indicates whether or not a functional unit is busy. A busy unit means that the execution of an issued instruction to that unit is not completed yet. For a busy unit, the table also identifies the destination register and the availability of the source registers. A source register for a unit is available if it does not appear as a destination for any other unit.

The destination register status table indicates the destination registers that have not yet been written to. For each such register the active functional unit that will write to the register is identified. The table has an entry for each register.

During the operand fetch stage, the scoreboard monitors the tables to determine whether or not the source registers are available to be read by an active functional unit. If none of the source registers is used as the destination register of other active functional units, the unit reads the operands from these registers and begins execution. After the execution is completed (i.e., at the end of execution stage), the scoreboard checks for WAR hazards before allowing the result to be written to the destination register. When no WAR hazard exists, the scoreboard tells the functional unit to go ahead and write the result to the destination register.

The main component of the scoreboard approach is the destination register status table. This table is used to solve data hazards between instructions. Each time an instruction is issued for execution, the instruction's destination register is marked busy. The destination register stays busy until the instruction completes execution. When a new instruction is considered for execution, its operands are checked to ensure that there are no register conflicts with prior instructions still in execution.

Control Hazard

In any set of instructions, there is normally a need for some kind of statement that allows the flow of control to be something other than sequential. Instructions that do this are included in every programming language and are called branches. In general, about 30% of all instructions in a program are branches. This means that branch instructions in the pipeline can reduce the throughput tremendously if not handled properly. Whenever a branch is taken, the performance of the pipeline is seriously affected. Each such branch requires a new address to be loaded into the program counter, which may invalidate all the instructions that are either already in the pipeline or pre-fetched in the buffer. This draining and refilling of the pipeline for each branch degrade the throughput of the pipeline to that of a sequential processor. Note that the presence of a branch statement does not automatically cause the pipeline to drain and begin refilling. A branch not taken allows the continued sequential flow of uninterrupted instructions to the pipeline. Only when a branch is taken does the problem arise.

In general, branch instructions can be classified into three groups: (1) unconditional branch, (2) conditional branch, and (3) loop branch. An unconditional branch always alters the sequential program flow. It sets a new target address in the program counter, rather than incrementing it by

1 to point to the next sequential instruction address, as is normally the case. A conditional branch sets a new target address in the program counter only when a certain condition, usually based on a condition code, is satisfied. Otherwise, the program counter is incremented by 1 as usual. In other words, a conditional branch selects a path of instructions based on a certain condition. If the condition is satisfied, the path starts from the target address and is called a target path. If it is not, the path starts from the next sequential instruction and is called a sequential path. Finally, a loop branch in a loop statement usually jumps back to the beginning of the loop and executes it either a fixed or a variable (data-dependent) number of times.

Among the preceding branch types, conditional branches are the hardest to handle. As an example, consider the following conditional branch instruction sequence:

i_1

i_2 (conditional branch to i_k) i_3

.

.

.

i_k (target)

i_{k+1}

Figure shows the execution of this sequence in our instruction pipeline when the target path is selected. In this figure, c denotes the branch penalty, that is, the number of cycles wasted whenever the target path is chosen.

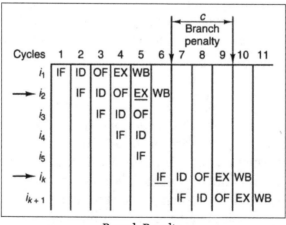

Branch Penalty

To show the effect of the branch penalty on the overall pipeline performance, the average number of cycles per instruction must be determined. Let t_{ave} denote the average number of cycles required for execution of an instruction; then:

$t_{ave} = P_b *$ (average number of cycles per branch instruction) +

$(1 - P_b) *$ (average number of cycles per nonbranch instruction),

where, P_b denotes the probability that a given instruction is a branch.

The average number of cycles per branch instruction can be determined by considering two cases. If the target path is chosen, 1+ c cycles (c = branch penalty) are needed for the execution; otherwise, there is no branch penalty and only one cycle is needed.

Thus average number of cycles per branch instruction = $P_t(1+c) + (1- P_t)(1)$, where P_t denotes the probability that the t target path is chosen. The average number of cycles per nonbranch instruction is 1. After the pipeline becomes filled with instructions, a nonbranch instruction completes every cycle. Thus,

$$t_{ave} = P_b\left[P_t(1+c)+(1-P_t)(1)\right]+(1-P_b)(1)=1+cP_bP_t.$$

After analyzing many practical programs, Lee and Smith have shown the average P_b to be approximately 0.1 to 0.3 and the average Pt to be approximately 0.6 to 0.7. Assuming that P_b=0.2, P_t = 0.65, and c=3, then:

$$t_{ave} = 1+3(0.2)(0.65)=1.39.$$

In other words, the pipeline operates at 72% (100/1.39 = 72) of its maximum rate when branch instructions are considered.

Sometimes, the performance of a pipeline is represented in terms of throughput. The throughput, H, of a pipeline can also be expressed as the average number of instructions executed per clock cycle. Thus

$$H = 1/t_{ave} = 1/(1+cP_bP_t).$$

To reduce the effect of branching on processor performance, several techniques have been proposed. Some of the better known techniques are branch prediction, delayed branching, and multiple prefetching. Each of these techniques is explained next.

Branch Prediction: In this type of design, the outcome of a branch decision is predicted before the branch is actually executed. Therefore, based on a particular prediction, the sequential path or the target path is chosen for execution. Although the chosen path often reduces the branch penalty, it may increase the penalty in case of incorrect prediction.

There are two types of predictions, static and dynamic. In static prediction, a fixed decision for prefetching one of the two paths is made before the program runs. For example, a simple technique would be to always assume that the branch is taken. This technique simply loads the program counter with the target address when a branch is encountered. Another such technique is to automatically choose one path (sequential or target) for some branch types and another for the rest of the branch types. If the chosen path is wrong, the pipeline is drained and instructions corresponding to the correct path are fetched; the penalty is paid.

In dynamic prediction, during the execution of the program the processor makes a decision based on the past information of the previously executed branches. For example, a simple technique would be to record the history of the last two paths taken by each branch instruction. If the last two executions of a branch instruction have chosen the same path, that path will be chosen for the current execution of the branch instruction. If the two paths do not match, one of the paths will be chosen randomly.

A better approach is to associate an n-bit counter with each branch instruction. This is known as the counter-based branch prediction approach. In this method, after executing a branch instruction for the first time, its counter, C, is set to a threshold, T, if the target path was taken, or to T-1 if the sequential path was taken. From then on, whenever the branch instruction is about to be executed, if $C \geq T$, then the target path is taken; otherwise, the sequential path is taken. The counter value C is updated after the branch is resolved. If the correct path is the target path, the counter is incremented by 1; if not, C is decremented by 1. If C ever reaches $2^n - 1$ (an upper bound), C is no longer incremented, even if the target path was correctly predicted and chosen. Likewise, C is never decremented to a value less than 0.

In practice, often n and T are chosen to be 2. Studies have shown that 2-bit predictors perform almost as well as predictors with more number of bits. The following diagram represents the possible states in a 2-bit predictor.

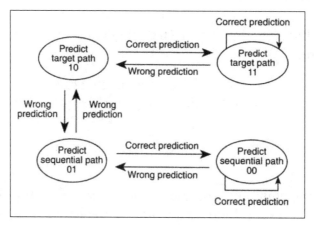

An alternative scheme to the preceding 2-bit predictor is to change the prediction only when the predicted path has been wrong for two consecutive times. The following diagram shows the possible states for such a scheme.

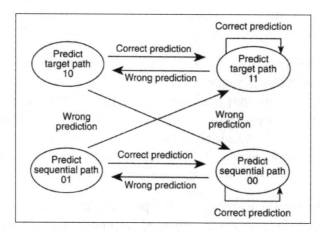

Most processors employ a small size cache memory called branch target buffer (BTB); sometimes referred to as target instruction cache (TIC). Often, each entry of this cache keeps a branch instruction's address with its target address and the history used by the prediction scheme. When a branch instruction is first executed, the processor allocates an entry in the BTB for this instruction. When a branch instruction is fetched, the processor searches the BTB to determine whether it holds an entry for the corresponding branch instruction. If there is a hit, the recorded history is used to determine whether the sequential or target path should be taken.

Static prediction methods usually require little hardware, but they may increase the complexity of the compiler. In contrast, dynamic prediction methods increase the hardware complexity, but they require less work at compile time. In general, dynamic prediction obtains better results than static prediction and also provides a greater degree of object code compatibility, since decisions are made after compile time.

To find the performance effect of branch prediction, we need to reevaluate the average number of cycles per branch instruction in equation (t_{ave} = P_{b*} (average number of cycles per branch instruction) + (1 - P_b) $_*$ (average number of cycles per non-branch instruction)). There are two possible cases: the predicted path is either correct or incorrect. In the case of a correctly predicted path, the penalty is d when the path is a target path, and the penalty is 0 when the path is a sequential path. Note that, in figure, the address of target path is obtained after the decode stage. However, when a branch target buffer is used in the design, the target address can be obtained during or after the fetch stage. In the case of an incorrectly predicted path for both target and sequential predicted paths, the penalty is c. Putting it all together we have,

Average number of cycles per branch instruction =

$$P_r\left[P_t(1+d)+(1-P_t)(1)\right]+(1-P_r)\left[P_t(1+c)+(1-P_t)(1+c)\right],$$

where, P_r is the probability of a right prediction. Substituting this term in equation (t_{ave} = P_{b*} (average number of cycles per branch instruction) + (1 - P_b) $_*$ (average number of cycles per non-branch instruction),

$$t_{ave} = P_b\left[P_r(P_t d + 1)+(1-P_r)(1+c)\right]+(1-P_b)(1)$$
$$=1+P_b c - P_b P_r c + P_b P_r P_t d.$$

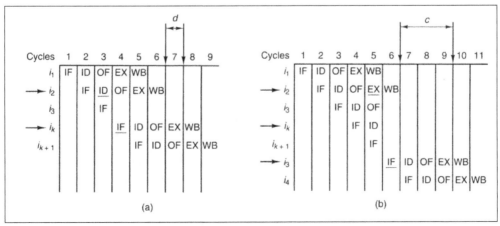

(a) (b)

Branch penalties for when the target path is predicted: (a) The penalty for a correctly chosen target path (b) The penalty for an incorrectly chosen target path

Assume that $P_b = 0.2$, $P_t = 0.65$, $c = 3$, and $d = 1$. Also assume that the predicted path is correct 70% of the time (i.e., $Pr = 0.70$). Then:

$$t_{ave} = 1.27.$$

That is, the pipeline operates at 78% of its maximum rate due to the branch prediction.

Delayed Branching

The delayed branching scheme eliminates or significantly reduces the effect of the branch penalty. In this type of design, a certain number of instructions after the branch instruction is fetched and executed regardless of which path will be chosen for the branch. For example, a processor with a branch delay of k executes a path containing the next k sequential instructions and then either continues on the same path or starts a new path from a new target address. As often as possible, the compiler tries to fill the next k instruction slots after the branch with instructions that are independent from the branch instruction. NOP (no operation) instructions are placed in any remaining empty slots. As an example, consider the following code:

i_1	Load	R_1,	A		
i_2	Load	R_2,	B		
i_3	BrZr	R_2,	i_7		-- branch to i_7 if $R_2 = 0$;
i_4	Load	R_3,	C		
i_5	Add	R_4,	R_2,	R_3	-- $R_4 = R_2 + R_3$
i_6	Mul	R_5,	R_1,	R_2	-- $R_5 = R_1 * R_2$
i_7	Add	R_4,	R_1,	R_2	-- $R_4 = R_1 + R_2$.

Assuming that k=2, the compiler modifies this code by moving the instruction i1 and inserting an NOP instruction after the branch instruction i_3. The modified code is:

i_2	Load	R_2,	B		
i_3	BrZr	R_2,	i_7		
i_1	Load NOP	R_1,	A		
i_4 i_5	Load Add	R_3, R_4,	C R_2,	R_3	
i_6 i_7	Mul Add	R_5, R_4,	R_1, R_1,	R_2 R_2	

As can be seen in the modified code, the instruction i_1 is executed regardless of the branch outcome.

Multiple Prefetching

In this type of design, the processor fetches both possible paths. Once the branch decision is made, the unwanted path is thrown away. By prefetching both possible paths, the fetch penalty is avoided in the case of an incorrect prediction.

To fetch both paths, two buffers are employed to service the pipeline. In normal execution, the first buffer is loaded with instructions from the next sequential address of the branch instruction.

If a branch occurs, the contents of the first buffer are invalidated, and the secondary buffer, which has been loaded with instructions from the target address of the branch instruction, is used as the primary buffer.

This double buffering scheme ensures a constant flow of instructions and data to the pipeline and reduces the time delays caused by the draining and refilling of the pipeline. Some amount of performance degradation is unavoidable any time the pipeline is drained, however.

In summary, each of the preceding simple techniques reduces the degradation of pipeline throughput. However, the choice of any of these techniques for a particular design depends on factors such as throughput requirements and cost constraints. In practice, due to these factors, it is not unusual to see a mixture of these techniques implemented on a single processor.

Further Throughput Improvement of an Instruction Pipeline

One way to increase the throughput of an instruction pipeline is to exploit instruction-level parallelism. The common approaches to accomplish such parallelism are called *superscalar*, *super-pipeline*, and very *long instruction word* (VLIW). Each approach attempts to initiate several instructions per cycle.

a) Superscalar: The superscalar approach relies on spatial parallelism, that is, multiple operations running concurrently on separate hardware. This approach achieves the execution of multiple instructions per clock cycle by issuing several instructions to different functional units. A superscalar processor contains one or more instruction pipelines sharing a set of functional units. It often contains functional units, such as an add unit, multiply unit, divide unit, floating-point add unit, and graphic unit. A superscalar processor contains a control mechanism to preserve the execution order of dependent instructions for ensuring a valid result.

The scoreboard method and Tomasulo's method can be used for implementing such mechanisms. In practice, most of the processors are based on the superscalar approach and employ a scoreboard method to ensure a valid result.

b) Superpipeline: The superpipeline approach achieves high performance by overlapping the execution of multiple instructions on one instruction pipeline. A superpipeline processor often has an instruction pipeline with more stages than a typical instruction pipeline design. In other words, the execution process of an instruction is broken down into even finer steps. By increasing the number of stages in the instruction pipeline, each stage has less work to do. This allows the pipeline clock rate to increase (cycle time decreases), since the clock rate depends on the delay found in the slowest stage of the pipeline.

An example of such architecture is the MIPS R4000 processor. The R4000 subdivides instruction fetching and data cache access to create an eight-stage pipeline. The stages are instruction fetch first half, instruction fetch second half, register fetch, instruction execute, data cache access first half, data cache access second half, tag check, and write back.

A superpipeline approach has certain benefits. The single functional unit requires less space and less logic on the chip than designs based on the superscalar approach. This extra space on the chip allows room for specialize circuitry to achieve higher speeds, room for large caches, and wide data paths.

Very Long Instruction Word (VLIW)

The very long instruction word (VLIW) approach makes extensive use of the compiler by requiring it to incorporate several small independent operations into a long instruction word. The instruction is large enough to provide, in parallel, enough control bits over many functional units. In other words, VLIW architecture provides many more functional units than a typical processor design, together with a compiler that finds parallelism across basic operations to keep the functional units as busy as possible. The compiler compacts ordinary sequential codes into long instruction words that make better use of resources. During execution, the control unit issues one long instruction per cycle. The issued instruction initiates many independent operations simultaneously.

A comparison of the three approaches will show a few interesting differences. For instance, the superscalar and VLIW approaches are more sensitive to resource conflicts than the superpipelined approach. In a superscalar or VLIW processor, a resource must be duplicated to reduce the chance of conflicts, while the superpipelined design avoids any resource conflicts.

To prevent the superpipelined processor from being slower than the superscalar, the technology used in the superpipelined must reduce the delay of the lengthy instruction pipeline. Therefore, in general, superpipelined designs require faster transistor technology such as GaAs (gallium arsinide), whereas superscalar designs require more transistors to account for the hardware resource duplication. The superscalar design often uses CMOS technology, since this technology provides good circuit density. Although superpipelining seems to be a more straightforward solution than superscaling, existing technology generally favors increasing circuit density over increasing circuit speed. Historically, circuit density has increased at a faster rate than transistor speed. This historical precedent suggests a general conclusion that the superscalar approach is more cost effective for industry to implement.

Technological advances have allowed superscalar and superpipelining techniques to be combined, providing good solutions too many current efficiency problems found in the computing industry. Such solutions, which attempt to take advantage of the positive attributes of each design, can be studied in existing processors. One example is the alpha microprocessor.

Arithmetic Pipeline

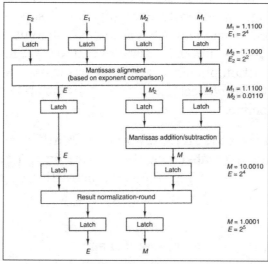

A pipelined floating-point adder

Some functions of the arithmetic logic unit of a processor can be pipelined to maximize performance. An arithmetic pipeline is used for implementing complex arithmetic functions like floating-point addition, multiplication, and division. These functions can be decomposed into consecutive subfunctions. For example figure presents a pipeline architecture for floating-point addition of two numbers. The floating-point addition can be divided into three stages: mantissas alignment, mantissas addition, and result normalization.

In the first stage, the mantissas M_1 and M_2 are aligned based on the difference in the exponents E_1 and E_2. If $| E_1 - E_2 | = k > 0$, then the mantissa with the smaller exponent is right shifted by k digit positions. In the second stage, the mantissas are added (or subtracted). In the third stage, the result is normalized so that the final mantissa has a nonzero digit after the fraction point. When necessary, this normalized adjustment is done by shifting the result mantissa and the exponent.

Another example of an arithmetic pipeline is shown in figure. This figure presents a pipelined architecture for multiplying two unsigned 4-bit numbers using carry save adders. The first stage generates the partial products M_1, M_2, M3, and M_4. figure represents how M_1 is generated; the rest of partial products can be generated in the same way. The M_1, M_2, M_3, and M_4, are added together through the two stages of carry save adders and the final stage of carry look ahead added.

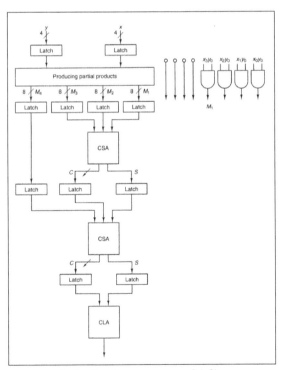

A pipelined carry save multiplier

Pipeline Control: Scheduling

Controlling the sequence of tasks presented to a pipeline for execution is extremely important for maximizing its utilization. If two tasks are initiated requiring the same stage of the pipeline at the same time, a collision occurs, which temporarily disrupts execution.

Reservation Table

There are two types of pipelines: static and dynamic. A static pipeline can perform only one function at a time, whereas a dynamic pipeline can perform more than one function at a time. A pipeline reservation table shows when stages of a pipeline are in use for a particular function. Each stage of the pipeline is represented by a row in the reservation table. Each row of the reservation table is in turn broken into columns, one per clock cycle. The number of columns indicates the total number of time units required for the pipeline to perform a particular function. To indicate that some stage S is in use at some time t_y, an X is placed at the intersection of the row and column in the table corresponding to that stage and time. Figure represents a reservation table for a static pipeline with three stages. The times t_0, t_1, t_2, t_3, and t_4 denote five consecutive clock cycles. The position of X's indicate that, in order to produce a result for an input data, the data must go through the stages 1, 2, 2, 3, and 1, progressively. The reservation table can be used for determining the time difference between input data initiations so that collisions won't occur (Initiation of an input data refers to the time that the data enter the first stage of the pipeline).

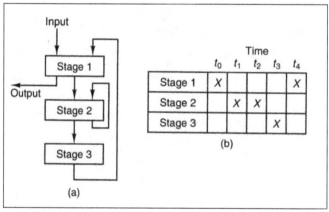

A static pipeline and its corresponding reservation table

Latency

The delay, or number of time units separating two initiations, is called latency. A collision will occur if two pieces of input data are initiated with latency equal to the distance between two X's in a reservation table. For example, the table in figure has two X's with a distance of 1 in the second row. Therefore, if a second piece of data is passed to the pipeline one time unit after the first, a collision will occur in stage 2.

Scheduling Static Pipelines

1. Forbidden list: Every reservation table with two or more X's in any given row has one or more forbidden latencies, which, if not prohibited, would allow two data to collide or arrive at the same stage of the pipeline at the same time. The forbidden list F is simply a list of integers corresponding to these prohibited latencies. With static pipelines, zero is always considered a forbidden latency, since it is impossible to initiate two jobs to the same pipeline at the same time. (However, as shown later, such initiations are possible with dynamic pipelines.) For example, the reservation table in figure has the forbidden list. Each element of this list can be figured by calculating the distance between two X's in a particular row.

2. Collision vectors: A collision vector is a string of binary digits of length N+1, where N is the largest forbidden latency in the forbidden list. The initial collision vector, C, is created from the forbidden list in the following way: each component ci of C, for i=0 to N, is 1 if i is an element of the forbidden list. Otherwise, ci is zero. Zeros in the collision vector indicate allowable latencies or times when initiations are allowed into the pipeline.

For the preceding forbidden list, the collision vector is:

$$C = c_4 c_3 c_2 c_1 c_0$$
$$= (1\ 0011\ )$$
$$43210 \qquad = \text{latency}.$$

Notice in this collision vector that latencies of 2 and 3 would be allowed, but latencies of 0, 1, and 4 would not.

3. State diagram: State diagrams can be used to show the different states of a pipeline for a given time slice. Once a state diagram is created, it is easier to derive schedules of input data for the pipeline that have no collisions.

To create the state diagram of a given pipeline, the initial state is always the initial collision vector. If there is a zero in position c_i, then an initiation to the pipeline is allowed after i time units or clock cycles. Figure represents a state diagram for the pipeline of figure. The collision vector 10011 forms the initial state. Note that the initial state has zero in positions 2 and 3. Therefore, a new datum can be initiated to the pipeline after two or three clock cycles. Each time an initiation is allowed the collision vector is shifted right i place with zeros filling in on the left. This corresponds to the passing of i time units. This new vector is then ORed with the initial collision vector to generate a new collision vector or state. ORing is necessary because the new initiation enforces a new constraint on the current status of the pipeline. Whenever a new collision vector is generated from an existing collision vector in the state diagram, an arc is drawn between them. The arc is labeled by latency i. The process of generating new collision vectors continues until no more can be generated.

Within a state diagram, any initiation of value N+1 or greater will automatically go back to the initial collision vector. This is simply because the current collision vector is shifted right N+1 places with zeros filling in on the left, producing a collision vector of all zeros. When a collision vector of all zeros is ORed with the initial collision vector, the initial collision vector is the result.

4. Average latency: The average latency is determined for a given cycle in a state diagram. A cycle in a state diagram is an alternating sequence of collision vectors and arcs, $C_0, a_1, C_1, ..., a_n, C_n$ in which each arc a_i connects collision vector C_{i-1} to C i, and all the collision vectors are distinct except the first and last. For simplicity, we represent a cycle by a sequence of latencies of its arcs. For example, in figure, the cycle $C_0, a_1, C_1, a_2, C_0, ,$ where $C_0 = (10011)$, $C_1 = (10111)$, a_1 is an arc from C_0 to C_1, and a_2 is an arc from C_1 to C_0, is represented as cycle C=(2,3), where 2 and 3 are the latencies of a_1 and a_2, respectively.

The average latency for a cycle is determined by adding the latencies (right-shifts values) of the arcs of the cycle and then dividing it by the total number of arcs in the cycle. For example, in figure, the cycle C=(2,3) has the average latency:

$(2 + 3)/2 = 2.5.$

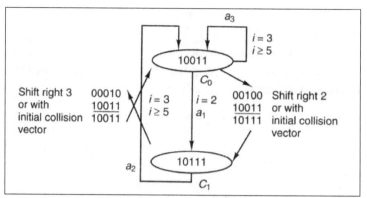

State diagram of a static pipeline

5. Minimum average latency: A pipeline may have several average latencies associated with different cycles. The minimum average latency is simply the smallest such ratio. For example, the following are the average latency cycles for the state diagram in figure.

$(2+3)/2 = 2.5$ from cycle C_0, a_1, C_1, a_2, C_0
$(2+5)/2 = 3.5$ from cycle C_0, a_1, C_1, a_2, C_0
$3/1 = 3$ from cycle C_0, a_3, C_0
$5/1 = 5$ from cycle C_0, a_3, C_0

Therefore, the minimum average latency (MAL) is 2.5. Although the cycle with the minimum average latency maximizes the throughput of the pipeline, sometimes a less efficient cycle may be chosen to reduce the implementation complexity of the pipeline's control circuit (i.e., a trade-off between time and cost.) For example, the cycle C=(2,3), which has the MAL of 2.5, requires a circuit that counts three units of time, then two units, again three units, and so on. However, if it is acceptable to initiate an input datum after every three units of time, the complexity of the circuit will be reduced. Therefore, sometimes it may be necessary to determine the smallest latency that can be used for initiating input data at all times. Such latency is called the minimum latency. One way to determine the minimum latency is to choose a cycle of length 1 with the smallest latency from the state diagram. Another way is to find the smallest integer whose product with any arbitrary integer is not a member of the forbidden list. For example, for the forbidden list, the minimum latency can be determined as follows:

Minimum latency	Times an integer	Product	Result
1	* 1	= 1	No good
2	* 1	= 2	OK
2	* 2	= 4	No good
3	* 1	= 3	OK
3	* 2	= 6	OK
4	*1	= 4	No good.

Therefore the minimum latency for this pipeline is 3.

Scheduling Dynamic Pipelines

When scheduling a static pipeline, only collisions between different input data for a particular function had to be avoided. With a dynamic pipeline, it is possible for different input data requiring different functions to be present in the pipeline at the same time. Therefore, collisions between these data must be considered as well. As with the static pipeline, however, dynamic pipeline scheduling begins with the compilation of a set of forbidden lists from function reservation tables. Next the collision vectors are obtained, and finally the sate diagram is drawn.

1. Forbidden lists: With a dynamic pipeline, the number of forbidden lists is the square of the number of functions sharing the pipeline. In figure the number of functions equals 2, A and B; therefore, the number of forbidden lists equals 4, denoted as AA, AB, BA, and BB. For example, if the forbidden list AB contains integer d, then a datum requiring function B cannot be initiated to the pipeline at some later time t+d, where t represents the time at which a datum requiring function A was initiated. Therefore,

$$AA = (3,0),\ AB = (2,1,0),\ BA = (4,2,1,0),\ \text{and}\ BB = (3,2,0).$$

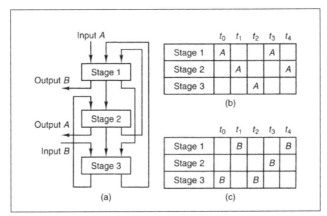

A dynamic pipeline and its corresponding reservation tables

2. Collision vectors and collision matrices: The collision vectors are determined in the same manner as for a static pipeline; o indicates a permissible latency and a 1 indicates a forbidden latency. For the preceding example, the collision vectors are:

$$C_{AA} = (0\ 1\ 0\ 0\ 1) \qquad C_{BA} = (1\ 0\ 1\ 1\ 1)$$

$$C_{AB} = (0\ 0\ 1\ 1\ 1) \qquad C_{BB} = (0\ 1\ 1\ 0\ 1).$$

The collision vectors for the A function form the collision matrix M_A, that is,

$$M_A = \begin{bmatrix} C_{AA} \\ C_{AB} \end{bmatrix}$$

The collision vectors for the B function form the collision matrix M_B:

$$M_B = \begin{bmatrix} C_{BA} \\ C_{BB} \end{bmatrix}$$

For the above collision vectors, the collision matrices are:

$$M_A = \begin{bmatrix} 01001 \\ 00111 \end{bmatrix}$$

$$M_B = \begin{bmatrix} 10111 \\ 01101 \end{bmatrix}$$

3. State diagram: The state diagram for the dynamic pipeline is developed in the same way as for the static pipeline. The resulting state diagram is much more complicated than a static pipeline state diagram due to the larger number of potential collisions.

As an example, consider the state diagram in figure. To start, refer to the collision matrix M_A. There are two types of collisions: an A colliding with another A (the top vector) or an A colliding with a B (the bottom vector.) If the first allowable latency from C_{AA} is chosen, in this case 1, the entire matrix is shifted right 1 place, with zeros filling in on the left. This new matrix is then ORed with the initial collision matrix M_A because the original forbidden latencies for function A still have to be considered in later initiations.

If the first allowable latency for vector C_{AB} in matrix M_A is chosen, in this case 3, the entire matrix is shifted right three places with zeros filling in on the left. This new matrix is then ORed with the initial collision matrix for function B, because the original collisions for function B are still possible and have to be considered. This shifting and ORing continues until all possible allowable latencies are considered and the state diagram is complete.

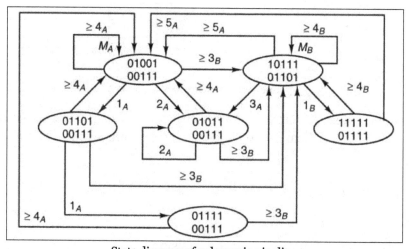

State diagram of a dynamic pipeline

Decreasing the MAL of a Pipeline using Delay Insertion

Sometimes it is possible to modify the reservation table of a pipeline so that the overall structure is unchanged, but the overall throughput is increased (i.e., the MAL is decreased). The reservation table can be modified with the insertion of delays or dummy stages in the table. Insertion of a delay in the table reflects the insertion of a latch in front of or after the logic for a stage. For example, figure represents the changes in a reservation table and its corresponding pipeline before and after delay insertion.

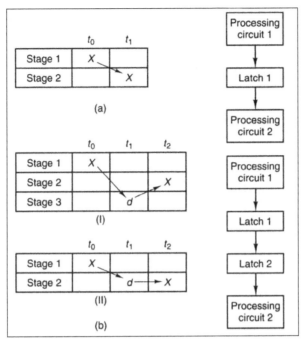

Changes in a reservation table and its corresponding pipeline before and after delay insertion:
(a) Before insertion of delay, (b) Inserting a delay between the two stages.

Given a desired cycle, the technique for delay insertion places some delays in certain rows of the original reservation table. Such delays may force the marks on certain rows to be moved forward. The location of the delays is chosen such that each row of the table matches some criteria of a cycle that the designer wishes to have. To understand the process of delay insertion, consider the reservation table shown in figure. As indicated, there is at least one row with two marks (X's), which means that for each input there is a stage that will be used at least two times. Therefore, we wish to modify this reservation table in such a way that MAL becomes 2.

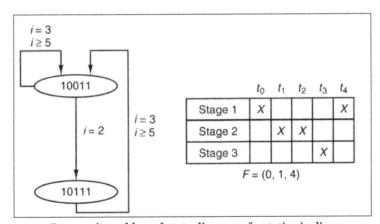

Reservation table and state diagram of a static pipeline

In general, the lower bound for the MAL is greater than or equal to the maximum number of marks in a row of the reservation table. The lower bound can be achieved by delay insertion, which increases the time per computation. To have a MAL = 2, we start with a cycle, say C = (2), and determine the properties of a reservation table that supports it. To do this, we need to define the following parameters.

1. Lc, the latency sequence, is the sequence of time between successive data that enter the pipeline. For cycle C=(2),

$$L_c = 2, 2, 2, 2, 2, \ldots$$

2. I_c, the initiation time sequence, is the starting time for each datum. The ith ($i>0$) element in this sequence is the starting time of the i th initiated data, so it equals the sum of the latencies between the previous initiations. For the preceding L_c,

$$I_c = 0, 2, 4, 6, 8, 10, \ldots$$

3. G_c, the initiation interval set, is the set of all distinct intervals between initiation times. That is, Gc = { t i- t j for every i>j }, where t i and t $_j$ are the ith and j th elements in the initiation time sequence, respectively. For our example,

$$G_c = 2, 4, 6, 8, \ldots$$

Note that G_c determines the properties that a reservation table must have in order to support cycle C. If an integer i is in G_c, any reservation table supporting cycle C cannot have two marks with distance of i time units (clocks) in any row. For example, for our cycle C, distances of 1 or 3 are possible because they are not in G_c. In general, it is easier to consider the complement of G_c. This is denoted by H_c and defined next.

4. H_c, the permissible distance set, is the complement of set G_c (i.e., $H_c = Z - G_c$, where Z is the set of all non-negative integers). For our cycle,

$$H_c = 0, 1, 3, 5, 7, \ldots$$

Therefore, any reservation table that supports a cycle C should have marks with distances that are allowed in H_c, that is H_c showing permissible (but not mandatory) distances between marks. In other words, if a reservation table has forbidden list F, then the cycle C is valid if,

$$F \subseteq H_c \quad \text{or} \quad F \cap G_c = \Phi$$

Since the set H_c is infinite, it is hard to deal with in the real world. Thus we try to make it finite by considering H_c (mod p), where p is the period of the cycle C, that is, and the sum of the latencies. This is an accurate categorization of all permissible distances, since the latency sequence repeats with period p. For our example,

$$H_c(mod2) = \{0, 1\}.$$

To facilitate the process of testing or constructing a reservation table, the following definition and theorem are given in:

1. Definition: Two integers i, j ε Z_p, where Zp is the set of all nonnegative integers less than p, are compatible with respect to H_c(mod p) if and only if $|i - j|$(mod p) ε H_c(mod p). A set is called a compatible class if every pair of its elements is compatible.

2. Theorem: Any reservation table to support cycle C must have rows with marks at the following times:

$$z_1 + i_1 p, z_2 + i_2 p, \ldots,$$

where, $\{z_1, z_2, ...\}$ is a compatible class of H_c (mod p) and $i_1, i_2, ...,$ are arbitrary integers.

We can apply this theorem to some compatible classes in order to construct all possible rows for a reservation table that supports a particular cycle.

In our example, one compatible class is $\{0,1\}$. Considering the original reservation table, the first row has two marks at time 0 and 4. When the positions of these marks are matched against the compatible class $\{0,1\}$, the first mark (position 0) matches, but not the second. Adding 2 * p (i.e. 4) to the second element (i.e.: 1) gives us $\{0,5\}$, so we can delay the second mark by one time unit. For the second row, we add 1 * p (i.e., 2) to each element $\{0,1\}$, so the new positions for the marks become 2 and 3.

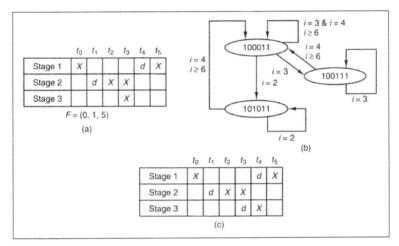

Figure represents a modified reservation table. This table is based on the assumption that input data to the stage 3 is independent from the result of stage 2. Figure represents an alternative solution in which there is assumed to be dependency between stages 2 and 3.

Permissions

Index